What Do Lawyers Do?

An Ethnography of a
Corporate Law Firm

What Do Lawyers Do?

An Ethnography of a Corporate Law Firm

SECOND EDITION

John Flood

QUID PRO BOOKS

New Orleans, Louisiana

Published in 2013 by Quid Pro Books. A previous edition of portions of this work has been cited in dissertation form as "Anatomy of Lawyering: An Ethnography of a Corporate Law Firm."

ISBN 978-1-61027-161-5 (pbk.)
ISBN 978-1-61027-210-0 (hbk.)
ISBN 978-1-61027-162-2 (eBook)

QUID PRO BOOKS
5860 Citrus Blvd.
Suite D-101
New Orleans, Louisiana 70123
www.quidprobooks.com

Publisher's Cataloging in Publication

Flood, John.
    What do lawyers do? : An ethnography of a corporate law firm / John Flood.
        p. cm. — (Classic dissertation series)
    Includes bibliographical references.
        ISBN 978-1-61027-161-5 (pbk.)

1. Lawyers—United States—corporate law. 2. Attorney and client—United States. 3. Law firms—globalization. 4. Practice of law—United States—sociological aspects. 5. Law partnership—United States. I. Title. II. Series.

KF300 .F83 2013   344.023'1.724

                                                                    2013266804

CONTENTS

ACKNOWLEDGMENTS

The book owes debts to many. First, I am very grateful to Jack Heinz who guided me and created an environment where I could do this research. Jack introduced me to the lawyers at Tischmann and vouched for me. I am also grateful to Howard S. Becker and Art Stinchcombe for their advice and counsel.

There is one person to whom I owe much and that is William Twining who not only originally gave me the freedom to explore this field but also knew everyone I ought to meet who worked in it. That meant helping me go to the United States, Yale and Chicago, the American Bar Foundation and Northwestern, where I encountered a different kind of research and approach to the field.

The book has had a kind of samizdat existence for a number of years as "Anatomy of Lawyering: An Ethnography of a Corporate Law Firm." I'm grateful to Alan Childress for persuading me to revise the book and take it out of the shadows with Quid Pro Books, and to many others over the years, including Robert Rosen, who offered similar encouragement.

My final thanks go to the lawyers at Tischmann and Weinstock whose firm is no more, having been merged into a much larger law firm. I think it was inevitable.

JF

July, 2013

LIST OF TABLES

LIST OF FIGURES

FOREWORD

What do lawyers do?

This important question—rather surprisingly—has not been systematically explored. Detailed studies describe the work of divorce lawyers, criminal defense attorneys, prosecutors, legal services lawyers, and personal injury lawyers. But far less is known about exactly what business lawyers do. John Flood's brilliant ethnography of a corporate law firm helps to fill this gap, providing an in-depth analysis of corporate lawyers at work and addressing significant issues of professional work. Originally done in the late 1980s, this classic study has now been updated and still stands as a singular contribution to the field for its insights into the work of corporate lawyers.

Sociological research has shed light on the substantial differences among private lawyers representing individual vs. organizational clients, among lawyers working in firms of different sizes, and across different areas of legal practice. This significant work has focused primarily on the structure of the legal profession, showing the growth of the corporate law sector, increased legal specialization, and differences in income, prestige, firm size, and demographics for attorneys working in different legal fields. But what do these aggregate trends reveal about what lawyers actually do? A second approach to studying the legal profession adopts Everett Cherrington Hughes' concept of "work as social interaction,"[1] a perspective exemplified by Flood's book. Drawing on his extensive ethnographic fieldwork at an 80-person corporate law firm in Chicago, Flood shows how lawyers' interactions with clients, others in the firm, opposing parties and their counsel all shape what they do.

The book distinguishes between litigators and office (or business) lawyers, demonstrating how very different these two kinds of lawyers are. "Litigators essentially play a reactive role: a crisis occurs and someone is needed to remedy or to repair the damage. . . . Office lawyers . . . plan things so that crises do not occur. They are essentially proactive. One could say a business lawyer has failed when a litigator is brought in." (pp. 94-95). This profoundly simple distinction has enormous ramifications for

---

[1] Everett Cherrington Hughes, *Men and Their Work* (Free Press, 1958), p. 68.

lawyering, as the book points out. Flood's background in the United Kingdom with its sharp division of work between barristers and solicitors no doubt sensitized him to the importance of this distinction—one that often eludes U.S. law students and scholars who think that all of lawyering involves zealous advocacy with clients effectively directing their counsel. By contrast, office lawyers—deal makers, transactional lawyers, business lawyers —work with clients to help them resolve uncertainties and collaborate with opposing counsel as they draft documents and negotiate agreements.

The case studies of office lawyering in this book vividly challenge, for example, Daniel Markovits' recent argument about lawyerly fidelity to clients and adversary advocacy.[2] Indeed, Flood's scholarship, along with other empirical research on lawyers' work, spurred me to examine how and why legal ethics scholars so often distort the lawyer's role by assuming that all lawyers act as litigators. In my critique of Markovits' position, I suggest that he presents a one-dimensional model of lawyerly fidelity, one based on a corporate litigator. My review of the literature on what lawyers actually do shows that "lawyers vary enormously in loyalty, client control, and legal assertiveness according to client differences, the nature of legal roles (counseling or litigation), and area of practice. . . . Understanding the nature of lawyerly fidelity to clients thus requires disaggregating the legal profession and paying attention to the micro-level patterns in different communities of legal practice."[3]

Attention to ethical decision making across different legal arenas, using empirical research about what lawyers do in their work, reflects a recent trend in the field of legal ethics. Instead of professional ethics as formal bar rules in which one size fits all lawyers, scholars have been examining the "multiple normative frameworks [that] exist for guiding lawyers' decisions."[4] These frameworks include the informal norms and values within law firm cultures, as well as the distinct norms for office lawyers vs. litigators. Although Flood's book examines a single law firm, his detailed exposition of this firm provides a model for understanding what lawyers do. He charts specific activities—from the time spent on various tasks to the songs created by associates to complain at Christmas about their long working hours—to flesh out life at the firm. Moreover, he

---

[2] Daniel Markovits, *A Modern Legal Ethics: Adversary Advocacy in a Democratic Age* (Princeton University Press, 2010), and "Lawyerly Fidelity," *NOMOS*, Vol. 54 (2013), p. 55.

[3] Lynn Mather, "Lawyerly Fidelity: An Ethical and Empirical Critique," *NOMOS*, Vol. 54 (2013), p. 124.

[4] Lynn Mather and Leslie C. Levin, "Why Context Matters," in *Lawyers in Practice: Ethical Decision Making in Context* (University of Chicago, 2012), p. 11.

also suggests in its last chapter how the process of lawyering changes over time in response to changes in practice, business, and the economy.

One of the oft-noted drawbacks of the social interactional approach is its inability to deal with change in the workplace. Michael J. Kelly's book, *Lives of Lawyers Revisited*, resolved the problem by his going back fifteen years later to each of the law firms he studied to assess what had transpired in the interim.[5] The firm John Flood studied merged with another firm in 2003, thus precluding that option, but he examines the increase in law firm mergers and economic competition to assess the future of corporate law practice. In particular, he draws on recent changes in professional regulation in the United Kingdom to question the ability of corporate firms in the United States to remain globally competitive under current laws. By presenting the internal dynamics of a corporate law firm at one point in time, this book also invites a comparative study to document changes in terms of getting clients, hiring laterals, billing, power of different practice groups, and even communication within the firm.

The book offers another intriguing theme in questioning the role of *law* in what lawyers do. Early on, Flood writes, "in the practice of law one finds very little law. Instead, one sees substantial amounts of face-to-face interaction, or conversing on the telephone, but legal research and writing, as such, constitute a minor portion of lawyer's work." (p. 28). The conventional wisdom about legal negotiation has long been that it occurs in the "shadow of the law."[6] That is, legal entitlements and rights are the key bargaining chips that parties use as they seek to resolve their disputes. But scholars have built on Flood's point and found, as Herbert Jacob did in his study of divorce, a far more "elusive shadow of the law."[7] In transactional legal work, office lawyers create new legal institutions—contracts—using well-known legal terms and concepts. In some wonderful passages, Flood analyzes the dialogue between lawyers as they construct a loan deal by stitching together legal language. Such language provides the normative framework for the contract, but their references to different sentences or phrases are also deeply embedded in the social interactions and hierarchies among lawyers.

---

[5] Michael J. Kelly, *Lives of Lawyers Revisited: Transformation and Resilience in the Organizations of Practice* (University of Michigan Press, 2007); see also *Lives of Lawyers: Journeys in the Organizations of Practice* (University of Michigan Press, 1994).

[6] Robert H. Mnookin and Lewis Kornhauser, "Bargaining in the Shadow of the Law: The Case of Divorce," *Yale Law Journal*, Vol. 88 (1979), p. 950.

[7] Herbert Jacob, "The Elusive Shadow of the Law," *Law & Society Review*, Vol. 26 (1992), p. 565.

I hope that this provocative book will stimulate further ethnographic research on corporate lawyers. The themes it raises—differences between office lawyers and litigators, ethical decision making in the context of legal work, change in corporate practice in relation to the economy and professional regulation, and the role of law in what lawyers do—remain crucial for understanding the role of lawyers in society.

LYNN MATHER
SUNY Distinguished Service Professor,
State University of New York Buffalo Law School

October, 2013

What Do Lawyers Do?

An Ethnography of a
Corporate Law Firm

PART ONE

THE LAW FIRM

1

The Changing Face of Corporate Law Practice

Introduction

In the 1930s Carr-Saunders and Wilson wrote in the first important study
of professions:

> The attitude of the professional man to his client or his employer
> is painstaking and is characterized by an admirable sense of
> responsibility; it is one of pride in service given rather than of
> interest in opportunity for personal profit. (1933: 471)

Aside from the bias to the male sex, this sentiment, perhaps true in
the 1930s, has now a quaint, almost naïve tone. The modern professions
are completely different from the idyllic picture drawn above; and none
more so than the legal profession, one of the holy trinity of professions;
the church, medicine, and the law. The first has all but disappeared as
a profession, superseded by science (Barnes 1985). The remaining two,
however, have thrived, but undergone dramatic changes: both are now
subject to the norms of business rather than the standards of professionalism (cf. Starr 1982). It is part of the purpose of this chapter to show that
the practice of law has become a business like any other business activity.
As a result of this transformation, the norms and standards so often identified with the professions have eroded (Osiel 1990; Flood 2012a). Eli
Wald's (2012) recent work on the law firm in the 21st century helps to
show how our representation of law firms has evolved over the last forty
years or so, yet many practices within law firms have endured.

In the next part, I outline some of the demographic changes that have
taken place in the legal profession and the reasons for them. This is followed by a discussion of how the corporate law firm operates, using examples of anti-trust litigation and the restructuring of an international corporation. These provide both an entry and a counterpoint to the particular
type of corporate law firm I shall be discussing throughout the remainder
of this book. Though the scale will be different, the substance is essentially
the same.

The Demographic Profile

The legal profession in the United States is huge and until the great recession of the early 21st century has been growing rapidly. If we look at the growth of the lawyer population against that of the general population in the U.S. since 1870, we see that from 1870 to 1970 the two have paralleled each other fairly closely, except for two slight rises in 1900 and 1940. In 1870 lawyers numbered 40,000; by 1900 the number had nearly tripled to 115,000; and by 1970 the number had reached 300,000, from which point it has skyrocketed to more than twice that figure (Halliday 1986). In 1985, for example, there were 655,191 lawyers, an increase of 21 percent since the beginning of the decade (Curran 1985; Galanter and Palay 1992). The vast majority of these, over 70 percent, were in private practice. This works out to one lawyer for every 513 members of the population. By 2008 there were 1,180,386 (ABA 2006). In 2000, 74 percent were in private practice (ABF 2004). The legal profession in the United States is one of the largest, if not the largest, in the world.

The present legal profession population is by no means a homogeneous mass. The majority of lawyers are in private practice (74%), with just under half of them in solo practice (ABF 2004). The next largest proportion (18%) is found in law firms of 51 and above lawyers (ABF 2004). These proportions represent a decline in solo practice being compensated by a rise in corporate practice. Whereas in 1960 solo practice claimed 64 percent of private practitioners, by 2000 more than half were engaged in firm practice.

Why the legal profession has grown so markedly still largely remains unsolved. But to some extent we can speculate that the twin forces of economy and state should have exercised considerable influence—through increased business activity and state regulation of affairs—on this growth in lawyers' numbers. Although Pashigian, however, argued, "size of government relative to the economy was found to have little effect on the demand for lawyers," such a possibility cannot be ruled out altogether (Pashigian 1978: 68; 1977). In place of an anticipated effect of governmental regulatory activity leading the demand for lawyers, Pashigian found that lawyer demand altered strongly with changes in real gross national product (GNP) (1978: 70). The two periods of lawyer population growth mentioned above were matched by surges in real GNP. If we take Pashigian's period, U.S. Census figures for GNP in 1970 prices show dramatic increases during the periods of heightened growth in the lawyer population. In 1870 the GNP was $7.4 billion; by 1900 it was nearly $19 billion; and between 1940 and 1945 the GNP rose from roughly $100 billion to over $200 billion dollars. By 1970 GNP had soared to around $980 billion dollars (U.S. Bureau of the Census I, 1975: 224). And if we examine the statistics for business enterprises over the same time span, we also see some positive reinforcement for the expected increase in lawyers. In 1870 there were 427,000 business concerns, which number rose to 1,174,000 in 1900. From 1940, with 2,156,000 business concerns, there was a decline in the volume of businesses until 1946, 2,142,000, when 132,916 new businesses were incorporated. By 1970 there were 2,442,000 businesses, a decline from a peak in 1960 of 2,708,000 (U.S. Bureau of Census II, 1975: 912-13). The two declines in the number of business concerns do not necessarily negate the economic argument, as lawyers would generate work from bankruptcies as well as business incorporations. Moreover, the drop in the number of businesses may be a result of mergers and acquisitions between corporations rather than reflecting a diminution in the general level of business activity. Whilst any speculation of these figures in relation to the growth in the number of lawyers must at best be tentative, they lend some support to the notion that increases in business activity call for commensurate increases in the numbers of lawyers.

Other scholars have suggested the numbers of lawyers relate to the quantity of law produced (Galanter and Palay 1992; Priest 1993), whereas Clark (1992) believes it is within the role of lawyers as agents who engage in normative ordering. As such they respond to changes in the wider society. Clark (1992: 301) identified four trends: greater internationalization; greater diversity in the population; changes in wealth levels; and greater involvement of the workforce in formal organizations.

One of the most startling moments throughout the twentieth century, and continuing since, has been the rise of the large corporate law firm. Though this type of firm is in a minority in absolute numbers,[1] its influence is overarching. Some firms are now composed of more than 4000 lawyers: the largest law firms in the world, DLA Piper, Clifford Chance and Baker and McKenzie, have offices in most of the major cities of the world. Like the corporations they serve, these large firms are also huge enterprises in their own right. In 1985, Skadden, Arps, Slate, Meagher and Flom had gross revenues of $169 million (*American Lawyer* Nov. 1986: chart). By 2010 its gross revenues topped $2 billion (AmLaw 200 2010; Caplan 1994). Its growth has been dramatic and remarkable. Since, historically, elite lawyers have been in the vanguard of the development of the American legal profession (Gordon 1983)—as in forming the Association of the Bar of the City of New York in 1870 and the American Bar Association in 1878 (Pound 1953: 254)—and typically have clustered in large corporate

---

[1] In 1985 law firms of 51 lawyers or more accounted for 1.2 percent of all firms (N = 42,318), but the same firms employed 11.2 percent of all private practitioners (Curran 1985: 4-5). In 2000 the percentage had risen to 2 percent with 18 percent of all private practitioners (ABF 2004).

firms, their importance in both the polity and the economy cannot be overestimated. The era of "mega-lawyering", as Marc Galanter has called it (1983: 152), is qualitatively different from that which preceded it. Big firms are similar in scope and size to the organizations for which they work (Heinz and Laumann 1982: Nelson 1988; Heinz et al 2005; Flood 2007, 2012a). How far the large corporate law firm has been successful and will remain so is under question, but perhaps its imminent demise is premature (Ribstein 2010).

Carlin's study of solo practitioners in Chicago (1962; 2011) showed those kinds of lawyers having to muddle through with limited resources and time at their disposal (see also Sarat and Felstiner 1986; Seron 1996; Travers 1997; Mather et al 2001). The nature of their work was routine, monotonous and unchallenging. Their ethics, at best, were questionable; the quality of their services dubious; and most important, their clients were usually unable to evaluate them or the quality of services they rendered. To a large degree, corporate lawyers cannot be criticized for similar failings. Their staffs are large; their clients, often in-house counsel, are knowledgeable; but their ethics, as with solo practitioners, may be doubtful. Having separated large law practice from other types, I now turn to describing some of the features of large law firms practice.

The Structure of Corporate Law Firms

Corporate law firms are broadly divided along the lines of partners—the members and owners of the firm—and associates who are employed by the partnership.[2] To explain how the system operates, I will start with the associates and progress upwards to the partners.[3] Associates are hired from law school: there is no intervening period of apprenticeship, for shortly after graduating from law school the associate will take the state bar examination and, on passing, will be admitted to the bar.[4]

Associates are the profit generators for a firm. They are billed out at roughly two and a half to three times what they are paid. So an associate

---

[2] *Black's Law Dictionary* (Rev. 4th ed.) defines "partnership" as: A voluntary contract between two or more competent persons to place their money, effects, labor, and skill, [...] in lawful commerce or business, with the understanding that there shall be a proportional sharing of the profits and losses between them.

[3] Besides these two categories, law firms hire enormous staffs of paralegals, law clerks, secretaries, librarians, messengers, and accountants.

[4] Note that each state administers its own bar examination and determines the rules for eligibility of entry. In most states, passing the examination entitles one to begin practice immediately. However, some states, such as Vermont, for example, require several months of clerking in an attorney's office as a prerequisite to unrestricted practice.

who is paid at the rate of $100 per hour will be charged to clients at $300+ per hour. Normally associates are required to bill up to 2,300 hours per year, which is an enormous amount when considering there are only 8,800 hours total in a year. Up to a quarter of that must be spent in *chargeable* time, which means associates generally have to work 70+ hours or more a week in order to generate the billable time.[5] Such demands often place intolerable burdens on associates, but they also allow the firm to monitor who will be a promising candidate for promotion to partner.[6]

The associate probation system is credited to Paul Cravath (Swaine 1946) who devised a rotation system within the firm for associates that entailed intensive training in different departments while working with a partner and senior associates. Complex matters would be divided into smaller tasks for associates to do. No billable hourly accounts were required; only that the associates complete the task on time.

As an associate travels up the tenure ladder, approximately seven years long, he or she is given more and more responsibility for handling more aspects of the case and for handing out work to junior associates. Whereas a firm may take in a class of twenty or thirty associates in one year, seven or ten years later only one or two will realize the prospect of partnership. This realization, open to all, combined with the murderously long hours, impels the majority of associates to find alternatives to the large law firm after about three years.[7] The usual alternatives are smaller firms, sometimes in a different city, or state or federal government posi-

---

[5] Chargeable or billable time is that time spent on work directly for client. It can also include travel time to and from clients, courts, etc. But it excludes the time, say, spent reading the latest cases from the Supreme Court in order to keep up with the latest developments, even though one of those cases may be of benefit to a client. It also omits the vexed question of realization rates, i.e., how much of that billable time is convertible into actual bills and how much must be absorbed by the firm as non-chargeable. When the recession hit in 2008, Citibank, which was one of the main funders of or lenders to law firms, began to exercise the covenants in its loan agreements because realization rates were, among other things, too low.

[6] In a speech at Indiana University School of Law, Mr. Justice Rehnquist said large firms, by increasing salaries, had become "substantially more concerned with profit maximization than were the firms when I practiced.... One might argue that such a firm is treating the associate very much as a manufacturer would treat a purchaser of 100 tons of scrap metal: If you use anything less than 100 tons that you paid for, you simply are not running an efficient business" (*New York Times*, March 23, 1987: 20). Law firms have been described as classifying their lawyers as "finders, minders, and grinders". *Finders* are the partners who bring in the work; *minders* distribute and monitor the production of work; and *grinders* are those who do the actual legal work.

[7] Three years is the optimal time because an associate has benefited from his or her association with the large firm, but has left sufficient time before the time for partnership, three or four years, for another firm to review him or her carefully before deciding whether to grant partnership.

tions. Many associates thus use the status and prestige of having worked in a large firm as a passport to a more secure job later on (Galanter and Palay 1992; Galanter and Henderson 2008).

If an associate is granted tenure as partner, he or she may at first be only an income partner. That is, the partner still receives a salary, as opposed to a share of the profits, but can attend partners' meetings, although without a vote. This stage can last for up to four years, when the partnership decides whether to convert the income partner into a fully-fledged equity partner with a draw of the profits and full voting rights. The main difference between partners and associates is that associates are expected to carry out tasks assigned to them. Partners, though they do undertake many assignments for senior partners much in the same way an associate might, are expected to contribute to the firm's stability and growth by finding new clients, i.e., they have to become "rainmakers".

Firms have two basic ways of remunerating partners, namely, lockstep and merit. The former is remuneration based entirely on seniority without regard to how many clients one controls (see Starbuck 1993; Lazega 2001), although there are hybrids which mix lockstep and merit. Pure merit pay (or eat what you kill), however, rewards an individual partner on the basis of how many clients that partner is responsible for and how many hours the partner bills in a year. More and more, firms are switching to the latter mode of remuneration. One reason for this change is that, whilst in previous years partners stayed with the firm they first made partner at, inter-firm mobility has increased tremendously. Firms such as Finley, Kumble, Wagner, Heine, Underberg, Manley, Myerson and Casey were largely composed of lateral hires from other firms on the promise of greater earnings than could be expected under the lockstep tradition. Its dependency on this non-organic growth and its need for short-term profits led to its eventual implosion (Eisler 1990).

Firm loyalty is in decline. Firms are also not averse to removing partners who do not generate sufficient work for the firm. Besides, those who prove incompetent for one reason or another, those who have specialized in a particular field are especially vulnerable. For example, specialists in air transport regulation have suffered since the Reagan administration deregulated the field. Moreover, the recession of the early 21st century has hastened the decline of enduring ties in law firms as they retrench and move towards more corporate structures (see Sterling and Reichman 2010; Wald 2010).

The Work of Corporate Law Firms

What then do large law firms do? In some respects this has been a difficult question to answer for the simple reason that, except for journalistic accounts, few data exist. The kinds of fields of law in which these lawyers practice tell us little about what they actually do. But some sketch of these fields should be drawn for heuristic purposes. Most large firms' expertise is in corporate work, e.g., complex contracts, international business, and large-scale litigation. Regardless of the dispute over whether there has in recent years been a litigation explosion (Galanter 1983), large law firms are geared to running large lawsuits continuing over a period of years.

In his book *The Partners*, Stewart (1983) presents in detail several cases of law firms' involvement in transactions and litigation, e.g., the refinancing of Chrysler, and the IBM anti-trust suit. Both of these examples demonstrate the peculiar talents of the large corporate law firm. Despite its age the book's cases are still highly relevant today.

Large-scale litigation requires intensive use of manpower over extended periods of time. The IBM anti-trust suit involved legions of lawyers in what was effectively one case that lasted for the better part of a decade (Stewart 1983: 53-113). IBM was charged with monopolizing the hardware part of the computer industry under section 2 of the Sherman Act.[8] The U.S. government suit came on the heels of several private actions instituted by smaller computer firms.[9] The effect of this multiplicity of suits was to put IBM under siege; different types of organizations spread across the country attacked it.

IBM relied on its outside counsel, the elite firm of Cravath, Swaine and Moore, to handle the litigation. Given the multiplicity and geographical diversity of the suits, IBM, through Cravath, had to employ other law firms to act as local counsel, though at all times Cravath held the position of lead counsel. As such, it devised and controlled the strategies adopted in the litigation. Cravath set up its litigation headquarters at the then White Plains head office of IBM. As the cases progressed, more and more associated were drafted onto the IBM case.

The private and government actions against IBM effectively interlocked, so that a win in one would redound to the benefit of the other. When the first suit, a private one brought by Control Data Corporation (CDC), was started, Cravath replied with a series of discovery requests that overwhelmed (i.e., they demanded enormous numbers of documents) the lawyers on the other side.[10] When CDC made its own discovery requests,

---

[8] 15 U.S.C. § 2 (1890).

[9] Private actions are brought under section 1 of the Sherman Act. For a more prosaic rendition of an anti-trust case, see Ellis and Meeks (1977).

[10] Discovery is the process whereby each side to a dispute is required by law to hand over copies of documents requested by the other side. A lawyer's work product is usually exempted. Document production is often a precursor to deposing potential

Cravath gave CDC's lawyers more documents than they could absorb. As Stewart points out, there was a crucial difference in the methods of the two sets of lawyers. Cravath had known what was in each of the documents it had produced; conversely, CDC's lawyers did not read every document they handed to Cravath. When the Cravath team combed the CDC documents, they discovered evidence of a plan by CDC to join a consortium that would have acted to fix prices and arrange markets to suborn IBM. When CDC's lawyers realized the information Cravath possessed, they agreed to settle.

At this stage only two partners and four associates were assigned to the litigation. When Cravath lost one of the cases against Telex with a $350 million verdict against IBM, IBM insisted that more lawyers be put on to the cases. In all, there were three partners, about twenty associates, and a considerable amount of help from IBM. The verdict against IBM stimulated the government into pressing forward its case. As discovery progressed, Cravath took somewhere in the region of a thousand depositions of witnesses. The government asked for 760 million IBM documents. Although the government sought a trial date in 1974, it was not until 1976 that the trial proper began, seven years after the U.S. Attorney General signed the complaint. Part of Cravath's strategy was to set up an office in the Southern District of New York near the trial court and to form teams around the broad issues of the case, such as "market structure" and "acts and practices", which would prepare the appropriate parts of the case as those witnesses came to testify. Only the partners, however, were allowed to speak in court.

While the government case was in progress, so were other private suits against IBM. Cravath was forced to set up satellite teams constructed out of its government team. These satellite teams travelled around the country as and when trials began. Some of these private actions were on trial for several months. Perhaps this is one of the salient points about this type of litigation: it drags on for years. Again, for example, one of the government witnesses spent a total of seven months on the witness stand.

By 1980, Cravath had won all the private cases, either at trial or on appeal, and by 1981 it had presented its case in the government matter. At this time the Reagan administration had taken over from that of President Carter. The new administration was characterized by a libertarian, free-market economic policy, and in contrast to the previous administration's intervention into the marketplace, the government entered settlement

---

witnesses in a case. The theory behind discovery is to accelerate the suit and to avoid surprises at trial: it removes, again in theory, the game element from a trial, but as we shall see, it frequently introduces its own game elements. See also Brazil (1980).

discussions rather than drag the case out interminably. In 1981 the case was dismissed.

Even within a large firm such as Cravath—currently with about 500 lawyers—such an intensive and extensive series of interconnected cases takes an enormous toll on a law firm. There is a danger that a single client comes to dominate the firm. And as client loyalties are becoming diluted as corporations are taking more legal jobs in-house, to rely on one or a few large clients can prove risky. Moreover, a single case like the IBM suit can distort the growth of a law firm. For while the case is in progress many associates are hired into the litigation department, there is a danger that once the case is finished there may be a shortage of work for them. Some of these dangers reappear in the next example of Chrysler Automotive Corporation's restructuring.

At the end of the 1970s, Chrysler was facing imminent collapse. The automobile company had not changed its production from heavy, thirsty motorcars suitable to the period of cheap gasoline to lighter, more efficient models. As a result, the company's inventory was too high and its sales were dismally low; in 1979 Chrysler lost $1.1 billion dollars (Stewart 1983: 201-44). In order to prevent a massive bankruptcy, Congress passed the Chrysler Corporation Loan Guarantee Act of 1979. The act stipulated that if certain conditions were met, the government would guarantee funds for Chrysler.

To shepherd the company through the labyrinth of these conditions, Chrysler hired Debevoise and Plimpton, a large Wall Street law firm. The central requirement of the restructuring of Chrysler was that all of Chrysler's and Chrysler Finance Company's (a subsidiary that financed customer loans) debtors relinquish the primacy of their interests in favour of the government. Manufacturers Hanover Corporation, a large bank, was the main debtor, with over $55 million in debts outstanding. But there were also around 400 other banks, large and small, in the U.S., Canada, Europe, and Japan that were owed large sums of money. Any one of them could claim a default on Chrysler's part and force Chrysler into bankruptcy, which would inflict huge loans on all creditors. It was in everyone's interest to keep Chrysler afloat.

Debevoise was taken on in part because it had no major bank as client and was therefore free of any potential conflicts of interest. As with the IBM anti-trust litigation, the Chrysler restructuring would require an enormous commitment of labor from Debevoise. Unlike Cravath, Debevoise had a firm rule that no single client could claim more than 15 percent of the firm's resources: it was obvious to the partnership that Chrysler would breach this rule. Nevertheless, the law firm agreed to be lead counsel for Chrysler.

In negotiation with banks in four parts of the world, Debevoise encountered many cultural and political problems. The Japanese concept of honor demanded that Japanese banks help Japanese corporations when they were in trouble. Thus the Japanese failed to understand why the American banks were not assisting Chrysler. They suspected the government of providing better conditions for American banks than Japanese ones. The Canadian banks' loans were secured by rights to the assets of Chrysler's subsidiary, unlike most of the American banks' loans, which were unsecured. The Canadian banks were determined to keep this advantage. Their first step was to freeze $50 million dollars of Chrysler's deposits in Canada. The American banks were convinced that the Canadians were receiving an unfair benefit and Debevoise had to persuade them not to scuttle the entire restructuring because of the freeze. Eventually, Debevoise had to assign a senior partner full-time to the Canadian negotiations.

The only true bargaining counter Debevoise possessed was the threat that Chrysler would go bankrupt, thereby defaulting on its loans. At certain stages in the negotiations with the banks and the U.S. Treasury, the threat appeared imminent without the willing agency of Chrysler. Chrysler was fast running out of money. A transfusion of $100 million from Peugeot, although having the appearance of a loan, had to be dressed as a sale; Peugeot could not have first priority on the stock which the "loan" was secured against since the U.S. government had priority over all others. Added to these difficulties was the problem Debevoise had in determining the exact size of Chrysler's likely loss for the year. Every time the figure was established, it changed for the worse, but some degree of accuracy was essential to satisfy both the Treasury and the Securities and Exchange Commission that the prospectus would be truthful.

When Debevoise reached a tentative agreement with the banks and the Treasury, it began the drafting of the documents that would tie the entire deal together. One hundred and fifty lawyers from ten law firms worked on the drafting. One lawyer described the process this way:

> This drafting was done in the course of three nearly 24-hour days. Lawyers would slump over the tables, then go out for few hours of sleep. But what was going on was not real negotiating. The basic terms of this deal had all been already agreed upon by the banks and by Chrysler. We were just implementing them, we were technicians. We were arguing over whether a clause should be restrictive or non-restrictive, whether we should say 'any' or 'all', whether a semicolon should replace a period. It takes a peculiar kind of mind to enjoy this sort of thing—one that likes to look for typos. (Stewart 1983: 228)

Though the great majority of the banks agreed to the terms, three attempted to go their own route by filing lawsuits which Debevoise had to delay. The firm finally had to invoke the help of the Treasury Secretary to dispel the banks' fears. Piece by piece, the transaction was coming to a close: the European and Japanese banks agreed, but the Canadian banks would not. Ultimately, it took the efforts of both the U.S. and Canadian governments to reconcile the differences. When the loan guarantee application was accepted by the Treasury, the closing could occur. Because this closing would require hundreds of signatories signing thousands of documents, it was spread over three law firms in Wall Street.

The lawyers here are portrayed as highly sophisticated technicians. They are supposed to construct complex transactions so that every contingency is accounted for. It may be drafting a series of interlocking documents as in the Chrysler case or manipulating procedural matters so as to confound the opposition as in the IBM litigation. Cravath and Debevoise could quickly introduce large quantities of lawyers to cope with exigencies. This ability can easily overwhelm, and is often intended to, the opposing parties' lawyers, whether they be private practitioners or government lawyers. Either a problem can be dragged out for an extended time as in IBM, or it can be telescoped as in Chrysler.

These two examples illustrate the capacities of and the exigencies faced by large corporate law firms. Individual lawyers and the firms they work for must tolerate immense pressures over extended lengths of time. In both situations discussed, the firms were profoundly affected by the changes wrought by the nature of these cases. Both firms breached intra-firm rules—creating separate offices for IBM and committing more than 15 percent of the firm's resources to Chrysler—that had guided their development. But firms such as Cravath and Debevoise exist to serve the needs of capital. Though they may desire to retain a certain *status quo ante*, they are not, however, immune to the economic pressures that capital exerts, for good or ill. Business and the professions are held to different standards and treated differently by the state. But given the intricate web of connections that exist between the professions—especially those of law and accountancy—and commerce and industry, it is surprising that the professions have managed to maintain for so long the idea that they are unsullied by the norms of business and consequently should possess the privilege of regulating themselves without community interference.[11]

---

[11] An interesting, but related, sideshow was presented during the federal investigation of the state judiciary ("Operation Greylord") in Cook County, Illinois. Every lawyer who gave information about corrupt activities did so only after he was threatened with prosecution. See also Auerbach (1976) and Foster (1986).

In some respects, large law firms are coming to resemble their clients. Whereas law firms grew by taking in a class of associates each year, training them, and eventually conferring the mantle of partner on them, they now merge with and take over other law firms in order to acquire missing expertise and extend their client bases (Stevens 1987: 37-68). Partners are raided by other firms for their client-acquisition abilities. Firms, which were once considered stable entities since partners remained with the same one for life, are now becoming shifting congeries of profit centers that will exist only as long as expedient. "The picture [...] painted", Stevens writes of Finley, Kumble, the *primus inter pares* of this recent development in law practice, "[is] of a lateral-transfer and merger addict [which] has assembled a sloppy collection of disconnected legal practices into the McDonald's of law" (1987: 56; cf. Eisler 1990). The senior partner of Skadden, Joe Flom, said the following about the development of his large firm:

> We are building a series of boutiques, or specialists, in individual areas with enough overall strength in terms of quantity so that we can put 30 or 40 people to work on an emergency basis without destroying the continuing business of the firm. Now, a lot has been said about how dehumanizing it is to have a large firm. That is not necessarily so. What you have really is a series of smaller firms working toward a common end. If you are lucky and get the people working together on a transactional basis, it works quite well. When I say transactional basis, and I think this is the essence of where corporate practice is going, people are coming in for specific transactions. They are not looking for somebody to hold their hand and are not looking for somebody who is in the same clubs that they are in. They are looking for somebody who will do a particular job, and do it well. (Federal Bar Council 1984: 95-6)

Who, then, are lawyers beholden to? Where do their fiduciary interests lie? The answer may not be easily found: though lawyers move from firm to firm with their clients, they use the client base they have established as a resource to assist them in gaining and maintaining power within the context of the firm. Power gives them the ability to claim more money, more lawyers working on their clients matters, and to set policy in the firm. There is an intertwining of needs and benefits that feed into and reinforce each other. One commentator, Peter M. Brown, expressed the sentiment in this way:

> The large law firm has now become an American institution in itself. Lawyers in big firms are no longer accountable to individual clients. Rather, they are accountable to their law firm. Law firms are the entity, not the individual. The objective of the large law firm is simply to make money and to grow bigger in order to

make more money. To a large extent, the client has been left out in the cold. (Federal Bar Council 1984: 90)

If such is the case, and the evidence strongly suggests that the over-commercialization of the elite bar has taken place, the privileges accorded to the traditional concept of the bar are no longer appropriate and the conventional modes of community response to the legal profession are historically out of kilter with modern reality. For example, the statement by Carr-Saunders and Wilson at the beginning of this chapter is old-fashioned in tone but describes nothing that we can recognize in the late twentieth or early twenty-first centuries. Parson's theory of professions is also seriously outmoded in this context, especially in relation to the necessary key attributes of professions of universalism (e.g., equality of treatment) and collectivity orientation (i.e., service to the community) (Parsons 1968: 536; 1954: 34-50, 370-86). Neither of these features is a salient characteristic of large law practice (Gordon 2002). Rather, Becker drives home the point more straightforwardly, that the name "profession" is a label invoked for specific purposes, in this case, the preservation of self-regulation (Becker 1970; also see Larson 1977). Joe Flom succinctly put these points into context when he said:

> It is true that the large law firms are not as gentlemanly today as the practice of law was in 1948 when I got out (of law school). I maintain that is a very good thing because we have to remember that gentlemanliness is often a euphemism for the club syndrome. It is also an excuse for keeping things the way they were and is also very often an excuse for maintaining inadequate standards or incompetence. (Federal Bar Council 1984: 94)

But we might question whether in fact there have been any fundamental changes in the attitudes about the professionalism of lawyers. In the seventeenth century, some of the American colonies attempted to exist without lawyers. Virginia passed the following draconian statute:

> Whereas many troublesome suits are multiplied by the unskill-fullness and covetousness of attorneys, who have more intended their own profit and their inordinate lucre than the good and benefit of their clients: *Be it therefore enacted*, that all mercenary attorneys be wholly expelled from such office, except such suits as they have already undertaken, and are now depending, and in case any person or persons shall offend contrary to this act to be fined at the discretion of the court.[12]

---

[12] Act VII of November, 1645, 1 Hening 302.

Even Alexander Hamilton, one of the Founding Fathers of the Republic, after the Revolution sought out the most lucrative clients who happened to be Tories, the very people who resisted democracy (Finkelman 1984). Another highly esteemed American, Daniel Webster, was not above using his position as chairman of a Senate committee on war reparation in favor of his clients (Gordon 1984). Thus, even in the early days of the Republic, the seeds of modern corporate practice, with their concomitant professional infelicities, were being sown.

To some extent, external regulation of the bar has already occurred. Both the Internal Revenue Service and the Securities and Exchange Commission have issued rules on what constitutes proper behavior for those attorneys who practice before them. Moreover, they now take disciplinary action against lawyers who infringe their practice rules (Routh 1984). External regulation of this kind, however, is anathema to the concept of a self-regulating profession. But within the confines of the bar itself, the trends show a disquieting move. Complaints to state bar disciplinary agencies involving lawyers' fees jumped from 39,000 in 1984 to 54,000 in 1985.[13] Although calls for national regulation are made, the US legal profession is deaf to this particular siren call (Davis 2009).

Finally, though the examples only hint at this phenomenon, the practice of corporate law has become heavily routinized and commoditized. The documents drafted by the teams of lawyers at Debevoise were mostly taken from standard forms ever present on the computer. Although changes are made to fit the specific situation, no document is drafted from point zero. Much of the discovery process involving many highly priced associates entails examining boxes of intra-company memoranda to determine whether they should be seen by the other side, which requires little in the way of legal skills.[14] Much of this kind of work is now performed by paralegals who are considerably cheaper than associates (Holme 1969; Johnstone and Wenglinsky 1985; Rasmussen and Sedlacek 1999; DeStefano 2012). The general counsel to Arthur Young and Company, one of the former Big Eight accounting firms, asserted, somewhat presciently: "While I cannot empirically prove my next statement, in twenty years of having been exposed to the law, I believe that 65 percent of what most lawyers do can be done by nonlawyers and should be done by nonlawyers—whether that is a computer, a paralegal or some other support staff" (Federal Bar Council 1984: 107). The introduction of large-scale legal process outsourcing has brought his forecast to fruition.

---

[13] *U.S. News,* March 2, 1987: 27.

[14] It is precisely these activities that have given rise to the growth of legal process outsourcing to countries like India, and also corporate clients' refusals to pay for first year associates (Krishnan 2009; Aggarwal 2011).

Large law firms, corporate practice, mega-lawyering, big law, whatever we call the Leviathan, is a response to the needs and contingencies of capitalism in the late twentieth and early twenty-first centuries. The ethos of professionalism that Carr-Saunders and Wilson could write about so strongly in the 1930s no longer has much meaning within the present organization of law practice. New forms demand new modes of arrangement and theorizing. Perhaps the words of Carl Liggio—reminiscent of Niklas Luhmann when he wrote that "communication between lawyers [....] laid down in the form of [....] texts presumably has far-reaching consequences for the chances of forming a profession, but also creates specific dangers for the coherence of the profession" (Luhmann 1975: 117)—are an apposite conclusion to this part:

> In my judgment, we cannot be professional unless we pay attention to the business of the law. There is too much out there, too many growing complexities in our practice that strain our abilities to practice in the cottage industry manner of the past. Laws are getting too complex and multiple, the information that we have to deal with is too massive. Unless we try to approach it in a very orderly and proper format, we will lose our professionalism. What do I mean by that? Most lawyers think of themselves first and foremost as lawyers, when in reality, they are a very small part of a much larger profession or industry. That industry is the industry of information management. (Federal Bar Council 1984: 106)

This study will examine, among other things, lawyers' interactions with clients and other lawyers. In my view, this necessarily entails the study of rationality and reason. If the idea of rationality entails action in pursuit of goals, then in essence we have described the practice of lawyering.[15] Or have we? Parsons wrote that the professions adhered to the "primacy of the values of cognitive rationality" (1968: 536). But our current conceptions of the rationality of professions rest, however, on an unsure footing. Macroscopic analysis of the professions has all but swamped

---

[15] The following quotations indicate what I intend by the concept of rationality. "[The] rationality of the animal man consists in his unique capacity to articulate [the aims of survival and thrival] and contemplate diverse and effective means of achieving [them]; applying reason to tasks. The resulting wonders we call man's work: his societies, cultures and civilizations. They embody the principle of learning from experience—not relying on instinct or programming, not continuing on as before, not merging aim and achievement, not proceeding blindly. This is what applying reason to tasks amounts to" (Jarvie 1984: 23-4). "[S]cientific rationalities are neither stable features nor sanctionable ideals of daily routines, and any attempt to stabilize these properties or to enforce conformity to them in the conduct of everyday affairs will magnify the senseless character of a person's behavioral environment and multiply the disorganized features of the system of interaction" (Garfinkel 1967: 283).

an understanding of the microanalysis of professional practices that constitute professional and social interaction.[16]

In this study I will be looking at the development of rationality as a constituent feature of what lawyers do, the power relationships between lawyers and clients, and the process of lawyering.

Theory and Intellectual History

Because I am focusing on a "profession" that works for "clients" in a "rational" way, I will elaborate the theoretical and background features which inform these concepts. Schon, in his book *The Reflective Practitioner* (1983), argued that the prevailing paradigm for understanding what professionals do has been "technical rationality". Technical rationality depends upon stable institutional contexts, based on systematic knowledge, science, of course, being the ideal (Schon 1983: 23). Whereas technical rationality may fit the scientific ideal—and that is a contentious statement in itself (Lynch 1985)—in the case of the professions, especially those that do not depend on hard science, there are strict limits to the efficacy of the model of technical rationality. The classic deductive, scientific model depends on the *ceteris paribus* assumption, that all other things are held equal; that is, we can isolate and test for effects in specific variables. We avoid interaction effects. In law, despite Langdell's attempt to render the study of law and science in the classical sense (Stevens 1983; Chase 1985), interaction effects are unavoidable. Inert data are not within the reach of lawyers. Clients, legislatures, and Acts of God intrude in the solution of problems. Problem solving for lawyers, then, is a constantly shifting activity, reactive more than proactive, subject to the unknown. In the place of technical rationality, Schon inserted the idea of "knowing-in-action". He wrote:

> Once we put aside the model of Technical Rationality, which leads us to think of intelligent practice as an *application* of knowledge to instrumental decisions, there is nothing strange about the idea that a kind of knowing is inherent in intelligent action. Common sense admits the category of know-how, and it does not stretch common sense very much to say that the know-how is *in* the action—that a tightrope walker's know-how, for example, lies in, and is revealed by, the way he takes his trip across the wire, or that a big-league pitcher's know-how is in his way of pitching to a batter's weakness, changing his pace, or distributing his energies over the course of a game. There is nothing in

---

[16] On the arguments over the relative merits of micro- and macro-sociological research, see Collins (1980) and Giddens (1984).

common sense to make us say that know-how consists in rules or plans which we entertain in the mind prior to action. Although, we sometimes think before acting, it is also true that in much of the spontaneous behavior of skillful practice we reveal a kind of knowing which does not stem from a prior intellectual operation. (Schon 1983: 50-51)

One of the aims of this study is to attempt to capture the working of knowing-in-action as it relates to lawyers. By showing what lawyers actually do in practice, we begin to see what they attach significance to and what therefore, is entailed in being a lawyer. And this difficulty, of not knowing, under which we labor as lawyers, researchers and educators has been succinctly captured by Twining (1985: 1): "[W]hat is involved in teaching, learning and assessing individual professional skills is under-theorized and under-researched". He illustrated his thesis in this manner:

> Some years ago in Hong Kong I participated in an ... heated argument, between leading lawyers in the Commonwealth, about the thesis, advanced by an Australian silk,[17] that all basic professional skills are ineffable, unteachable and only capable of being picked up by trial and error on live clients. Among the most striking features of these debates were the following points:
>
> 1. Almost none of the protagonists had any competence in educational theory;
>
> 2. There was little or no empirical evidence for most of the assertions that were made by any side;
>
> 3. There seemed to be no coherent or articulated theory as to what constitutes basic lawyering skills nor as to how far these are intellectual skills that can be abstracted or otherwise identified in a manner that would make it possible and suitable for them to be taught, learned, or tested systematically in educational institutions. (Twining 1985: 1-2)[18]

Inasmuch as we know anything about the practices of lawyering, as distinct from the structural analyses of the profession, Twining is right in his view. We are woefully ignorant about what goes on in the real world of lawyering. The majority of research on the legal profession has to a large extent taken for granted what lawyers actually do (cf. Abel and Lewis 1989). This has led to a partial research program that has concentrated on

---

[17] A silk is a senior barrister who has been awarded the title of Queen's Counsel by the Lord Chancellor.

[18] I should add that Twining's remarks are set within the context of a debate about formal direct training in professional skills and problems of evaluating the effects of such training; but his argument, nonetheless, is relevant here.

the social structure of lawyers without specifying what it is lawyers do, or how lawyers relate to their clients. Indirectly, then, he highlights the fact that research on the legal profession has followed two paths over the past. On the one hand, there is the structural analysis, as I mentioned before, which has been the dominant force in the field. On the other, there is interactional analysis. I think it relevant for the purposes of this study to distinguish these strands clearly, so that the reader will see where the present contribution fits in with the current state of research. The structural approach is best exemplified by Heinz and Laumann's magisterial study of Chicago lawyers (1982), which surveys the Chicago bar in considerable depth as to its religious, ethnic, and class backgrounds, but lacks an analysis of what lawyers actually do. The picture presented to the reader is fixed. The interactional approach differs in that it attempts to produce a dynamic picture of the processes involved in being a lawyer. Mann's study (1985) of white-collar defense lawyers is a good exemplar of this approach.

The Structural Approach

The dominant paradigm in structural research has a long lineage, which can be seen in the works of the "Economics of the Legal Profession" surveys in the early 1930s—e.g., Garrison (1935) and Twining (1968)—through Blaustein and Porter (1954), through those of Carlin (1962; 1966) and Smigel (1969), to those of Heinz and Laumann (1982) and Heinz et al (2005). *The American Lawyer* (Blaustein and Porter 1954) was an early study in synthesizing the multi-faceted research that had been carried out in the seven years prior to publication. Besides being synthetic, it also had a distinct policy orientation. Much of its findings were the result of survey research, and, in addition, it had no discernible theoretical structure. But it laid a foundation for further research, without which we would be much the poorer.

The work of Carlin and Smigel represents the middle period of this chronology. In substance and methodology these studies were rather more sophisticated than Blaustein and Porter. Both authors were trained social scientists with some legal training.[19] Even though these studies are theoretically informed,[20] the theory does not generate, with the possible exception of Carlin, greatly enlightening explanations about lawyers in the social structure. Methodologically, Smigel's study is unsatisfactory for what it

---

[19] To be fair to Carlin, he is, in fact, both a lawyer and a sociologist.

[20] Smigel locates his work in the bed of organization theory (see, e.g., Whyte 1967); Carlin's books were concerned with the tensions inherent in status differentiation and the moral division of labor (see, e.g., Hughes 1958).

fails to tell us—e.g., what the life of a large law firm consists of—rather than what it does (cf. Auchincloss 1956). His perception of the Wall Street lawyer is superficial in its description of the persons and their work. However, this reflects the limited access researchers had to lawyers and law firms. Big law firms took great care to remain outside the limelight. Carlin's *Lawyers on Their Own* is far richer in its presentation of solo practitioners' work and their status contradictions.

The third and final phase of research on the legal profession is represented by Heinz and Laumann's *Chicago Lawyers*, which, as was Blaustein and Porter's work, was a landmark volume in research on the legal profession,[21] and their later revisions in *Urban Lawyer*. Theoretically and methodologically, this is research of the highest rank. The authors interviewed a large number of respondents over a range of topics: lawyers' work prestige of work, lawyers' values, and various background characteristics. One of the chief features of their study was an attempt to characterize the nature of the lawyer-client relationship. They found, for example, that the nature of legal work was determined more by "categories of client types rather than by doctrinal categories or other systematic theory" (1982: 35).

Heinz and Laumann argued there was a broad division between the corporate and personal business sectors; that there were two hemispheres containing different social, religious, and ethnic groups with different values who do different sorts of work for different types of clients. Theoretically, they rely on the conceptual framework devised by Terence Johnson in his work on professions (1972). The problem of autonomy of the professional practitioner, according to Johnson, is a function of the social distance that obtains between the producer and consumer. Johnson writes:

> There is an *irreducible but variable* minimum of uncertainty in any consumer-producer relationship, and, depending on the degree of this indeterminacy and the social structural context, various institutions will arise to reduce the uncertainty. Power relationships will determine whether uncertainty is reduced at the expense of producer or consumer. (1972: 41)

Adopting an historic perspective, Johnson found three main modes of resolution for the tension. First, he termed the situation where the producer controlled the relationship with the consumer "collegiate control" of

---

[21] Although I refer to the *final* phase here—and for heuristic purposes the focus of this discussion is the American legal profession—I should point out that there is a substantial body of research on the legal profession which has been conducted outside the United States as well as that which has adopted a comparative perspective. See, e.g., Dias et al (1981) and Abel (1985; 1988; 2003).

which "professionalism" was a sub-type. Second, "patronage", of which corporate patronage is a form, was used to describe circumstances where the consumer determined the nature of the relationship. Finally, Johnson labeled the category where a third party intervenes in the relationship between the producer and consumer to resolve the tension as "mediation", the most pervasive being the intervention of the state (1972: 45-6; see also Bystydzienski 1979).

Following Johnson, then, Heinz and Laumann argued that fields of practice developed within the corporate sector and were chosen as a result of client demand rather than producer determination. They found that the client determined goals and lawyers merely advised on the technical aspects of achieving them (Heinz and Laumann 1982: 365-73). In the personal business sector, clients were one-shot players who were largely unable to determine outcomes (cf. Rosenthal 1974). Here, the lawyers were in control—almost. If they were, there would be a nice inversion of the expected outcome, that is, corporate lawyers in a patronage based relationship and personal sector lawyers as the true professionals. Instead, Heinz and Laumann hedge by characterizing the personal sector as subject to some forms of external control and therefore nearer, perhaps, to mediation (1982: 362-5).

Their analysis, however, is light on the configurations of power in society. The role of the state is absent from Heinz and Laumann's conception of the lawyer-client relationship. The state not only intervenes between lawyers and clients[22] (as it does between doctors and patients (Berlant 1975)), but also support and reinforces the credentialing system (Freidson 1986). Thus, Johnson's mediative category is probably more comprehensive than Heinz and Laumann would like it to be. And though they refer to the phenomenon of the large law firm, they ignore the tensions within such bureaucratically organized institutions (Larson 1977, but cf. Halliday 1983, and Nelson 1988; Lazega 2001). That these organizations—large law firms—although nominally collegial, are in fact often similar to the corporations they serve, as I mentioned earlier, both in form and values, may not necessarily bespeak of a struggle of control, but rather an amicable accommodation of mutual ends. Part of the problem is Heinz and Laumann's attempt to impose a cross-sectional analysis on a theory that depends on historical explanation.

Macrosociological structural research does, however, give rise to many hypotheses about, in this case, the legal profession. It is enormously suggestive and forms a solid bedrock on which to build further research. Without it, we would be much the poorer. Nevertheless, it can only explain

---

[22] The state intrudes into more than just the personal sector (e.g., Katz 1982; 1985). It affects the relationship between corporate client and lawyer (Mann 1985).

some aspects of this field. In order to grasp a complete view, we need the fruits of the next approach, namely, the interactional approach.

The Interactional Approach

This approach has a much shorter ancestry than the structural. Whereas the structural approach builds on three decades of work, the interactional approach has only about one decade's worth of research behind it. Starting with Rosenthal (1974), the literature moves with Macaulay (1979) and Hosticka (1979) to Mann (1985), Griffiths (1986), and Sarat and Felstiner (1986); but also see Macaulay (1984), Cain (1983, 1985), Maynard (1984), Travers (1997), Mather (2003), and Scheffer (2010).

The interaction approach concentrates on different units of study than does the structural. Instead of taking aggregations of units and analyzing them, the interactionist researcher focuses on relatively few subjects and their intersubjective meanings. This is, in part, due to the desire to understand the components of the relationships actors form. Such an end requires two features: that theory to some extent arise from the research rather than being applied a priori; and that labor intensive kinds of research strategy be used.[23]

Rosenthal (1974) investigated the interaction between personal injury lawyers and their clients to discover if active client participation in the case increased damage awards. His original intention had been to study at first-hand the consultations between lawyer and client: he was unable to do so (cf. Danet et al 1980). Instead, Rosenthal intensively interviewed clients and lawyers, which created a rich picture of what occurred between the actors in the personal injury process. Hosticka (1979), however, was able to take the necessary next step and actually observe the interaction between legal services' lawyers and clients. Whilst providing no data from the interactions themselves, he provided a thick description which attempted to determine who controlled the progression of topics within the discourse.

Mann (1985) and Sarat and Felstiner (1986) displayed the talk between lawyers and clients as a resource for analysis. Mann himself became a participant-observer in a white-collar defense firm, which handled such

---

[23] On the first point regarding theory, Cain would disagree: "[M]ethodology must always be subordinate to theory. Existing theory and/or hunches about how theory might be developed and/or the sociological imagination tell us where to look and roughly what to look for. This applies, or should apply, even if we are considering a completely unexamined institution or set of practices." (Cain 1985: 139); conversely, see Glaser and Strauss (1967), who prefer to see theory generated as part of the research process.

cases as securities fraud, tax fraud, and bankruptcy fraud among others. In addition, he interviewed a wide spectrum of white-collar defense lawyers. Combining these data, Mann draws a finely grained picture of how white-collar defense is accomplished: we receive a perspective on the means lawyers and clients adopt to work or not with each other. Power, as conceptualized above, is displayed not just as a function of coercion—who calls the shots—but also as a function of knowledge as well as economic advantage.

Sarat and Felstiner concentrated on one interview to examine the ways "that clients are instructed in the meaning of law and the meaning of social relations contained in law and legal practices" (1986: 96). Their clients are less sophisticated than Mann's, being people who wish to divorce and who possess little or no knowledge of the legal process or system. Sarat and Felstiner show how lawyers tread a delicate line between wanting to "educate" clients and simultaneously "distance" themselves so they can avoid being blamed in case of error. Their lawyers also wanted to remain in control of the lawyer-client relationship and dictate their clients' strategy. Cain (1983), in her pilot study of English solicitors, constructed a theory of lawyers as "conceptive ideologists", based on Marx (1976), as guardians of a translation process that clients' problems have to undergo in order to receive the sanction of the law. It is through interactional studies such as these that knowledge of the legal profession and legal system is constructed, and that we learn how the diverse constituent elements constitute a system that, for all practical purposes, functions.[24]

There are two sub-types of interactional analysis that should be mentioned here. One is the journalistic type, less theoretical, of which Stewart's *The Partners* (1983) is the key exemplar. Stewart, a former *American Lawyer* writer, takes several cases handled by large, Wall Street type law firms and dramatizes the accounts of the conduct of the cases. This sort of writing is a product of the journalism of the *American Lawyer*, and also the *National Law Journal* and the *Legal Times* of Washington, which has burrowed its way into the bowels of corporate law firms, often to their annoyance.[25] But, sensational as it often is, such work is nonetheless extremely rich and suggestive for researchers interested in corporate lawyers and lawyering (see Flood 1996).

The second sub-type—the economic approach—is a theory-driven answer to the question: what do business lawyers do? (Gilson 1984) This work grows out of economic theory's concern with transaction costs (Wil-

---

[24] See also Heumann 1977, Mnookin and Kornhauser 1979, and Blumberg 1967.

[25] For example, the *American Lawyer* started by always being able to obtain copies of secret documents prepared by PwC which analyzed and compared the earnings of lawyers and law firms on Wall Street.

liamson 1979), but unfortunately it has no empirical base and tends to treat transactions as games. For example, Gilson expresses his hypothesis in this way: "My hypothesis—the business lawyer as transaction cost engineer—thus asserts the dual claim that skilled structuring of the transaction's form can create transaction value *and* that business lawyers are primary players at the game" (1984: 255).[26] This concentration on games places the interactions between lawyers and clients in an ironic light. It moves us away, however, from the embeddedness of social action that needs to be revealed and displayed (Garfinkel 1967: 35-75). Gilson's work has been followed up in different areas.[27] Okamoto (1995) further posited that business lawyers act as reputational intermediaries and this distinguishes them from other lawyers, and he has taken this work into teaching transactional lawyering (2009), which has culminated in a new online approach, called 'LawMeets' (www.lawmeets.com). Bernstein (1995) applied Gilson's ideas among Silicon Valley lawyers to show, using Suchman's (1994) work on Silicon Valley lawyers, that lawyers indeed created value for clients. Flood and Sosa (2008) have used Gilson to understand cross-border lawyering.

In general, the interactional approach brings us close to the continually unfolding, contingent nature of social interaction. Rather than producing a snapshot of a particular moment, this approach creates a dynamic, emerging picture of actors in motion tackling the rigors of life from moment to moment. It is a necessary element of any comprehensive study of how law firms function.

Two points we can take away here. First, the macrosociology of the professions sensitizes us to issues within particular professions and across professions and occupations, but there are inadequacies. Second, and, this cuts across both the structural and interactional perspectives, theory-driven approaches have a tendency to limit vision, since we lack basic knowledge about what people actually do in their occupations. Therefore, an inductive approach is a useful condition for the creation of theory. That is, more data-driven analyses are needed (Cicourel 1975). The inductive endeavor, however, has only a recent history in the sociology of the professions and inside the scope of the legal profession we are ignorant about large fields of practice. If we compare the situation to that of the sociology of the medical profession, the discrepancy is immediately appar-

---

[26] According to Gilson, capital asset pricing theory allows for no transaction costs. Moving from theory to the real world demands that such costs be accounted for. The concept of the transaction cost engineer is one who will reduce the friction caused by such costs to a minimum (1984: 251-53).

[27] See especially the 1995 symposium issue, "Business Lawyering and Value Creation for Clients," of the *Oregon Law Review* (vol. 74, no. 1).

ent (Strong 1979, and Fisher and Todd 1983). In part, this is due to the peculiar nature of the lawyer-client relationship, where loss of liberty, loss of property, the burden of stigma, and the disclosure of secrets, are real possibilities and can disable in more subtle ways than illness (see Danet et al 1980 and Rosenthal 1980).[28]

Introduction to the Research Setting

My own research was undertaken in a business law firm in Chicago.[29] The law firm, which I call Tischmann and Weinstock, was medium-sized and practiced in most areas of law including corporate, litigation, real estate, securities, labor and EEOC, estate planning, ERISA, and tax. Its clients ranged from large corporations and real estate funds through closely held businesses and wealthy families requiring sophisticated tax and estate planning to small businesses and individuals. In 2003 the firm merged with another long-established corporate law firm bringing to a close a hundred year history.

The idea to research a corporate law firm developed out of work I had done on barristers' clerks in England, and also my reading of Heinz and Laumann's *Chicago Lawyers* which had brought to my attention the fact that the corporate hemisphere was a virtual *tabula rasa* regarding re-search and that scholars of the legal profession could do no more than speculate about it. In addition, social research had displayed a tendency to study "down" at the expense of "up", that is, concentrate on the less privi-leged and less powerful members of society (cf. Marcus 1980 and Slovak 1979).

Two effects flow from the downward direction of research. One, we simply know less about powerful institutions. Since policy-making, for example, tends to be directed to those below, there is a more of a "need" to know about the poor and deprived rather than the wealthy. Two, one could perhaps argue that the kinds of practice corporate lawyers engage in are more intellectually stimulating and wide ranging than those of personal sector lawyers. Heinz and Laumann differentiated fields of law by practice characteristics comparing the corporate and personal business clusters.

---

[28] I am omitting two further approaches that have been used extensively in recent years: Bourdieu's field theory, and Latour's Actor Network Theory. See Dezalay and Garth (1986) and Latour (2010).

[29] My agreement with the firm included the proviso that confidentiality would be re-spected, so the names that follow in the examples are pseudonyms. In addition, I have altered certain features of the case studies—with no effect to the analysis—to preserve confidentiality. My fieldwork was conducted during the period 1984 to 1986 with some later returns and conversations with Tischmann's lawyers.

The range of fields of law greater in the corporate clusters, and they scored higher than the personal clusters on such characteristics as "high on technical expertise" and "high change in law". My general focus in the research was primarily on such matters as: what do lawyers actually do? What kind of relationships do lawyers form with clients? What sorts of clients does a law firm have? How do lawyers transact business with other lawyers? Are corporate lawyers as lacking in autonomy as Heinz and Laumann indicate? These questions could be at best only tentative and the answers seemed to me to be best sought through participant-observation (Johnson 1975; Douglas 1976; Katz 1982; Flood 1983, 2005). Following this route would limit me in answering the macro questions, but since I was mainly concerned about formulating data-driven analyses rather than theory-driven ones, it made sense to me to adopt a method that brought me close to the subjects of my research. Thus, the questions listed above were raised more to sensitize me to certain issues without blinding me to others that might arise during the research.

One point about the difficulties associated with participant-observation is that, by its very nature, it demands closeness with one's subjects that is not found in other methods. And as Danet et al (1980) so poignantly described, lawyers are among the most difficult of professionals to get close to. Few have done so. The main stumbling block, of course, is the potential breach of lawyer-client confidentiality. When I first approached the law firm with the idea of doing research, this was the first item on the agenda in our discussion. My proposal to overcome the hurdle, which was accepted by the firm, was for them to hire me as a temporary associate, thus bringing me within ambit of the lawyer-client privilege. Mann (1985), in his study of white-collar defense lawyers, adopted the same tactic. It, perhaps more importantly, brought me within their insurance policy (Chambliss and Wilkins 2002). Although my academic training is in law, both in Great Britain and the United States, I am not admitted to practice in either place, unlike Mann who was admitted to the New York Bar.[30] Sarat and Felstiner (1985), however, employed no such device to gain entry. They instead spent considerable time discussing their project with prospective lawyer subjects, but remained at all times outsiders.

As a result of this relationship, I was able to observe and participate in the work of the firm. Most cases I only saw parts of rather than their whole "lives".[31] I collected my data by taking notes in the meetings and

---

[30] At times during the research, I felt the absence of the correct symbols created some small difficulty for me. For example, if I wrote a brief, I could not sign it.

[31] This is largely due to the nature of much of legal work, especially litigation, which progresses—if that is the *appropriate* term—in fits and starts over long periods. For example, in one case, a federal magistrate took 18 months to hand down a decision on a

talking with the lawyers involved. During this part of my research I was at the law firm almost every day, and hence I was able to keep track of the meetings and developments in the case studies (as well as follow other aspects of firm activity). As with any ethnography there is an element of serendipity involved and the selection of incidents relies on what the observer encounters. I spent much time wandering the corridors of the firm chatting to people to find out what was happening. I got two things out of this: people became used to having me around—even despite my odd accent—and I found out what was happening or about to happen. My time in the firm had to be reaffirmed constantly so that lawyers would let me sit in meetings and the like.[32] I enjoyed being a lawyer, as I was called on to do legal work occasionally. I used to like in particular that one partner had a part-share in a very good pizza parlor and he would order in pizzas.

This study is divided into two parts. Part I is the ethnography of the law firm. It depicts in broad strokes the ways in which the firm functions: structure, recruitment, work and getting clients. Part II is rather different in that I attempt to analyze in detail what corporate lawyers' work is. I make extensive and intensive use of case studies, which display lawyers' interactions with each other and with clients. It is this part that anatomizes lawyering by trying to show how work is accomplished. A central finding of the study is that in the practice of law one finds very little law. Instead, one sees substantial amounts of face-to-face interaction, or conversing on the telephone, but legal research and writing, as such, constitute a minor portion of lawyer's work.

---

motion to dismiss for summary judgment. That, of course, is beyond the lawyer's control.

[32] My admission to the firm was of course sanctioned by the senior partners, but because they gave permission didn't mean anyone else would necessarily be helpful. So I had to negotiate my presence around the firm constantly self-monitoring how I was being perceived. I found, for instance, that if I left the firm for a break I had to renegotiate my way back in. It didn't take long for one's presence to be forgotten. I therefore tried to avoid breaks while doing my observation.

2

The Structure and Work of the Tischmann Law Firm

Tischmann and Weinstock is a law firm with a substantial history in Chicago. Two Jewish lawyers began the firm at the turn of the century. By the 1920s it had grown to five partners and by the 1950s contained around 15 partners. In mid-1987 there were approximately 80 lawyers in Tischmann—45 partners and 35 associates—of whom about 85 percent were Jewish, 20 percent were women (predominantly associates), and none were from any other ethnic minority group. The firm ranked, at that time, in the third quartile of the 500 largest law firms in the United States.

In the way Wald frames it (2008a, 2008b), Tischmann was a classic Jewish law firm. Most of its lawyers were Jewish and they were prominent in the Jewish community. The firm was composed largely of two groups, the German Jews and the Russian Jews. The former considered themselves superior to the latter, which was reinforced because the Russian Jews agreed with this. The firm's clientele had been found initially within the Jewish community. That community had its own country clubs, banks, and other forms of commercial life. Perhaps the only aspect of Tischmann that was not Jewish was that its lawyers were educated at non-religious affiliated law schools such as Chicago and Northwestern.

The firm is organized like most other law firms of comparable size. That is, it is departmentalized and governed by a management committee of "the great and the good" (i.e., the biggest rainmakers in the firm; see chapter 5 for details of rainmaker and governance). (Tolbert and Stern 1987; Empson 2013).

The Politics of Organization

The physical morphology of Tischmann is like that of most other law firms. The lawyers' officers are laid out around the external perimeter, with their secretaries outside their doors. The interior is taken up with the paralegals offices, file rooms, and the library. Although Tischmann occupied one and a half floors, it would soon take over the remainder of the second floor. The lawyers tended to cluster according to field. Litigators lined the east wall of floor one, with corporate and real estate dominating the east and south walls. The west wall had a mixture of labor, employee benefits, tax, and securities. Floor two was predominantly real estate, a big part of Tischmann's work.

The most prestigious walls along which to have one's office were the east and the north. They were preferred over the south and west because they had better views and were less powerfully affected by the sun. As to be expected, then, the three largest groups—corporate, real estate, and litigation—were arranged along these walls. The other variables that affected placement in the office were seniority and productivity. The most senior lawyers occupied the corner offices. These offices were large and light, having two sets of windows. One exception to this was the managing partner, who had a large office along the north wall of the second floor. When the merger between Tischmann and another law firm, Bernstein and Feldman, occurred, Tischmann took over part of floor two, on which it had an option but had not occupied previously. In so doing, a new corner office was created. Another senior partner who, until the merger, had occupied the southeast corner office on floor one, agreed to move to the new corner office to allow one of the incoming partners to take over his old office. During the remodeling one of the walls of the senior lawyer's office was moved in about one foot to accommodate an accountant's office next door (which is even smaller than an associate's office). He was livid, taking this minuscule loss of space as a reduction of his status. At one stage he was demanding the wall be moved back to its original position, which would have left the next-door office unusable. Also if partners were not generating many clients or billing sufficient hours, they could find themselves being relocated to inferior positions, or being prevented from relocating to a better one. The geopolitics of office placement were important considerations in establishing esteem and status within a law firm.

Another matter of success within a law firm was membership on an office committee. There were six internal committees at Tischmann: management; Finance; Office Administration; Associates; Practice Development; and Professional Conduct. I classify the Recruitment Committee as an external committee since its members spent most of their time and attention focused outside the office. Each committee had around seven members. The most important of the committees was the management Committee: it took all the major decisions that affected the firm and its members. Among other things it decided partners' draws, who would be partner, who would be a capital partner, and acted as a clearing house for the other committees.

The Finance Committee ambit included preparing the annual budget and setting the billing rates for the attorneys. The Office Administration Committee supervised the office manager and support staff (i.e., secretaries and messengers). The Associates Committee reviewed associates' work and recommended their salaries and bonuses; it also coordinated its work with the Recruitment Committee. The Professional Conduct Committee supervised pro bono cases taken by the firm.

The committee which was the least successful was the Practice Development Committee. One reason for this, according to the managing partner, was that it was staffed by successful lawyers who already have enough business. In his opinion it should have had members who had no business and therefore need to find it. In sum, the most important committees were the first three, management, finance, and office administration. Membership on one of these committees was a symbol of success within the firm.

Lawyers' Work

The core areas of work in Tischmann were corporate, real estate, litigation, estates and probate, securities, labor, and tax. Chapter 4 presents a detailed breakdown of who does what kinds of work in the firm. The most successful areas were real estate and corporate. Litigation mainly existed to service other areas. There is, however, another way to examine lawyers' work.

Using the lawyers' time records for two two-week periods in 1985, I compiled an index of lawyers' task (see Harbaugh and McDonald 1977; Hellman 1991). The index, generated from the time records, contains the following categories (with examples of specific elements in parentheses): compiling (documents); conference with (lawyers, other persons); drafting (agreements); meetings (depositions, clients); office administration (billing); omissions (vacations, illness); preparation (negotiations); recruiting (interviewing); research (cases); reviewing (draft contracts); revising (closing documents); sending out (plans); teleconference with (lawyers, other persons).

The main activity of lawyers is talking on the telephone with persons other than Tischmann lawyers (31.1%). If we add talking with other Tischmann lawyers by telephone the percentage rise to 32.5 percent. The second largest activity is talking face to face with other Tischmann lawyer (12%). Talking with Tischmann lawyers and others takes up 18.1 percent of lawyers' billable time. If we sum time spent at meetings outside the office (2.6%), office meetings (0.7%), telephoning and talking face to face, we find lawyers spend 53.9 percent of their chargeable time talking. Writing, however, takes up only 20.8 percent (16.3%—drafting; 4.5% revising). Certain tasks are carried out by specific types of lawyers. For example, partners rather than associates attend meetings, and then mostly mid-level and senior partners. Similarly, talking with other Tischmann lawyers is done more by senior and mid-level partners than by associates.[33] Research is an activity mainly carried out by associates. Reviewing and revising are mostly done by senior people, ranging from senior associates to mid-level partners. Table 2.1 lists the largest frequencies for each category of tasks.

TABLE 2.1

Largest Frequencies for Each Category of Lawyers' Tasks

TASK	FREQUENCY	PERCENT
Telephone with external persons	4128	31.1
Conference with Tischmann lawyers	1598	12.0
Draft letters	1027	7.7
Review Documents	557	4.2
Draft documents	308	2.3
Attend meetings	238	1.8
Review files	216	1.6
Research	209	1.6
Review correspondence	203	1.5
Revise documents	183	1.4
Telephone with Tischmann lawyers	163	1.2
Review agreements	138	1.0
Send out documents	108	0.8
Revise agreements	105	0.8
Billing	91	0.7
Committee meetings	89	0.7
Vacation days	89	0.7
Interviewing	52	0.4
Prepare meeting	47	0.4
Prepare deposition	43	0.3
File documents	38	0.3

Across fields of law, the lawyers who talk most amongst each other, both face to face and on the telephone, are the litigators (18.5%) and the real estate people (17.9%), with the corporate lawyers trailing at 12.3 percent. The real estate lawyers do most of the writing. Considerable

---

[33] One of the problems associated with analyzing such self-reported data is not knowing if, e.g., the lack of associates' involvement with talking is due to the fact that they have not yet "learned" to count it as a reportable event (Garfinkel 1967; Parkes and Thrift 1980).

research remains to be done in this area, though aspects of it will be touched on in later chapters.

One final point should be added here. Tischmann undertakes considerable quantities of pro bono work for a range of clients from foundations to various civil rights committees. In one year, two partners contributed 1,000 hours to one pro bono case.

The Support Staff

Lawyers are only part of the structure of the law firm. In addition, there are secretaries, paralegals, messengers, librarians, word processors, accountants, data processors, mailroom clerks, and telecommunications people. All of them are vital to the proper operation of a law firm. An office manager is in charge of these personnel. The office manager also has a second function, which is sending and collecting bills. His two functions, collecting bills and overseeing personnel, sometimes cause conflict. From the partners' perspective, the office manager is there to protect and increase their profits. This means maintaining tight control over costs, of which salaries are the majority portion. Following the merger with Bernstein, when several secretaries followed their attorneys into Tischmann, office procedures were rationalized. All the support staff had to log in and out during the day. If they were late, their salaries were docked. Because they perceived their salaries already low, many secretaries left after having their salaries reduced. Much of the office gossip turned on how much of a "bastard" the office manager was, and who was about to suffer his wrath next. Some of the secretaries were aggrieved at how they were treated by the office manager. They felt he conveniently forgot the many occasions when they came in during weekends to help their attorneys, when he decided to dock their pay for some infraction.

Connected with the role of secretaries is the state of office technology. My study of Tischmann coincided with the transfer to personal computers. All documents were being moved away from a central pool to the individual secretaries. The centralized word processing pool was recognized as a disaster, especially for the associates who drafted most of the larger documents. The most typical complaints about the pool were delays in producing the documents, too many errors, and accidental erasure, especially when deadlines approached. In one instance, a junior partner had to append a motion requesting the late filing of a brief caused by a word processor malfunction. Fortunately, the court granted the request. Such complaints were always being brought up at associates' meetings. As a result of the complaints, the management committee decided to hire a consultant who recommended that the central pool be retired and that each secretary have her own PC.

There were 11 paralegals at Tischmann: three in litigation, four in probate, and five in real estate. Their role is to carry out most of the routine matters, e.g., filling in forms, checking court dockets, summarizing depositions, filing documents with various clerks in the city and county offices. Whereas associates' starting salaries were then in the region of $50,000 a year and more, paralegals rarely earned more than half that amount. And this is the main reason for their existence: they are inexpensive compared to associates. The job offered no real career opportunities. Unlike their British counterparts, they could not, after a certain time, become attorneys (Johnstone and Hopson 1967; Johnstone and Flood 1982; Francis 2011). Hence, most paralegals were women who stayed in the job for an average of three or four years. Out of the eleven, two were male.

The Merger

During the 1980s the firm merged, and also took on several lawyers from a different firm. The merger swelled the ranks of Tischmann immensely, adding some twenty lawyers. In some respects, to call the joining of the two firms a merger was a misnomer, since Tischmann took over Bernstein, in a friendly fashion. At the time of the merger, Bernstein was desperately seeking a "White Knight" (i.e., a protector) to help solve its problems. Bernstein had been losing many of its mid-level attorneys because the two senior partners refused to hand over significant responsibility for clients to the other partners, nor would they encourage their partners to generate their own clienteles, preferring instead to have the firm's other lawyers work for them. The loss at the middle level created another problem. Bernstein held an expensive lease on a suite of offices in the downtown area of Chicago. As the lawyers left, the remaining partners found themselves being slowly bankrupted by the lease, and moreover, were realizing how difficult it was to undertake clients' work with insufficient resources.

Tischmann knew that if it took over the ailing Bernstein, what it was really getting was, in the words of the managing partner, "the book of business of three elderly partners". It took the risk. The risk, however, entailed borrowing large sums of money from the bank, something Tischmann was not used to doing, being essentially an under-capitalized and self-resourced law firm as are many law firms. Financially, especially in the short term, the merger was not the success that Tischmann hoped it would be. Bernstein's accounts receivables never came up to expectations, and one of the elderly partners died nine months into the merger, creating doubt about whether his clients would stay with Tischmann. As the managing partner said, "We needed him to stay alive for eighteen months at least to have the clients commit to us." The merger also exacerbated the already poor partner-associate ratio at Tischmann, giving Tischmann twice as many partners as associates. (After the merger, a few former Bernstein lawyers were pruned from the stock. See Chapters 4 and 6 for more discussion of this topic.)

The experience of the merger was bitter for some of the Tischmann partners. They objected to borrowing money to finance the process of merging, and they felt cheated by the poor state of Bernstein's accounts receivable. Since that time the managing partner resisted further merger proposals until 2003 when Tischmann itself was taken over by a much larger firm.

3

Recruiting New Lawyers

The lifeblood of any law firm of size is the steady stream of new recruits. Without them the firm will wither and die (Dinovitzer 2004). A law firm is a flow; it is a constantly changing flux of people joining an organization, leaving to go to another, leaving to become judges or other public officials, becoming partners, and so on. A firm may be known for its senior partners—in some cases, the "name" partners (those senior partners whose names compose the name of the firm)—but they have to be supported by an infrastructure of "minders and grinders" (the junior partners and associates who essentially create the profit for the senior partners). The very best grinders, which every firm wants, for the corporate bar are in limited supply. The consequence of this is that the elite corporate bar spends tremendous amounts of time and money on recruiting new associates.

The recruiting process is tied to the law school academic year, which usually begins late August. Law firms typically conduct in-school interviews near the start of the academic year. Choosing which schools to interview at is not a simple matter. The pattern looks like a set of concentric rings with the highest density at the center, and becoming more scattered towards the periphery. At the centre is the city in which the firm is located. In Tischmann's case, Chicago has a range of schools from the top five national elite all the way to the local proprietary schools unaffiliated with any university. The difficult choice is which schools to interview at outside Chicago.

Tischmann's usual source of recruits has always been the law schools at the University of Chicago and Northwestern University, with a preference for the former.[34] In recent years, however, with increasing competition in the market for graduates from elite law schools, Tischmann has begun to hire graduates from the higher echelons of the regional and local law schools.

Tischmann has a recruitment committee, of about eight people, which is supposed to reflect the various departments and levels in the firm (Kanter 1983). Thus, it includes litigators, real estate lawyers, corporate

---

[34] Here's a teaser. There is a law professor at a West Coast law school who graduated from Chicago and was an associate with Tischmann.

counsel, partners, associates, and a paralegal. Every matter related to recruiting is filtered through this committee.

The committee's first assignment is to decide how many recruits they would like to hire and where they will interview for them. This is not an easy task because the recruiting process is multi-layered; they can be planning up to four years in advance. No firm likes to hire a new associate, if possible, without having advance knowledge of that associate's capabilities. And paper credentials are insufficient, though necessary, to satisfy the calculus. In order to survey the potential pool more critically, the firm takes on summer associates. These are students either in their second year of law school or, less usually, in their first year. Typically, if a summer associate is competent, he or she will be offered a job following graduation.

So, the committee balances several factors simultaneously: the number of offers it has outstanding to previous summer associates, the number of associates entering after having done a clerkship for a judge, and the number of summer associates it would like to have for the next summer. This calculus may be compounded further by the prospect of lateral hires entering the firm.[35] On top of this, it has to decide where to interview. Tischmann still hankers after the elite schools, so the committee likes to include Harvard and Michigan on its roster. In fact, Michigan has become a key school for Tischmann to recruit from. Although only a few of its lawyers are from there, the reputation of the school, combined with its relatively close proximity to Chicago, makes it an attractive potential source of recruits.

As I mentioned earlier, Tischmann has suffered competition for high quality recruits from the larger firms. This has resulted in Tischmann having to canvass more widely than before and carefully choose out of state law schools to interview potential recruits at. Schools such as Minnesota and Wisconsin-Madison have thus risen in attractiveness.

The next step in the recruiting process is to interview students at the school. These interviews follow a standard format at most schools. The firm submits a resume and invites students to sign up for interviews on a particular day. If the school has a lottery system because certain firms are exceedingly popular, then the student enters that. However, law firms will sometimes circumvent the lottery because it may not draw what they consider "the best and the brightest".

The interviews last for twenty minutes. The applicants dress up in business suits, even though simple observation shows they spend most of their time in jeans and casual wear, which they change back into once the

---

[35] A lateral hire is an attorney who enters the firm after having practiced elsewhere.

interview is over. Nevertheless, the appropriate symbols must be articulated precisely. The students will have submitted their resumes with lists of courses taken, with grades; law review position, if any; and previous employment.

The interviews, though cursory at best, concentrate on the student resume and the personality of the student: does he or she look like the right type of person to fit in Tischmann? When the members of the recruiting committee have completed the preliminary round of interviews and given pizza parties at the schools (the pizza party at Michigan is an important event symbolically, even though the first year they held it only a handful turned up, fewer, in fact, than the lawyers present) they meet to decide who should be called back.

The "call back" is when the operation changes from being a wide canvass to an intensive probe. The committee design large charts, which when read from left to right, show the candidate, expected date of graduation, who interviewed him or her, who is supposed to monitor the candidate (called a "click person"), and whether an offer has been made and accepted. The call back is still, however, an intermediate stage where the firm is in constant competition with others for the same candidates.

"Bringing them through" the firm or office, another name for the call back, is a long and tedious process. The candidate is brought into town the night before, if from out of town, and appears at the office the next day at nine o'clock. The committee's paralegal takes charge of the candidate and tells him how to fill in his expense forms for flights and hotel and then introduces him to an associate who will be his "mentor" for the day. The committee will have arranged about seven or eight interviews with a range of partners and associates.

Arranging these interviews is usually delegated to the paralegal. To her—paralegals are usually women—it is an unpleasant chore. The problem is that the paralegal is at the bottom of the totem pole in the firm and therefore has little persuasive power and no coercive power at all. It is easy to refuse a paralegal or fob her off with an excuse, and many lawyers do this. The result is that there is a pool of "regular" interviewers, those who for one reason or another, e.g., civic duty, not much work to do, will undertake to do interviews either in the normal course of events or to fill in. This is often a contentious point with the members of the recruiting committee, who feel cheated by their colleagues who are not contributing their fair share of work for the firm's future.

The interviews are draining affairs for the candidates because they are invariably asked the same questions over and over again, and each time they must attempt to retain a certain freshness of answer. The task is not always so easy for the interviewers, either, because given the nature of the entrants to the legal profession, many of the candidates appear equally qualified (Warkov with Zelan 1965; Zemans and Rosenblum 1981; Heinz and Laumann 1982; Dinovitzer 2004). To a large extent, candidates are viewed as fungible commodities. Unless the candidate has some outstanding feature on his resume, the interview can be hard work for both interviewer and interviewee. Each interviewer fills in a standard form giving details about personality, intelligence, drive, etc.

At lunch, the candidate is taken out by three or four associates. This is still part of the process: how well does the candidate act in a social situation? When the remainder of the interviews are completed in the afternoon, the candidate leaves. For the candidate, the worst part of the process is over; if successful, he will merely have to sit back and let himself be wooed.

The next step for the committee is to gather in the interview forms, read them, and try to reach a decision on the suitability of the candidate. In addition, they review the reports on the candidates' writing samples. Each candidate is asked to submit a legal memorandum, a brief, or some other piece of legal writing, which one associate, who was a part-time teacher at a local law school, read, commented on and graded.

At this stage the comments can be very brutal. A candidate not only has to measure up academically, but also in personality. The "wrong attitude" can be a barrier. One of the interpretative tasks the committee has to perform is to determine what weight to assign to the remarks of the various interviewers. One senior partner would list his comments extensively, but always finish with the recommendation that the candidate not be hired. His reason was that Tischmann could not expect to compete with the larger firms. Instead he thought the firm should hire laterals only after they had been with larger firms for two or three years. The committee always regarded his recommendations with derision.

Another partner was viewed as a consistently regular interviewer whose comments were valued. But because the committee chair felt this partner had done too many interviews, with the danger that this judgment could become stale, he was taken off the interviewer list temporarily. Some interviews, though, are known to be overly sympathetic, others unduly critical and harsh. And of course these elements are found within the committee as well. One committee member was very insistent that only the brightest and most aggressive should be hired—"no wimps"—since they would ultimately make the best lawyers. Others in the committee pointed out that to have nothing but clones of this particular partner around the office would make the place insufferable. There were other qualities that people should have, (but not necessarily in lawyers, he claimed). After the various issues have been hammered out and determinations have been made as to who is good and desirable and who is not, the committee begins the courtship ritual of making offers.[36]

In some respects, this is the most risky part of the process. In the elite bar, law firms are in a sellers' market. Since students with the good resumes will be sought after by several firms, Tischmann has to be able to sell itself as a special organization. Given that it is a medium-sized general practice firm, there are certain factors that are out of its range. It cannot provide the large, "sexy" cases that the large firms do,[37] or rather not as many and as regularly; and it might not be able to compete in salary with the larger firms, though the differences will be marginal. The firm competes by claiming that we consist of people who know each other, who engage in a variety of work which we will share with you, and you will stand an excellent chance, assuming you do good work, of making partner. Thus, the collegial spirit of the firm is made paramount, accompanied by the characteristic that it is somewhere where good work will be recognized and rewarded.

The candidate and firm then begin to court their way to a resolution. This means the firm puts pressure on the candidate to accept an offer quickly. Once the offer is accepted, all others received by the candidate are redundant. In the normal course of events, an acceptance of an offer by a second year student effectively means that the law student will hope to return to the firm as a first year associate following graduation from law school. Special problems occur among those who are first year students, third year students, and those who wish to split their summer between two firms and perhaps two cities.

If the firm is unable to fill its quota of second year students in the "summer program", it then looks to first year students. These, to some extent, are gap fillers. They cannot fill the role that the second year students do, since they are not necessarily going to come back for their second summer nor return as associates. They do provide publicity value, since they can be expected to spread the good word that Tischmann is a good firm at which to spend the summer. One year Tischmann had the problem of having a preponderance of first year students over second years. This was in large part due to their insistence on recruiting at only those schools they had traditionally relied upon for candidates. Once they started interviewing students from a wider range of schools, that particular problem evaporated.

---

[36] There were no black lawyers at Tischmann. I never heard anyone saying we won't hire blacks but its Jewish ideology seemed to prevent their being considered. See Wilkins and Gulati (1996).

[37] The large, sexy case might not be desirable as the experience of the antitrust suit against IBM showed in Chapter 1.

Even with a steady supply of second year students, the supply might not match the demand for summer associates in a particular year. Although there may be commitments from the current crop of second year summer associates to appear the following year as first year associates, there will be some attrition. Filling the shortfall requires the firm to hire third year students straight into positions as associates.

Taking a third year student without prior knowledge of his work is considered a risk. The central question is: why didn't he or she get a job in the firm where they spent their summer? There are, of course, a range of answers: she did not like the work the firm did, e.g., insurance defense work (boring); he decided to move to a different city; or, the firm did not like him. Tischmann's recruitment committee always put this possible answer high on their list, and a member of the committee who knows someone at the "summer firm" is deputed to call and find out why the student was not given a job: "Was he a jerk?"; "Couldn't he cut it?"; and so forth. If the answers are favorable, and the students writing samples are good, then the committee courts the candidate.

Since the competition for students is keen, the committee designates a member to monitor a student, i.e., be a "click" person as the committee calls it. The click person calls regularly to enquire if the student needs any further information, whether the student would like to talk to anyone in the office about aspects of practice, and most importantly, whether the student has yet made up his mind about the offer. This courting can take weeks.

Once a student accepts an offer, his resume is circulated around the firm. And once the summer class is full, the committee tries to work out possible places for the summer associates to sit. One of Tischmann's major problems has been a great shortage of space, so that where to put the summer associates frequently becomes a game of musical chairs. The ones most often displaced are the paralegals, who are shunted into conference rooms or forced to double or triple occupy rooms.

One of the concepts behind having second year law students spend the summer in the law firm is that their time should be programed. The "summer program" provides that the summer associates should receive a cross-section of work from within the firm and be told how well or poorly they are doing. Rarely do such programmatic intentions last. The summer associates find themselves spending most of their time in the library researching legal problems and writing memoranda, which is not very different from what they do in law school.

With a firm the size of Tischmann, other problems arise. In order to establish a program, the committee set up a group that would receive all assignments to summer associates and distribute them according to the summer associates' needs and the demands that were currently placed on them. No attorney was supposed to hand out a project directly to a summer associate. This system invariably crashed after a while and the summer associates began to receive their assignments directly from partners and associates. As a result, some associates became overloaded.

In addition, reviews of work were often neglected or skimpy. If anything, the difficulty of maintaining a normal practice and trying to set up a program for inexperienced summer associates are virtually incompatible unless the firm is prepared to devote adequate resources to the program. Thus, some of the larger firms in this field have been able to run more successful programs. Since Tischmann runs its business with the philosophy that lean is best, there have been few people to spare for the problems that summer associates encounter.

One problem Tischmann found itself encountering was the phenomenon of "split summers", which entails a summer associate agreeing to work at two law firms in one summer, often in different cities. Law firms have traditionally disliked split summers on the grounds that neither the student nor the firms have long enough to evaluate the other. But, given the shortages of elite associates, there is little law firms have been able to do besides plead with them not to split summers.

Proms and Parties

Summer clerkships are rarely a realistic experience of what working in a law firm will be like (White 1983: 59). The summer associates are not asked to work hard; indeed, they are forbidden to work long hours. They are expected to taste the entire menu of what the firm has to offer in the way of different kinds of work. For this they are paid extremely well. Some of the larger firms in New York and Los Angeles include housing and car rentals in their packages to summer associates.

In addition to these benefits, the firm tries to sell itself to the summer associates by providing a range of social activities for them. Tischmann holds its "prom", a formal dinner and dance for the attorneys and their spouses and significant others during the summer, so that the summer associates can participate. The firm tries to make the location interesting: one year the prom was held on a boat while sailing on Lake Michigan; and another was held at a country club. The firm picnic, to which the entire firm is invited, is also held during the summer. In addition, summer associates are taken to baseball games and invited to parties held at partners' homes over the course of the summer.

Throughout the summer the lawyers in the firm monitor the progress of the summer associates. They gossip continuously about them. By the end, the recruitment committee has a fairly clear picture of whom they would like to offer a full-time position to on graduation. However, being given an offer does not preclude a student from interviewing elsewhere during the third year to see if another offer might not better the original.

The recruitment process, then, is both expensive and time consuming. Those most affected are the mid-level and senior associates and the junior partners; some, but not many, mid-level partners may also be involved. At Tischmann, it is the fourteenth most demanding task that lawyers are involved with, taking up 0.4 percent of their time. To summarize this process, it is basically a long, involved courtship ritual where two actors, law student and firm, dance around each other for up to two years (from the first interview on campus to final hiring) before mating.

4

The Care and Feeding of Associates and Partners

Introduction

In 1899 Paul D. Cravath became a partner in the firm of Seward, Guthrie and Steele, which was eventually to become Cravath, Swaine and Moore. Seven years into his partnership, Cravath initiated the "Cravath system" (Swaine 1946). The Cravath system became to law firms what Langdell's case method was to law schools (Stevens 1983). It was the first systematic approach to law firm staffing and resource allocation, which ultimately would influence recruitment and staffing in law firms around the country.

The Cravath system was simple in its design: it required that the best law school graduates be employed, then trained rigorously and broadly, and if they showed promise and achievement, they would be made partners in the firm. The system opposed the practice of hiring men (as virtually all lawyers were in those days) who had been trained elsewhere, for Cravath believed they would have habits of mind that would be inconsistent with the ones he was trying to inculcate.

Cravath's ideas were radical for their times. He insisted that associates be paid a salary, and, with the prospect of a partnership before them, they would work hard and consistently for the firm. If at the end of their probationary period, usually six years, they did not display sufficient mental ability, combined with personality, judgment, and character, they would be asked to leave. But the firm would help them find employment elsewhere, especially in the corporate departments of their clients, thus building up a strong network of Cravath people who would remain loyal to the firm.

The system also required that associates be trained thoroughly within the firm. But, as Cravath noted,

> At the outset of their practice Cravath men are not thrown into deep water and told to swim; rather, they are taken into shallow water and carefully taught strokes. The Cravath office does not follow the practice of many other offices of leaving small routine matters entirely to young men fresh from law without much supervision, on the theory that a man best learns how to handle cases by actually handling them. Under the "Cravath system" a young man watches his senior break a large problem down into its component parts, is given one of the small parts and does thoroughly and exhaustively the part assigned to him—a process

> impracticable in the handling of small routine matters. Cravath
> believed that the man who learns to analyze the component
> parts of a large problem involving complicated facts, and to do
> each detailed part well, becomes a better lawyer faster than the
> man who is not taught in such detail. Matters involving small
> amounts often involve difficult, complicated law problems, and a
> man may be misled, perhaps made careless, by being allowed to
> handle such a matter without adequate analysis and supervision.
> (Swaine 1946: II, 4-5)

Fundamentally, the system has not changed much; the same principles still hold in firms in general (cf. Galanter and Henderson 2008). In order to understand the nature of legal work, one must understand how that work is organized within the institution of the law firm. This chapter therefore is in part an external view of the nature of law firm work and is complementary to what comes later in Part II. Although the system still obtains, its application has altered in the intervening years with incoming associates divided into two groups—those that will receive training and those that will not. The former have the opportunity to win partnership while the latter are not on track (Wilkins and Gulati 1996; Dinovitzer 2004). Here I focus on the training group.[38]

In the previous chapter I described how the firm went about hiring its new associates. It is no longer appropriate, as it was when Robert Swaine was writing his memoir of Cravath, Swaine and Moore, to address associates as "men". Eleven out of eighty lawyers in Tischmann are women, though at the time of the fieldwork, only two were partners and junior partners at that. When new associates join the firm, the others feel a sense of relief. They can now shift some of their "grunt" work onto the new ones, they are one year nearer to the partnership decision, and they are symbolically more integrated into the firm than before. They now have someone to tell war stories to.

Starting Work

Most of what summer associates do is research legal problems and write memoranda appraising the results, which are then criticized by the lawyers who assigned them the problem. There is some possibility that summer associates will also assist in the drafting of briefs and corporate documents. Much of what first year associates do is similar, only this time the responsibility is greater. They are beginning to establish reputations, which are quickly formed, about their skills and personalities. In Tisch-

---

[38] For more information on the deprofessionalization of legal work see Brooks 2011.

mann, with its tradition of running a "lean outfit" (i.e., staffing a project parsimoniously), responsibility comes early to associates, and they find themselves heavily involved in matter from the beginning. This is especially the case among the litigation attorneys. One first year associate was brought into an arbitration where he undertook not only the fact searching and question preparation for witnesses, but also the brief writing. The case consumed enormous quantities of his time.

Giving a tyro associate that kind of responsibility demands that the attorney who is in charge of the matter closely supervises the associate's work so that the associate does not go astray or commit some terrible mistake (cf. Fox 1957, 1959; Bosk 1979). In this particular arbitration, two partners—one junior, the other senior—both of whom were heavily committed to other cases in addition to this one, supervised the associate. The result was that the associate worked on his own for much of the time—without much feedback—unsure if he was doing everything correctly or not.

At one point in the arbitration, a brief was due. The associate had been working on the brief for a week, drafting and redrafting, until he had his final draft prepared. The senior partner had demanded that he be shown the final draft before it was sent to the arbitrators—the junior partner being in the Far East on another matter at that time—so that he could make any final revisions. The day before the brief was due, the associate took it to the senior partner, but he was absent from the office and would not be back until well after the last possible time for mailing. The associate was frantic with worry. He did not want to send it out in defiance of the partner's instructions, but he had to file it. He felt he would be damned either way. Eventually he was able to find another partner who was not involved in the case but was knowledgeable about arbitrations, who agreed to review the brief for him.

Ideally, no associate should ever fall into this kind of trap. But associates are in an awkward situation: on the one hand they are there to be trained, on the other they are there to generate profit for the partnership. The Cravath system attempted to find a point to equilibrium between the two, but present day law practice has to a large extent abandoned part of Cravath's principles.

Competition is so great that the training component has fallen away and the extraction of surplus has become paramount. Instead of observing how problems are broken down into their components, associates are frequently assigned a piece of a problem with no knowledge of how it fits into the general picture. In addition to being deprived of a general purview, associates are being forced to elect a specialty fairly soon after arriving at a firm. In many cases, they are asked to state a preference *before* joining the firm. Again, these developments run counter to Cravath's ideas of how to rear associates.

Tischmann used to believe that associates should try several areas of practice before settling on one or two. Dual specialties are quite common: a lawyer may practice in both, say, real estate and litigation. Table 4.1 presents a breakdown of all the specialties and their combinations by status of lawyer found within Tischmann. Note that there are six categories, namely senior, middle and junior partners, and senior, middle and junior associates.

TABLE 4.1
Fields of Practice by Lawyer

Fields of Practice*

Status	Corporate	Litigation	Real Estate	Securities	Labor
Senior Partner	6	2	1	0	0
Mid Partner	2	2	2	1	1
Junior Partner	0	0	2	0	0
Senior Associate	0	4	1	1	0
Mid Associate	1	1	2	0	0
Junior Associate	0	2	1	0	0
	Employee Benefits	Tax	Estate Planning	Real Estate Litigation	Labor Litigation
Senior Partner	0	0	0	0	0
Mid Partner	0	0	3	1	0
Junior Partner	0	0	0	0	1
Senior Associate	1	0	1	0	0
Mid Associate	1	0	0	1	0
Junior Associate	0	0	0	1	1
	Tax & Corporate	Estate Planning & Tax	Corporate & Securities	Real Estate & Corporate	Tax & Estate Planning
Senior Partner	1	0	1	1	1
Mid Partner	0	0	1	1	0
Junior Partner	0	0	0	1	0
Senior Associate	0	1	0	0	0
Mid Associate	0	0	0	1	0
Junior Associate	0	0	0	0	0

	Corporate & Real Estate	Estate Planning & Employee Benefits	Securities & Corporate	Real Estate & Tax	Securities & Labor
Senior Partner	0	0	0	0	0
Mid Partner	0	0	0	1	0
Junior Partner	1	1	0	0	0
Senior Associate	0	0	0	0	1
Mid Associate	0	0	1	0	0
Junior Associate	0	0	0	0	0

* Key: In the joint specialties, the first is the major and the second is the minor.

Although the firm used to be relatively relaxed about associates' choices, the old guard was of the opinion that litigation was not a proper choice for a true Tischmann lawyer. One associate was asked by the senior partner why, as a graduate of the University of Chicago Law School, he chose to go into litigation, which was not the right kind of work for a gentleman lawyer to be in.

In fact, the tensions between the different departments of the firm affect the associates profoundly. To a young associate, certain areas of practice are "sexier" than others. For example, litigation is often perceived as exciting, whilst estate planning is considered dull though steady. Associates' initial desires about what area of practice to enter may be sharply modified by what the firm chooses to emphasize as its specialties.

In the 1970s, litigation became a necessary part of law practice. Businesses were engaging in litigation more rather than deciding issues purely on a business basis. Tischmann had thrived without a litigation partner for many decades, and resented having to import one. The partner eventually chosen came out of a much lower status law school (Chicago-Kent), and was an Irish Catholic. As litigation became part of the normal life of practice, a litigation section developed with a full complement of partners and associates. The litigation attorneys mostly came from Northwestern University Law School rather than the University of Chicago, whether by design or accident is unknown (cf. Kingston and Lewis 1990; Garth and Martin 1993). Nonetheless, when the litigation department at Tischmann established itself, it was greedy for associates. In this respect, it came into conflict with the other main growing area of practice, namely, real estate.

Real estate had always been a staple of Tischmann, but the rainmaking abilities of one particular partner brought in substantial clients with complex business transactions to be taken care of. These types of transactions need the services of a number of associates. Eight associates work in the real estate field, and, during the latter part of my fieldwork, more were being hired. It was by far one of the most profitable fields in the firm. Moreover, this profitability gave the associates a better chance of becoming partner than most of the other fields, since the partners in the area had considerable clout. The partners in real estate constituted the second largest group (12) after the fifteen corporate partners.

Legal work in real estate involves little law, but requires great attention to detail, especially in the reading of leases. A transaction concerning the sale of a shopping mall involves the close examination of many leases and sub-leases to understand what everyone's liabilities are and if there are any potential conflicts. (See Chapter 7 for further discussion of this topic.) This is work that can be broken down into easily manageable units. Such work, therefore, because it is straightforward is ideal for associates and junior partners. When associates have to negotiate with other lawyers, they can be at a disadvantage because of their junior status. One associate who was helping to arrange the financing of a purchase of a shopping mall for a client found that he was dealing with a crusty partner from another firm who sent the associate on what the associate considered were all kinds of wild and pointless goose-chases. As much as he disliked the partner, there was nothing he could do except complain to his supervising partner. The matter was too valuable to jeopardize.

Associates can have an even worse time coping with partners in their own firm, than with those in others. Knowing when and how to correct a partner in a meeting is a talent that requires great delicacy in its exercise. For if a partner gives the wrong information, often the associate will be blamed for not supplying the correct answer. One senior associate described the following experience with a senior partner:

> George Brown [the partner] will not give way on an argument. Once he and I were in a conference with an [IRS] agent. They were arguing over some point that I knew George was wrong. I happened to be sitting on the same side of the table as the agent and was trying to signal to George that he was wrong, but he wouldn't listen. Finally, they decided to check the [Internal Revenue] Code. Where we were sitting they only had an old copy of the Code, which supported the things George was saying. And the agent was so flustered that he couldn't find the relevant section. So we got our way because George had upset the agent.

In this case the associate was fortunate, as was the partner, but sometimes events do not turn out so well. In another example, a junior associate was acting as "third chair" to a partner during a cross-examination that the partner was conducting.[39] The client was also in attendance. The associate had spent many hours drafting the questions that the partner would want to ask on cross-examination, and then had briefed the partner on the rationale behind them. The cross-examination was proceeding well until near the end, when it appeared to both the client and the associate that the partner was about to wind up his questioning without asking two important questions.

The client spoke to the associate, asking him to bring the lacuna to the partner's notice. At first the associate tried to persuade the second chair lawyer to pass on the message. She refused. The only recourse left to the associate was to speak to the partner directly, about which he was anxious. He nevertheless plucked up his courage, and whispered to the partner that he should ask these questions. The partner abruptly stopped and demanded a recess so that he could find out "who was actually conducting this cross-examination, himself or his associate". As soon as they were outside the room, the senior partner lambasted the associate for embarrassing him in front of the arbitrators and the client, even though the client was standing by at the time. To cap it all, the senior partner returned to the room and asked the particular questions he had missed.

The associate felt torn between doing his best for the client and not upsetting the partner. It was a sharp lesson in realizing that loyalty to the firm takes precedence over that for the client. The matter was compounded by the fact that it was close to review time.[40]

Each year every associate is reviewed twice by the partnership, for work performance and collegiality. These reviews are started by a survey where every partner must answer questions, with respect to each associate they worked with, on the quality of the associates' work and what they were like to work with. The Associates Committee then reviews the surveys and arranges interviews with every associate to discuss the substance of the reviews. The review process both allows the firm to monitor the progress, or lack thereof, of the associate and allows the associate to determine his or her standing within the firm, suggesting answers to questions such as, "Will I make partner?" and "Should I start looking for another job?" The reviews are also used as a basis for deciding the amount of the associate's salary increase. The interviews are occasions where the associates can state their sides of the issues, such as whether they are getting enough feedback on their work, and whether they are receiving sufficient

---

[39] The term in quotes is lawyers' talk for denoting hierarchy on a case. "Third chair" means that there were three lawyers involved, where the senior partner was first chair and the junior partner was second chair.

[40] The second chair understood precisely how the senior partner in this situation would react to being "corrected", which was why she refused and let the junior take the fallout.

training or are being left to flounder. Reviewing associates, then, is a two way process which theoretically should lead to an improved set of working relationships. But of course, that is an ideal.

The associate in the preceding example mentioned his predicament with the partner at the cross-examination to his interviewers during his review. Initially, the partners who interviewed him were concerned that the associate had been placed in an untenable situation. They advised him to talk to the senior partner, which he did. Later he was called back to discuss the result with his interviewers. He was told that the situation was difficult, and that he would have to swallow his pride and apologize to the partner for stepping out of line and embarrassing him. The associate was shocked by this result, but realized that it was useless for him to do other than what had been requested. All he could do would be to avoid working with the partner again and learn a different scheme of situational ethics.

Not infrequently, the decision to change from one area of practice to another is taken on the basis of congeniality and compatibility with other attorneys in the firm or the lack thereof. Partners sometimes act like "prima donnas," believing that the world will immediately respond to their whims. Young female associates are sometimes considered by partners to be there to satisfy sexual as well as business needs.[41] One associate complained about a partner who would never give him complete instructions. The partner would explain the problem in just enough detail for it to appear relatively solvable. When the associate started his research, he found he lacked several facts that were material to his needs. Since the partner spent much of his time out of the office, it was difficult for the associate to complete his assignment by the deadline, with the result that the partner criticized the associate, calling him untrustworthy to his other partners. Consequently the associate decided to move into another field, and began seriously considering offers from head-hunters to move to other firms.

One area of potential conflict between partners and associates is that of secretaries. Tischmann's policy is to have a partner and associate share a secretary. The typing demands of each vary, with partners requiring more letters to be typed, and associates needing more memoranda and briefs typed. The following Table 4.2 shows the distribution of writing demands by status. These figures are taken from the time records kept by the attorneys in the firm. Twenty-five types of writing were counted, e.g., drafting memoranda, briefs, letters, contracts, motions, agreements, etc. The frequency totals below show the number of times an attorney recorded a writing activity during a four-week period.

---

[41] This is not peculiar to the U.S. The big London law firms had their share of sexual predators, as I have learned from talking to female associates and partners in the UK.

TABLE 4.2

Distribution of Writing Tasks by Status

Junior Associate	Mid Associate	Senior Associate	Junior Partner	Mid Partner	Senior Partner
64	430	332	348	643	311

The figures for the partners are high because significant portions of their time are spent writing correspondences. For junior partners, the percentage is 71.3 percent; for mid-level partners it is 47.1 percent; and for senior partners it is 32.2 percent. Correspondence writing is an activity that, on the whole, one would not expect to be delegated to associates since it entails direct contact with clients, which is the partners' prerogative. If then we remove correspondences from the figures, the bulk of writing in terms of memoranda and briefs is carried out by associates, especially mid-level and senior associates. Junior associates spend more time doing legal research.

Problems arise with sharing secretaries because associates are usually the ones writing to deadlines, whether statutory or imposed by a court or a client. In addition, their documents are on average longer than the correspondences written by partners. A particular difficulty for an associate is to get the services of a secretary for a sufficient length of time to produce the document. The main obstacle is the partner "pulling rank" and having the secretary abandon the associate's work in favor of his or hers. In fact, this is a perennial complaint of associates, both among themselves, and at associates' meetings. Nothing, however, seemed to be done to remedy the situation. It is a continual source of frustration that associates must accommodate.

Two partners at Tischmann were especially notorious for pulling rank. One continually badgered his secretaries so they always left, to be followed by a succession of temporaries. The other partner, in truth, wanted a secretary to herself. No associate was able to share with her. She preempted all her secretary's time. Eventually, she was paired with a paralegal who, in large part, worked for this particular partner. His use of the secretary was really an extension of hers.

Although associates sometimes feel they bear an intolerable burden of unsympathetic partners' wants, they are given license once each year to comment on their fate in the Christmas Party entertainment. They write a series of songs that tell of the angst of an associate. One, for example, was written in response to a memorandum that circulated on December 12 forbidding any associate to take off more than Christmas Day. The reason given by the management committee, though not stated in the memorandum, was that pressure of year-end work was becoming overbearing because too many associates were taking vacations at that time. Many partners subscribed to the sentiment of the memorandum; some even complained that associates should have no vacation for the first year or two. One associate sang the following song at the Christmas Party (two days after the memorandum was issued).

TRY TO REMEMBER
(To the tune of "Try to Remember")

Try to remember
That now it's December
And deals all close
To make some money

Your communication
That you seek a vacation
Is not perceived
As very funny

If you try to leave now
You will be deadmeat now
So stay away from climates
Too warm and sunny

Try to remember
That since it's December
You are staying.......
.... staying........
........staying.......
.........staying......

The next two songs speak of the general hardship associates suffer. The first is:

THE ASSOCIATES' LAMENT
(To the tune of "Let it Snow")

Oh, the weather outside is pretty,
But, why do I feel shitty?
Because I'm here making dough.
Might as well let it snow, let it snow.

Now the weather outside is frightful
But, I still have got a nightful,
Of documents and briefs to go.
Let it snow, let it snow, let it snow.

How I'd love to go out and play,
Have a life I can call my own,
But I'm stuck here to do this work,
And, all I can do is moan.

I'm writing this Goddamn pleading
While my life is quickly fleeting.
The best years of my life will go
To Smithley Doe, Smithley Doe, Smithley Doe
[a big client]

The final song is relevant to the main theme of this chapter, the progression from associate to partner:

I'M OUT SIX YEARS, GOING ON SEVEN YEARS
(To the tune of "I Am Sixteen, Going on Seventeen")

I'm out six years, going on seven years,
I should be next in line.
All the rumors I hear,
Say this is the year.
Hey—I think I'm doing fine.

I'm out six years, going on seven years,
Still maybe all's not great.
I wonder why
I just heard from Ty –
"Are you willing to relocate?"

I don't see why they'd pass me up,
I've worked myself half-dead.
Nevertheless, I've pondered why
My name's off the letterhead.

Aw, hell, I'll admit it,
I'll never make partner.
I've got nothing left to lose,
I guess I'll just take up singing
the Permanent Associate Blues.

Cravath also believed that beginning associates should be rotated through the different areas of practice, so that after two or three years the young man could make an informed choice about which field he would like to concentrate on. The luxury of freedom of choice is now accorded to only a few. Firms such as Tischmann demand an early choice from associates. Preferably associates will have decided in law school where their talents lie, be they in litigation, tax, and so forth. Those who are uncertain or have no preference are assigned to where the need is greatest. This is not to say that change is not permitted. One of Tischmann's biggest problems with associates has been keeping them in litigation. In the past three years, four associates have left the firm out of litigation, one was asked to leave, and two moved into other areas, notably real estate and securities.

The firm of Cravath, Swaine and Moore made the headlines during 1986 by raising the "stakes" for the corporate bar. Cravath decided they would raise associates' starting salaries by an average of $12,000 per year; and that they would achieve this without increasing the associates' hourly rates charged to clients. Virtually every corporate firm, from medium-sized to large (i.e., say the largest 500 firms in the country), was forced to follow suit. To do otherwise would have meant involuntarily withdrawing from the market for elite law students. Whereas Cravath could raise salaries without passing the costs along to their clients, most other firms could not. And since the partnership of a law firm makes its profit from its associates, a rise without an attendant increase in billable charges to clients would for the most part be impossible. The majority of firms are under-capitalized and therefore are unable to absorb such costs, or rather most partners would not be prepared to suffer a drop in income. They expect to see year on year increases in profits per partner (Heinz 2009).

The solution for most firms, Tischmann included, was to find a means of extracting more surplus from their associates. The core method is to demand more billable hours. In his study of four large law firms in Chicago, Nelson indicated that hours billed by associates varied according to type of work done, with litigators billing on average 110 hours more than those in different fields (1983: 219). The larger metropolitan firms have insisted on minima of between 2,000 to 2,200 billable hours a year. This requires associates to bill between 40 and 44 hours a week, necessitating a typical working week of around 70 to 80 hours.

On Becoming a Partner

The ostensible idea of every associate is "to make partner". This is the second principle of the Cravath system; the first being in-house training (cf. Smigel 1969). In a large firm such as Kirkland & Ellis or Sullivan & Cromwell, the odds against becoming a partner are very high. The entering classes of associates can be as high as 35 and 65,[42] out of which perhaps only a few will be anointed and Kirkland & Ellis only named ten new partners in 1987. Tischmann operated for many years on the principle that if an associate accomplished good work, he or she would make partner

---

[42] *Of Counsel*, April 20, 1987, p. 12.

without the stress found in the very large firms. Hence, Tischmann subscribed to the Cravath system intensely in order to have as long and as consistent a probationary period as possible. Of course Tischmann never had many associates come up each year for the partnership decision: the yearly average was two, no more than three. Only in one year did the firm raise more, i.e., six associates, into the partnership.

Until recent years, Tischmann existed with a one-to-one ratio of partners to associates. The current average among large firms is between one-to-two and one-to-three. Recent hirings, departures and the merger, however, drastically altered the ratio to two partners for each associate, which is the reverse of what it normally is. Even with this disparity, Tischmann needed to make some associates partners. If the firm was seen by potential recruits to be one that rejected able associates, its recruitment would suffer. This change in the partner-associate ratio brought about a change in the policy of making every associate who survived the probationary period into a partner. Some associates, mainly in litigation, were aware of these changes, even unarticulated. Over a span of two years three senior associates left for other firms each larger than Tischmann. One, admittedly, had been rejected for partner. But all three were concerned that their chances of rising into partnership were reduced by being in litigation. This, in part, was a function of the locus of power in the firm: it rested not with the litigators—unlike larger firms where litigation is often generally more respected—but with the corporate and real estate lawyers.[43]

The issue of the locus of power incorporates the problem of mentors. For associates to succeed, they need someone in authority who will vouch for them and argue their case whenever necessary. Choosing the right mentor is one of the first things associates must do, but the process is fraught with difficulty. The only way an associate can really make an informed decision is by knowing and working with a partner and establishing a bond with trust—which takes time. At the same time, the associate is being pressured to make an early decision about which area to specialize in. These two forces are incompatible with each other.

Some associates tried to cope with the problem by specializing in two areas, most commonly a mixture of litigation and real estate, or real estate and corporate. When sufficient time has been spent in a combination, the associate may opt, but not always, for one over the other. The advantage is that the associate is able to decide on an informed basis, and can still establish a relationship of depth with a partner in the time he has before partnership decisions are taken. The disadvantage is that the associate

---

[43] Compare Lazega's (2001) discussion of Montesquieu structures in the firm he studied in New England, which analyzes how different sets of partners must fight over scarce resources, namely associates.

risks the ire of the department he chooses to quit in preference for the other. The jilted department is left short-handed. Associates may be hired to fill specific gaps, but they cannot, within limits, be compelled to stay in that particular area permanently. If they can persuade other partners they possess skills that are cross-marketable, say from corporate to securities, and they are given assignments, then they can switch. This is not, however, a frequent occurrence.

Building a relationship with a mentor is a two-way affair. The associate must establish a bond with the right kind of partner, one who can persuade the other partners to accept his charge as one of them. The partner must be able to rely on the associate to produce the work on time and with no errors. In other words, the associate must prove that he or she is an invaluable extension of the partner's human capital. In Tischmann, the main areas are corporate, real estate, litigation, and estate planning, with securities growing into a significant area. The field most at risk was litigation, the one that is most secure was real estate.

For the first two or three years of practice, the associate is searching for the right mentor. Who not to choose becomes known very early. One associate remarked that being connected with one particular partner "was the kiss of death" as far as progressing in the firm. Consequently, that partner had great difficulty in having associates work for him. They tended to become conveniently very busy when he called. Other partners could be good fun or interesting to work with, but nevertheless lacked the necessary influence when it came time to promote the associate. One or two partners who were very powerful claimed many associates, almost to the extent of creating a firm within a firm. One associate joked that when the reigning managing partner left, the firm would change its name from Tischmann to Solomon & Associates to reflect its true composition, the primacy of the new managing partner.[44]

Approaching making partner is an anxious moment for an associate. When I first arrived at Tischmann, the probationary period was seven years, but there were rumors circulating among the associates that the period would be extended to eight or eight and a half years. The associates held their own meeting to discuss this issue. Five were particularly concerned because they had been with Tischmann for seven years already and were reluctant to wait another year. The associates elected a committee of three associates to speak to the partnership about the length of time. Two associates who were expected to come up for partner that year excluded themselves from the committee. The partnership reached no immediate

---

[44] The joke reflects the fact that if this partner left Tischmann he would take a substantial amount of business with him.

conclusion, but when the merger occurred, the norm was eased up to eight years.

The associates who were coming into the firm through the merger were unknown quantities to the Tischmann partners. Those Bernstein associates who had been promised partnerships in Bernstein before the merger were asked to wait another year to allow the Tischmann partners to evaluate them. This delay created considerable anxiety for the Bernstein associates.

As associates reach the partnership threshold, then, intensive lobbying among the partners occurs. Certain associates, because of a combination of mentor/patron and consistently well-regarded work, present no obstacle to making partner. Where the mentor has little "clout" within the firm, or the associate is a minor field, the decision becomes more contentious. One extreme instance is worth noting here.

Following the merger, six candidates were up for partner. In a firm of 80 lawyers, this meant nearly ten percent of the lawyers in the firm were about to be made partner in one sweep. The case for three of the associates was very strong. One of them, for example, was the fifth biggest rainmaker in the firm. Another was the main expert on company pension plans (an increasingly important element in corporate and other types of legal work). The remainder were characterized by a lack of any special features that would have made them indispensable to the firm and were thus considered fungible. Political considerations thus came into play. Each associate had his or her mentor sponsoring him or her for partnership. Two were Bernstein associates already assured of their rise in status. Tischmann did not have the right to prevent them from becoming partner, only to delay it. Two were essential to the firm for the reasons stated above. The remainder were arguable. One was a litigator who had tremendous support from part of the litigation section, which argued vociferously for her. The other was an estate planner and tax lawyer. Although support for him was weak, when the decision was finally taken to admit the litigator to the partnership, the partners felt compassion for the estate planner and, in a fit of sympathy, decided to admit him also. Hence, six associates became partners.

Partnership: On Being a "Member" of the Firm

One immediate difference between associates and newly elected partners is that they are no longer employees of the firm, but members. They are, in fact, self-employed. They now have to make provision for their own retirements and provide their own health insurance. One new partner calculated that, as a result of the new expenses, his earnings in the first year of partnership might just equal what he earned in his last year of being an associate. In some firms, though not Tischmann, the partners must pay for their own secretaries out of their own earnings or draws. Thus with the potential for greatly increased earnings and security of tenure comes the burden of the expenses of running a costly enterprise.

Chicago is renowned for a style of partnership, called "two-tier" partnership (Heintz and Markham-Bugbee 1986). Basically, the partners are divided into income and equity partners. The former—an intermediate step—receive a salary, but have no capital stake in the firm: they rise to this level after another four years. The latter are the true owners of the firm, in that they invest the capital and are liable for the firm's debts and ventures.

Tischmann operated a version of this system, termed the junior partner/senior partner alternative. In this system, all partners were equity holders, but the amounts held and the contributions that could be made to firm policy and decision making varied greatly with the level of seniority. The senior partners determined the amounts. This provided the senior partners with the facility to monitor continuously the performance of their junior partners. The juniors' capacity to sit on certain committees and to vote on issues was severely limited. As they proved themselves, they were awarded increasing amounts of equity and authority. Of course, if they were rainmakers (i.e., client-getters), no matter how junior they are, their draws would reflect that fact.

The managing partner was firmly of the view that this alternative was the correct one. He claimed that:

> I have problems thinking of someone on salary as a partner. The awarding of units [the measure of a person's stake in the partnership] determines who is where, anyway. And junior partners are really like associates: they do the same work. It's just a change of label.

The concept of security of tenure, according to the managing partner, was not as solid as say that of academics. He believed that making partner constituted no automatic right to tenure. Partners must continue to perform to "earn their keep". He also felt seven years was an inadequate length of time to evaluate someone's potential thoroughly. If someone is not performing appropriately after three or four years as a partner (when that person would be considered for full partner voting rights), then that person would have to find another post elsewhere. He said, "I can't keep someone around for twenty years and go home every day knowing I made a mistake." His view encapsulated the two-tier system. During my tenure with the firm, one partner, mid-level, was asked to leave, and another was put under threat of being asked to leave. Another applied to become of counsel to the firm, that is, a form of retirement.

During one year, the management committee conducted an experiment. They reviewed all partners as they review associates. The committee split into twos and each couple interviewed a third of the partners. Using the computerized statistics, compiled for billing purposes, they attempted to evaluate the strengths and weaknesses of each partner and indicate to the partner where improvements could be made, that is, how productivity could be improved. The idea was not well received and was not repeated. One partner, upset by the review, said he came to Tischmann, and stayed with it, because it was not like the large firms solely oriented to the "bottom line", but was instead collegial and congenial. Reviews, in his mind, contaminated those qualities.

The most contentious time for partners is the occasion of the determination of the size of their draws by the management committee (cf. Spangler 1986: 41). As with elections to partner, these decisions are taken just before Christmas when the partnership holds its largest meeting. The current spread of draws reflected a 3:1 ratio—approximately $300,000 to $950,000—from the most junior to the most senior. The management committee decided on the basis of hours billed and clients controlled.[45] For senior partners the latter was most important. (For further discussion of this aspect see Chapter 5.) For juniors, the hours billed, with a small rainmaking element, were the most significant element in the determination. Since Tischmann was top-heavy with partners, they had to be productive, especially to justify their higher billable rates.

The final determination of the draws was sent around to the partners several hours before the partnership meeting. The lists were handwritten, reflecting the fact that the management committee had only just finished its deliberations and that they were not yet fully final. The size of increase or decrease signified the senior partners' satisfaction or dissatisfaction with the partners' performance during the year. Not everyone accepted the decision, and challenges to the committee's decisions were made at the meeting, in public. For this, a partner needed to be certain of the strength of his or her case. When challenges were made the management committee reconstituted itself in the hallway outside the meeting and revised its decision. This was generally the ultimate decision.

Though lawyers may place their work first, their status within the firm was directly signaled by the size of their draws, which provided the only common measure of success and status within the firm (cf. Liu 2010). Some lawyers found inventive methods to set themselves apart from the mass. For example, the late Roy Cohn, former counsel to Senator Joseph

---

[45] Cf. Bauman's (1999: 47-50) description of Baker & McKenzie's "formula" for computing partner remuneration, which was far more byzantine than Tischmann's simple process.

McCarthy's House committee investigating Un-American activities during the 1950s, had an arrangement with his firm whereby it would pay *all* his expenses, including his homes in New York City and Connecticut, his Rolls Royce, his barber's bills, his meals and more (American Lawyer, June 1987: 101-6). By this time papers such as the *American Lawyer* were constantly reporting the migration of partners from firm to firm in search of bigger earnings. The concept of tenure for life as Cravath espoused it— "Every lawyer who enters the Cravath office has a right to aspire to find his life career there" (Swaine 1948: 7)—had collapsed.

5

Establishing and Maintaining a Client Base

Introduction

A lawyer is someone hired for a fee. Without clients who pay the fees lawyers cannot practice, unless they are in government or are members of corporate law departments. Clients, then, are the lifeblood of the law firm. But unlike blood, which reproduces itself in the marrow of our bones and replenishes itself on oxygen, clients do not possess those propensities for self-reproduction. Law firms, especially corporate ones, must therefore receive continuous transfusions of clients in order to exist and prosper. Such a state of affairs compels firms to compete vigorously both to find clients and then to keep them (cf. Pashigian 1977, 1978). This chapter explores some of the techniques that lawyers and law firms use to accomplish these aims.

Very little has been written on this topic. Bourn's study (1986) focused on how businesses found their lawyers, rather than the other way round. One of the most thorough investigations is Claude Rowe's *How and Where Lawyers Get Practice* (1955), which has a blurb that reads as follows:

> 780 LAWYERS' ANSWERS TO THE QUESTION: *"How and Where Do Lawyers Get Practice?"* –
>
> Containing the results of exhaustive discussions and conferences, in persons, with over fifteen hundred lawyers, in all capacities, including deans of law schools, judges, district attorneys, senators, congressmen, governors, and other officials. Including any aspects of or affiliations pertaining to securing business, clients, living, work, secrets of practice, how to maintain, increase, improve, keep, lose, how not to lose, when, why. All sources are revealed. Each answer is the individual's, purely and simply, and usually contains some new points, angles, cases and instances; all answers combined resulting in an absolutely complete cross-section answer. A value that characterizes and distinguishes this book.

Tischmann was more fortunate than some insofar as it was an established firm that had built up expertise in certain areas in which it had earned a strong reputation. Its client book, which listed all clients and the jobs being done was substantial; over 250 pages long. In the markets of the 1980s, however, a strong reputation was ultimately ephemeral, and Tischmann recognized this.

History of Clients at Tischmann

Tischmann had an advantage, which to some could also be a disadvantage, of being a minority firm in its early days. Jewish lawyers were barred from the mainstream, protestant firms, so they formed their own firms that served Jewish clients (Dinovitzer 2006; Wald 2008a, 2008b). In effect, for some years there existed an alternative Jewish economy. Exclusion by others brought cohesion within a group. In these early days, Tischmann was composed mainly of German Jews. They established their client lists through personal networks based on such institutions as the Standard Club in Chicago. Gradually, as the influx of Jews from Eastern Europe strengthened, East European Jews joined the firm and added their networks of clients to the others. Clients requested such services as incorporating companies, putting together real estate deals, and planning estates, but there was little litigation. Thus, Tischmann was primarily a facilitative law firm: its members counseled, negotiated, and advised rather than resolved conflicts.

One feature of the early period lingered through to the 1970s. Individual lawyers thought of clients as their personal clients, not those of the firm. Although the firm existed, the constituent lawyers did not always think of it as an entity to be continued with clients being served by generation after generation of lawyers. When a lawyer retired or died, he frequently made no succession arrangement for his clients' affairs to be handled by other lawyers in the firm. Firm consciousness, then, seemed to be a fairly recent and fragile phenomenon.

Clients, too, viewed their relations with lawyers in much the same fashion: their affairs were handled by an individual lawyer and not by the firm. Once it was established that although lawyers had "rights" in a client by virtue of having brought that client into the firm, the firm "owned" the client. Of course, there was no way this rule could be enforced against clients; they were free to deal with the situation anyway they wanted. Perhaps the consciousness of Tischmann as an entity was fully established when the firm decided not to alter its name according to the composition of the partners who ran the firm. The name would no longer reflect an assemblage of lawyers, but instead would symbolically identify the firm as an enduring entity.

In recent years, the trend towards the concept of the firm being the representative of the client received a setback. For example, through aggressive marketing, Finley, Kumble, Wagner, Heine, Underberg, Manley and Casey attempted to dominate the legal market by acquiring law firms and raiding others for their best "rainmakers". Stevens (1987:42) quoted the managing partner, Steve Kumble, as articulating his philosophy that:

> Lawyers bring in clients and law firms service them. I don't care what anyone says about a firm's history or traditions or any such nonsense. Except for a few clients who are still deep in the stone age, you don't get hired that way. Clients go with the lawyers they know, the lawyer they've worked with, the lawyer who delivers for them regardless of his firm's place in the pecking order. Sure you have to be able to service that client once he's on board, but it's the individual who gets him there. Those who fail to see this—and thank heaven there are many of them—overrate the power of the firm and underrate the power of the lawyers that make it work.

However, this was not a fail-safe strategy as Finley Kumble learned when it imploded under heavy debt obligations taken on to finance risky lateral hires (Eisler 1990).[46]

Getting Clients

The easiest method for a law firm to obtain clients is to inherit them. This method is painless and requires little original effort. What it does require is a patronage relationship so that a senior can devolve his "empire" onto a junior. The senior partner in Tischmann had one of the largest clients in the firm, which he had served for many years. As he began contemplating retirement, he started to give more and more responsibility to a younger, though senior, partner who had done a considerable amount of work for this client. Some of the lawyers in the firm were worried that the client, who was known to regard the senior partner in an avuncular light, might not transfer his regard to the new partner because he was younger and did not have the same gravitas or extensive counseling relationship with the client that the senior partner had had. Others thought the relationship would change to a more formalized one where the "new" lawyer would have a more "technical" relationship rather than the basically informal one that the retiring partner had enjoyed. Most considered it likely that the client would stay (or hoped he would) with the firm.

Sometimes problems existed where younger lawyers ought be inheriting clients and the older lawyers refrained from passing along responsibility. This lead to the younger lawyers defecting from the firm. Two senior

---

[46] The problem is a recurring one as the demise of Dewey & Leboeuf, a long established firm, demonstrated. The firm filed for Chapter 11 bankruptcy protection in May 2012 (Ax and Prasad 2012).

partners at Tischmann had such reputations. Their philosophy was that junior and middle range partners should serve the senior partners' clients rather than be concerned with clients of their own. This attitude frustrated the junior partners. They could see no future for themselves except as the lackeys of these partners. Any clients they tried to bring into the firm were characterized as "inferior" by these senior partners, who believed their clients were the *crème de la crème*. Compounding the feelings of frustration were the senior partners' views that no junior partner should have any responsibility for their clients; that is, the junior partners were relegated to the status of "minders/grinders". Thus the only solution for the junior partners was to leave and find firms that would encourage their drive and ambition.

The normal method of getting clients took place outside the firm. It entailed networking by joining clubs, being involved in business ventures, giving seminars to chambers of commerce, having a well-connected family, and more; but most of all it entailed being lucky. One partner, who had some of the most valuable clients in the firm, made his first connection with a big client riding in the elevator of his building. The story is partly apocryphal and had acquired the status of legend, but demonstrated the element of serendipity in businesses where personal relations are of paramount importance. A neighbor of his was complaining one day that he was unable to find a lawyer to handle a corporate problem his company—a real estate investment trust—was having difficulty with. The partner offered himself, and that became the start of a continuous supply of work from the company, which continued even when the neighbor moved to another part of the country. As the partner's reputation in this field of work grew, so did his array of clients. In the space of a few years he became one of the most powerful members of the firm, with his clients generating several million dollars' worth of business a year. He rationalized his success this way:

> Once you've got a major client, the rest follow like sheep. You can be a lousy lawyer, but if they like you, they'll come. It's the herd instinct. Look, if I'm general counsel of a large corporation, no one can criticize me if I retain Kirkland and Ellis [one of the largest firms in Chicago]. It doesn't have to do with how good they are, just how big they are. So you take a risk when you hire someone smaller.

Another partner had a cousin who was extremely successful in starting his own securities companies, whose legal business he passed to his cousin in the firm. As the cousin prospered, so did the lawyer. One side effect of having a cousin well known in the securities business was that other securities people knew of him and were willing to give their legal work to the lawyer-relative. While attending a securities conference one day, the lawyer enlisted two new clients because they knew his cousin and needed a Chicago lawyer. This lawyer also thought carefully about what kind of conference or seminar he would attend: "It's no good going to a seminar that is full of lawyers. I'm not going to get any business out of them. I need a place that's full of securities people and accountants; they're the ones who can bring me business." He would also sign himself up for conferences but not attend. "I don't need them, but when people look through the lists of participants they'll see my name and that of the firm. And with luck, if they need a securities lawyer, they'll call me."

Giving seminars can be an important way of legitimately publicizing the firm. One labor lawyer who was trying to develop a satellite practice in one of the suburbs was a frequent speaker at Chamber of Commerce seminars. When the lawyers were asked to present a paper at such a seminar, they would put together a package about the firm. It would list the lawyers and their fields, and try to emphasize the distinctiveness of the firm. With a general practice firm, proving distinctiveness is often hard to achieve. The brochure presents an interesting insight into how the firm perceives itself:

> Founded in 19—, Tischmann still maintains its original philosophy that its lawyers are both attorneys and counselors. We offer expert advice on legal questions and advice is given with an eye to the broader context in which the legal questions arise. By identifying both legal and non-legal considerations, we can recommend action which is not only legally sound, but which will produce the best overall results for our clients.

> In the firm's view, the ever-increasing complexity of doing business in today's regulatory climate increases the importance of the role of the lawyer as attorney and counselor. The practice of law can no longer be a "reaction" to problems as they arise. If possible, the lawyer should counsel and advise the client in hope of anticipating the many problems the client may face in the future. We feel that by careful and innovative lawyering, we have met and will continue to meet the challenges of today's law practice.

> The firm has a reputation for creative lawyering in which our lawyers find ways to accomplish the results the client seeks. While our lawyers have a broad range of experience, each has also developed special expertise in a specific substantive area of the law. As a result, each Tischmann client should expect to be in "one to one" contact with his or her personal lawyer who knows and understand the client's business. At the same time, each client knows that each lawyer is able to call upon the knowledge and experience of other lawyers in our office to provide the best planning and solutions to specific legal problems.

The brochures themselves rarely if ever produced a client, but personal contacts with the audience, say HR directors from local businesses, could succeed in bringing in clients. The particular partner involved in developing the suburban practice found that many businesses needed counseling on how to negotiate with unions that wished to become established. The suburbs have traditionally been a place where businesses go when they leave the city, often to avoid unions. The Chambers of Commerce, then, were ideal avenues for him to use to tap into this market. The partner also produced a newsletter for the firm which told the attorneys how the suburban practice was faring. Most of its six or so pages were given over to the fruits of client development and seminars given by the lawyers, e.g., "The seminars are definitely gaining exposure for Tischmann's suburban office and the number of clients is steadily increasing". There then followed a list of lawyers and clients brought into the fold. The seminar reports were glowing: "Bill Smith's [a Tischmann partner] November 1 seminar on 'Interest-Free and Other Below-market Loans' attracted a standing room only crowd for this office. Attendees were representatives from Merrill Lynch, Touche Roche, Porte Brown, Tempo Graphics, Royal Fuel, Detterbeck and Company, and Peacock Engineering."

Another common method for getting clients, according to the lawyers at Tischmann, was through being on the "other side" in a case. A partner with several large corporate clients said he acquired them this way. He had been involved in large real estate transactions and had handled them sufficiently well that the people on the other sides had sought him out for future deals. Attracting a client by this manner means that a client has "proof positive" of a lawyer's ability. It is comparable to a barrister's clerk's desire to have his barristers in court as much as possible where they may be seen and evaluated by solicitors (Flood 1983).

The most frequent form of client-getting by far, however, was through networking. Bourn (1986: 59) found that 75 percent of her sample of businesses located attorneys through networks of friends and colleagues. Typically, such a request is: "I need a lawyer who can handle a securities issue for me. Do you know anyone?" According to Bourn, the next largest category is that of personal knowledge, which is 29 percent, where the potential client actually knows the lawyer. The lawyers at Tischmann were plugged into many networks, not just Chambers of Commerce, but also charitable foundations, especially Jewish ones, schools, political activities, both Democrat and Republican, and bar associations. Besides formal membership in bar associations through joining sections and becoming officers in them, bar associations can sometimes produce unanticipated effects.

In 1984, for example, the American Bar Association held its annual meeting in Chicago, in part to inaugurate the new downtown bar center attached to Northwestern's law school. The occasion provided an opportunity for many Chicago law firms to act as unofficial hosts to out-of-town lawyers. Tischmann was among them. The majority of the firms were holding their receptions in hotels and restaurants. Tischmann, or rather the management committee, decided to hold a reception during the meeting, but something out of the ordinary. The firm held its reception on the top story of a luxury department store, Neiman Marcus. The same summer that the American Bar Center was opening, a new, very fashionable and expensive, luxury department store opened on Michigan Avenue—one of the main downtown shopping centers—near to the bar center. Tischmann reserved the top floor restaurant and part of the food hall.

In order to make the reception a success, Tischmann hired a consultant to help the lawyers use the reception as a vehicle for promoting the firm and gaining business. The first step was acquiring the lists of those attending the ABA annual meeting, and then combing them for people the lawyers knew. Those that were considered good "business prospects" were invited by the lawyers that knew them. In addition, a request was sent to every lawyer in the firm asking for a list of "notables" who should receive invitations. Ultimately, more than a thousand invitations, with handwritten envelopes, were sent. Corps of secretaries, messengers, and paralegals were dragooned into writing the envelopes.[47]

As the date for the reception approached, the consultant was brought into a breakfast meeting at the firm, which every lawyer was commanded via a three line whip to attend. The memorandum from the partner in charge of the party to all attorneys and summer associates was headed, "Re: Survival Techniques":

> Peter Smith, Director of Marketing and Director of Midwest Law Firms Group at XXX Accounting Company will be hosting a one hour meeting on Wednesday morning of this week at 8:30am in the 32nd Floor Conference Room at which he will be sharing some ideas he has in regard to creating the appropriate image at cocktail parties. Attendance by all is expected. We would like to be finished by 9:30am, therefore, please be there promptly at 8:30am.

Over sweet rolls and coffee, the senior partner in charge of the reception spoke about the importance of the occasion as a means of publicizing the firm and increasing its potential business. Many of the lawyers had

---

[47] The postage costs alone amounted to nearly $2,000.

mixed feelings about the event; it was expensive, the rental cost was $10,000, and it seemed an artificial way of generating business. The consultant then talked about how the party should be conducted. His main emphasis was on how to change the conversation from social talk to business talk, and then finding the appropriate moment to hand over a business card. He warned that no opportunity should be missed to switch a conversation from social to business; otherwise the talk would be "wasted".

About 230 of those invited agreed to come, but the partner in charge told the lawyers to write to those who could not attend, offering future assistance if ever needed. A few days before the reception, the event received some publicity from a local newspaper as one of the events to attend during the ABA meetings. The Tischmann lawyers faithfully followed their consultant's instructions and business cards were being exchanged at high speed during the reception.

After the reception, considerable follow-up work was needed. The partner in charge distributed another memorandum on the "ABA Party":

> Attached hereto are the following:
>
> 1. List of guests who attended the party;
>
> 2. List of guests who indicated that they would be in attendance but who did not come to the party;
>
> 3. Copy of three signatures from our guest books which we were unable to read—if anyone recognizes any of these please let my secretary know; and
>
> 4. Your guest list as submitted to the ABA Party Committee for placement on the computer.
>
> I find it difficult to prepare letters for others and, therefore, in lieu of my suggesting a form of letter, I would rather suggest that the following points could be covered in the letter and that the style of the same should be yours rather than mine:
>
> 1. Thank them for attending;
>
> 2. Possibly mention something either legal or otherwise relative to what you may have discussed at the party;
>
> 3. Possibly some reference to their work on an ABA committee; and/or
>
> 4. A possible line such as "looking forward to working with you in the future."

When, finally, the paperwork was removed to the file room, it occupied six expandable folders: the total cost of the reception was $18,000. In effect, the party was a public relations exercise that left the firm with no real way of establishing how much business had been generated.

Retaining Clients

Finding clients is only part of lawyers' concerns; they must also learn how to keep them in the stable. One method Tischmann employed to achieve this goal was staffing projects with the smallest number of people possible. When Stewart (1983) described the enormous numbers of highly priced associates Cravath deployed on the IBM antitrust suit, it becomes clear that part of the raison d'étre of a large law firm is its capacity to throw virtually unlimited cohorts of attorneys at a problem. Not only is Tischmann not in a position to do this, being less than a hundred lawyers, but as a senior partner said, "the firm should be a lean and mean machine." This policy had the benefit of keeping costs low for clients. Determining how price elastic the demand was for Tischmann's services is difficult. Many of the firm's clients were businesses that could not afford their own in-house legal departments, so they had to employ outside counsel. But these clients could switch to another firm of lesser caliber if billing rates became too high.

Tischmann was facing this problem, in part, as a result of the salary wars among the upper class of law firms. There was a trickle down effect across cities and firms when the highest echelon raises its salaries for its associates. Although the highest salaries were currently being paid by firms in New York, Chicago was affected, because the very large firms in most cities, such as New York, Los Angeles, and Chicago, were both able to and did pass on these raises in the form of higher billing rates to their corporate clients.[48] The medium-range firms such as Tischmann were not quite as fortunate in having the same kind of compliant clients. Forcing extra billable hours out of associates, say up to 2,200 per year, helped overcome some internal pressures caused by the raises but there was still a difficulty determining how to pass on that cost to the client. As one partner said: "No associate in Chicago is worth several hundred dollars an hour. It's ridiculous. If rates keep going up like this, I don't know what'll happen." To a degree, Tischmann fought the issue by keeping hourly rates relatively low; but the entire process was a balancing act between hours

---

[48] Soon after Skadden Arps opened its office in Chicago, most corporate law firms in Chicago found that they had to increase their pay to New York rates because Skadden did not distinguish between offices for remuneration purposes (Caplan 1994). As with Cravath's massive bump in associates' pay, a single firm's policies can have extensive effects throughout the legal environment.

billed, hourly rates, and levels of profit generated and expected in the form of partners' draws.

The dream of most lawyers was to find clients who would keep them for the remainder of their careers. Shearman and Sterling's representation of Citicorp, a client that generated millions of dollars in fees every year, was a paradigm. The trick was to capture a client, especially a corporate client, when it was small, and then grow with it. A partner at Tischmann who had a publicly held company for a client said he originally obtained the client because "the guy who runs it and I knew each other from years ago and grew up together." He felt he had nurtured the client through its formative years into its present state.[49]

Consequently, he was very protective of, and defensive about, the client. When the client became involved in litigation, the lawyer called in a litigation partner to assist him. He was, however, concerned about establishing clearly the line of authority from the outset: every decision had to go through him; the litigation partner would have no direct contact with the client. Moreover, the differences in approach between corporate attorneys and litigators perturbed him.[50] At one stage the litigator argued that they should seek fees from the court. The corporate partner was adamantly opposed because he did not want the client to think that fees would be taken care of by some external agency. "I like to be concise with clients," he said, meaning clients should be aware of whom and how much they will pay. He went on to say that if the liquidator wanted to work with him on this case they should share the same frame of reference: "We better be on the same beam."

This kind of extreme paternalism was normal among the senior lawyers. At least three were enmeshed in such relationships with their clients, and their success was thought to depend on this kind of paternalism, which also raised fears among the others about what would happen to the clients' relationships with the firm when these lawyers retired. This was brought to a head in one particular case when a senior lawyer died nine months after joining the firm as part of the merger. There were grave fears concerning whether the firm as a unit had developed sufficiently strong

---

[49] When looking through old records of Tischmann I found clients who were large household names. I asked where these clients were and the answer was that they had outgrown the firm and needed the expertise of the very big firms with their connections to the big banks. General counsel in these old clients had to forego their loyalty and move on.

[50] Despite the differences between US and UK lawyers, in some ways they are similar. Although there is no separate category of barrister, American litigators appear to behave in a similar fashion and are distinct from office lawyers.

links with this lawyer's clients to fill the void caused by his death.[51] But even paternalism has its limits. One senior partner had no problem being aggressive and forceful with clients who were contemporaries or younger than him. With older clients, however, he averred that "I am deferential; I let them tell me what to do; I won't argue with them."

Keeping clients happy is sometimes wearing for the lawyer, but it is part of the game of being a lawyer and therefore must be accepted. Very wealthy clients seemed to be the most capricious. Two partners, one senior, the other middle-range, visited a client in the suburbs to discuss a new theory they had developed for a case. The client made them drink about four scotches before they could really discuss matters; moreover they were worried whether he would adopt their ideas. At first he liked the idea, later he equivocated. The senior partner tried to reinforce his idea by saying, "it's no worse than Kirkland would do for you".[52] The same client once called the partner at 10pm to hear the partner's final speech in a case. They talked till 3am. The next day when the jury brought in a verdict in favor of the client, the client leaned over to the lawyer and said, "Well, at least you got that fucking right!"

Another wealthy client was involved in extensive litigation during the course of which he had discarded several lawyers. When a partner at Tischmann received the case, he thought it a "mixed blessing," never knowing whether the client would leave. During the discovery phase of the litigation, the opposing party requested some personal papers from the client. These papers included explicit, often critical comments about his lawyers, past and present. The issue was so sensitive that the papers were given to a paralegal, who was then locked in a room and instructed to "white out" (i.e., redact) all remarks about the partner.[53] Even the partner himself was forbidden to see the unexpurgated papers.

To keep clients, lawyers must both follow their demands and on occasion anticipate them. One large client felt it would be a good idea for Tischmann to open a branch at its mid-West headquarters in the suburbs. Tischmann complied. (The venture was unsuccessful, however, since it failed to generate much new business.) Another client, in cooperation with a partner, has been pressing for a branch office in another state, but the firm was wary about committing resources to the proposed plan because of

---

[51] The firm-wide view was that the partner should have waited 18 months in order to ensure the clients were incorporated into the firm's roster.

[52] The partner is here invoking the name of Kirkland & Ellis, a large Chicago law firm.

[53] The remarks about the current lawyer-client relationship were excluded from discovery on the grounds of lawyer-client confidentiality.

the failure of the other venture, and continued to debate the issue. It never opened the branch.

Anticipating clients' demands can best be illustrated by the following example. A partner who inherited, from a senior lawyer, a small but growing company as a client visited the company for its annual general meeting. While the lawyer was talking to the president of the company, the president told him that the company was implementing a change in structure, but that the actual legal work was being done by another lawyer from a different firm. The partner was shocked and asked why the work had not been given to him. The president said that he believed Tischmann had no expertise in this kind of work and so looked elsewhere. Because this type of structural change being sought was relatively new, the partner had not anticipated that his client would need this kind of work. No amount of persuasion on this part could make the president redirect the work to Tischmann. The firm still possessed the company as a client, but had failed to obtain a substantial and profitable piece of business from it.

The prototypical means of retaining clients is to cross-sell services to them. Thus, if a client comes to the firm with a single task in mind, such as a real estate transaction, the firm will attempt to entice the client into using the firm's tax, ERISA, or litigation departments as well, and, if possible, put the client on a retainer so there is a constant stream of money coming into the firm. But cross-selling is a delicate matter. If a client is, for example, referred to a lawyer in the firm because of some special expertise, the lawyer may not be able to cross-sell the client. One partner who was a specialist in an arcane area of tax law had many clients referred to him for that particular matter alone. It was understood, though never openly articulated, that he would never attempt to poach the clients, the sanction being that he would receive no more referrals. Even if, therefore, referred clients asked about other services in Tischmann, he had to refuse them for fear of upsetting the lawyer who had referred them. But if a client came without a referral, then the understanding was that open season had been declared.

There is another form of cross-selling that sometimes occurs between lawyer and client. A partner who did legal work for an investment bank was expected to refer the law firm's clients to the investment bank, thus establishing a symbiotic relationship. This kind of symbiosis was taken a step further when a big client of the firm asked the partnership to form a limited partnership with it to enter a real estate deal: the partnership had little choice but to comply (cf. Flood 2009).

"Making Rain"

Clients, as I said at the beginning of this chapter, are important because they are the lifeblood of a law firm. But clients have another attribute that benefits their handlers. Lawyers who bring in substantial numbers of clients are termed "rainmakers." One central consequence of being a rainmaker is to be granted power and wealth. Rainmakers control the firm and receive the largest draws. They win seats on the management committees of firms and thus obtain positions with the authority to help create and influence policy and the future direction of the firm (cf. Furlong 2012). At Tischmann there were seven lawyers on the policy committee, all of whom were substantial client finders and minders. They also constituted the highest remunerated group in the firm.

In this section I will show how although a lawyer may control a large number of clients, that degree of control does not of itself indicate whether a lawyer will be considered either a rainmaker or a member of the firm's elite. In Table 5.1 on the following page, I have rank ordered the lawyers in Tischmann by the numbers of clients attributed to them.[54] The attribution is made on the basis that a lawyer is considered in control of a client, i.e., belongs to the lawyer, when that lawyer is designated, in the client book, as the billing partner. Only in a few cases have some lawyers not actively generated their entire clientele. Instead, they have been granted clients by another lawyer for some reason. For example, when one large corporate client split into two entities, the original billing partner continued with one while the other part was assigned to another partner. In all other cases the lawyers generated their own business and therefore possess their own clientele. These clients are broken down into two categories—individual and corporate—which reflect the types of clients Tischmann handles. The lawyers, too, are separated into the status groups of senior partner, middle partner, junior partner, senior associate, middle associate, and junior associate. As might be expected senior partners control the bulk of the clients.

---

[54] These figures are drawn from the Tischmann client book. The client book is a listing of all clients and their respective billing partners. It is put together for clerical and billing purposes by the accounting department of the firm. Each client is given a code number that the attorneys and secretaries use for billing purposes. The book is reissued and updated as often as new clients are added to the roster.

TABLE 5.1

Numbers of Clients (Individual and Corporate) by Lawyer

Lawyer ID & Status*	Client: Individual	Client: Corporate	Lawyer ID & Status	Client: Individual	Client: Corporate	Lawyer ID & Status	Client: Individual	Client Corporate
1/SP	153	143	2/SP	137	68	3/SP	140	37
4/SP	82	50	5/SP	44	43	6/SP	44	43
7/SP	49	39	8/SP	54	22	9/SP	64	22
10/JP	57	23	11/SP	49	18	12/SP	47	18
13/MP	41	26	14/MP	26	46	15/SP	39	29
16/MP	38	28	17/MP	28	26	18/JP	19	26
19/MP	18	20	20/MP	93	13	21/MP	69	9
22/JP	44	2	23/JP	41	5	24/SP	23	12
25/JP	21	13	26/MP	17	11	27/SP	14	16
28/MP	6	29	29/SA	5	24	30/SA	14	1
31/MP	13	7	32/MP	12	6	33/MA	11	0
34/MA	10	1	35/JP	8	6	36/SA	8	5
37/SP	8	5	38/SA	8	0	39/SA	6	5
40/MP	5	8	41/MA	5	3	42/MP	4	9
43/JP	3	7	44/MA	4	5	45/SA	4	2
46/SA	3	0	47/SA	2	2	48/MA	0	4
49/MA	1	1	50/SA	0	1	51/SA	2	0
52/MA	1	0	53/JA	0	0	54/JA	0	0
55/JA	0	0	56/JA	0	0	57/JA	0	0
58/JA	0	0	59/MA	0	0	60/JA	0	0

Total of Individual Clients=1,594; Corporate Clients=939

* Key: Status categories are as follows: SP=senior partner; MP=mid partner; JP=junior partner; SA=senior associate; MA=mid associate; JA=junior associate.

These numbers, very crudely, indicate who are and who are not the rainmakers in Tischmann. The low numbers signify one of two things: that either the lawyers are relatively new associates who would not be expected to have any clients yet, or lawyers who have been unsuccessful at finding clients. The following lawyers have the most clients (that is, they have large numbers of both individual and corporate clients):

TABLE 5.2

Lawyers with Highest Percentages of Clients

Lawyer ID*	Percentages (numbers in parentheses)**	
	Client-Individual	Client-Corporate
1	9.6 (153)	15.2 (143)
2	8.6 (137)	7.2 (68)
3	8.8 (140)	3.9 (37)
4	5.1 (82)	5.3 (50)
5	2.8 (44)	4.8 (43)
6	2.8 (44)	4.8 (43)

* Key: Each of these lawyers is a senior partner as shown in Table 5.1.

** Figure in parentheses are actual numbers of clients controlled by each lawyer.

In the case of Lawyer 3, most of the clients are individuals (79%). What the numbers fail to indicate is who has the most active clients. Although one may have a large roster of clients, they may only bring in small amounts of work. To be a successful rainmaker, one must have clients who are sources of regular work. Thus, a lawyer could have only one or two clients, but these could be enormously profitable. So, while simple numbers help to paint a picture of who is likely to be successful within the firm, they do not tell us who is a consistent rainmaker: instead there is a *tromp l'oeil* effect about the numbers.[55]

The profile of who is a rainmaker can be obtained through somewhat different means, however. As I mentioned earlier, there is a certain congruence between the most successful rainmakers and the members of the management committee. In Table 5.1 above, the actual members of the management committee are Lawyers 1, 2, 3, 4, 5, 9, and 15. The mean number of their clients, both individual and corporate, is 150. The list excludes some who one might expect from the aggregate numbers of clients would be included, e.g., Lawyers 6, 7, 8, 10, 12, 14, 20, and 22. However, their mean number of clients is only 77.5, which is insufficient for inclusion on the management committee.

---

[55] For an insightful analysis of British lawyers' routines on billing, see Brown and Lewis 2011.

Admittedly, a management committee this large would be unwieldy, but there have to be good reasons for excluding such potential members. On the whole, individual clients do not carry as much weight as corporate ones. Many of the clients of Lawyers 7, 8, 22, and 28, are estate planning clients. That is, much of their legal work is done on a once-only basis or irregular repeat. The client supplies the relevant data and the lawyer draws up the appropriate plan; and unless the client's situation changes radically or there is an abrupt exogenous change—as with Tax Reform Acts—the plan is not altered. Hence, these lawyers' clients are not, in part, "continuous feed" or "repeat player" clients. Other reasons for exclusion from the management committee are self-selection through, for example, age (as in the case of Lawyer 7 who was in his eighties), poor health, and semi-retirement (as in the case of Lawyer 12).

To attempt to locate a rational basis for identifying successful rainmakers, I analyzed the time records of all the attorneys in Table 5.1 for two sample two-week periods in March and October. These records provided information on, amongst other things, which lawyers did what tasks for what clients and for which lawyers as billing partners (i.e., to whom the client belonged) and for how long. A task here is defined as an episode of work carried out on behalf of a client, e.g., a telephone call, or drafting a letter. Taking the two groups of lawyers with the highest numbers of clients in the firm, namely, the members of the management committee and the group of alternates, we can compute the group means of numbers of tasks per the management and alternates groups per the clients for each group. Table 5.3 illustrates the derivation of these means by showing the total numbers of episodes of work for the sample four-week period for each lawyer in the two groups.

TABLE 5.3

Work Episodes for Sample Four Week Period for Management Committee Group Lawyers and Alternate Group Lawyers

Management Group		Alternate Group	
Lawyer ID	Total Work Episodes	Lawyer ID	Total Work Episodes
5	2205	8	430
4	1385	7	346
9	754	6	338
2	633	10	328
1	588	14	157
15	415	12	140
3	327	10	33
		28	33
	Total 6307 (Mean 901)		Total 1805 (Mean 225.6)

Reading this table leads to certain conclusions about which lawyers—in terms of possessing business-producing clients or the lack thereof—would or would not be counted as major rainmakers in the firm. The management committee group is far ahead of the alternates group with a mean number of episodes of work per group of clients of 901 compared to the alternates' mean number of 225.6. Lawyers 20 and 22 are not deemed legitimate candidates because their level of tasks are so low (33 in each case), despite the relatively high number of clients on their rosters—93 individual, 13 corporate, and 44 individual, 2 corporate, respectively. Conversely, Lawyers 4 and 5 have extremely large numbers of tasks to their credit, 1385 and 2205 respectively: they also happen to be the two most powerful lawyers in the firm.

Those between the two poles who are on the management committee, except for one member, share a minimum of 400 tasks for the period. The exception is Lawyer 3, who has only 327 tasks with a preponderance of individual over corporate clients. His position is politically charged since he belonged to the firm Tischmann merged with and the two firms had to be represented on the committee. Lawyer 7 would have been the natural choice (with 346 total tasks), but he removed himself on the grounds of age and Lawyer 3 was the next in line. This also helps to explain why Lawyer 8 is no longer a member. He stepped down when the merger took place to allow the other firm to put its representatives on the committee, although he could have validly claimed a seat.

Putting aside this anomaly, 400 tasks in a four-week sample period would appear to be the threshold for membership on the committee. Clearly, then, Lawyers 6, 10 and 14 are not candidates. Another distinguishing feature is that, again except for one lawyer, the members of the management committee have at least one corporate client for which there are more than a hundred tasks in the sample four week period. Lawyers 4 and 5 demonstrate their pre-eminence in this area by having very high numbers of tasks per client. Lawyer 4 has two clients, Alpha and Beta, with 274 and 198 tasks per sample four-week period respectively. Lawyer 5, who is by far the most successful and powerful lawyer in the firm, has four clients who generate enormous amounts of work: Gamma with 848, Delta with 347, Epsilon with 256, and Zeta with 251 tasks in the sample four-week period. Lawyer 2 has at best 77 tasks for a single client, but this is counterbalanced by his having 633 total tasks, the fourth highest total. Lawyer 6 comes close with one corporate client generating 95 tasks, but his total is low at 338 tasks in the sample period.

Perhaps one anomaly is Lawyer 1, who had the highest number of clients, both individual and corporate, of any lawyer in the firm at 153 (individual) and 143 (corporate); but his number of tasks is only the fifth largest in the firm. His situation (along with Lawyer 20, who out of 93 individual/13 corporate clients, had only 33 tasks) illustrates the problem inherent in relying on number of clients as an indicator of one's business activity.

The numbers also show how reliant the lawyers are on a relatively small number of clients, despite having large numbers on their roster. For example, with the exceptions of Lawyers 1 and 3, the ten biggest clients per each lawyer in Table 5.3 account for at least 60 percent of each lawyer's business, in most cases higher. These lawyers, then, probably typical of most, have fairly concentrated practices: a few clients provide sufficient work for a successful practice. The two exceptions, Lawyers 1 and 3, have rather more diffuse practices. Their percentages are 57.9 and 58.4 respectively. These lower percentages are probably a reflection of the exceptionally large range of clients each possesses, especially individual clients.

The foregoing represents a sketch of the successful rainmaker: a lawyer who has corporate clients that generate continuously high levels of tasks that keep other lawyers within the firm in work. A lawyer who merely has a large number of clients on the books is not necessarily busy if most of those clients are moribund—a static picture can lie. Instead, one needs to examine the amount (flow) of work transacted through a lawyer. Lawyers having few clients who demand large amounts of legal work on a regular basis are easily more successful than lawyers who have many clients that require work only from time to time.

6

A Theory of Law Firm Organization as Crisis Management

In this chapter I argue that Tischmann was in the cusp of a crisis. As a medium-sized corporate law firm it was in a quandary. On the one hand, it faced competition from the large firms, both in attempts to steal clients and in raising key partners; and on the other hand, it had to cope with the difficulty of apportioning time among large and small clients, often to the detriment of the latter. It was suffering because it was at that point where it had to decide which way it wanted to go: Did it want to be a corporate big firm or a specialized boutique?

During a "Chicago Tonight" television show in 1986, John Calloway asked Don Reuben, senior partner of Reuben and Proctor, and Robert Olgivie, senior partner of Isham, Lincoln and Beale (both of Chicago), why the two firms, both medium-sized, were merging. Reuben, speaking for both, said that the two firms were in business, and that to do business profitably they had to be able to serve their clients and potential clients in the ways that large corporations expected. When Heinz and Laumann (1982) carried out their survey on Chicago lawyers in the mid-1970s, firms of 50 lawyers or more were considered large firms. By the standards of the late 20th century they are medium-sized to the low end of large. Reuben's firm had about 80 lawyers and Olgivie's around 115. In other words, they were both solidly medium-sized. Together they form a reasonably large law firm capable of satisfying most large corporate clients' needs. Reuben gave the example of a potential client who insisted that if Reuben and Proctor were to take on a particular piece of litigation, not only would the firm have to have sufficient computer capability, but it would also have to install matching computer systems with the client's New York office. Such investment is expensive, especially when the firm is in the middle range. The merger between Reuben and Proctor and Isham, Lincoln and Beale made that kind of an investment less onerous and kept the client within the firm's stable.

Tischmann had about 80 lawyers, and it was growing incrementally. It was, however, chasing larger clients than it had. This posed a problem since Tischmann has always run a "lean" operation: that is, the firm as-signed the least possible number of lawyers onto any particular case or matter. "Leanness" allowed the firm to concentrate on saving costs and hence increased productivity, leading to bigger profits, which also meant the firm could submit lower bills to its clients. It also meant that not too many associates are tied up in any one matter at any one time, and provided for something approaching a generalist environment for the lawyers, allowing them to practice in more than one area of law. In the larger firms specialization was the norm and teams of lawyers could be assigned to cases without influencing the staffing of any other division.[56]

Traditionally, Tischmann had had clients in the order of small to medium size corporations. In addition to that type of clientele, the law firm did work for wealthy individuals and families. Over the last five to ten years Tischmann had begun to attract some large clients, with whom leanness was not necessarily an essential factor in their relationship with the firm. Large clients expected to pay legal bills as a normal aspect of day-to-day business. One survey by the American Bar Foundation of corporate counsel (Martin 1987) found that the budgets for corporate legal departments ranged from $10,000 per annum to $90,000,000 per annum. Half of the survey respondents also reported that more than half of these budgets were spent on outside counsel: expenditures ranged from $0 to $69,300,000 (Martin 1987: 9-10).

Clients also expected a law firm to have a "normal" pyramidal composition, that is, an excess of associates, those who do the bulk of the work over partners. Tischmann had a further problem in this regard, since it had twice as many partners as associates. This is not the way a firm becomes and stays profitable.

How did Tischmann get into this situation? The firm had followed traditional lines for many years. It had recruited its associates from the main law schools in the Midwest, namely, University of Chicago and Northwestern University. The best and the brightest were taken on with the assurance, bar some calamity, that a partnership would follow after the usual probationary period of seven years. When growth was steady and predictable, as Tischmann's had been, such a policy was equitable and beneficial to all. When there were hiccups in growth, either in increases or declines, then the policy got out of kilter with the needs of the firm.

This is really a dialectical situation. The seeds of steady growth allied to a policy of ensuring tenure for everyone and hiring new associates every year contain their own poison of destruction. Eventually the organization gets too unwieldy and out of proportion. The prime ratio that ensures maximum profit begins to change and count against that end (cf. Galanter and Palay 1992).

---

[56] See examples in Chapter 1.

For example, when Tischmann's clients needed litigation counsel to handle disputes, the firm had to create a litigation section. And as litigation, itself, became a profitable line of work for law firms in general, there was more competition for that type of work in the legal market. Whereas Tischmann had created a section to deal with disputes generated by clients who were already in the firm, the section had never really sought to obtain litigation clients on its own account. Yet now it needed to do so in order to sustain its existence.

Tischmann overcame this hurdle by laterally taking on a litigation lawyer, since the litigator, who had his own stable of clients, was also a rainmaker. But the increase in litigation business engendered intense competition among corporate law firms. In order to get the large, profitable cases, one either needed to be a large firm or an exceptional rainmaker, such as Joe Flom of Skadden Arps (Caplan 1993) or Marty Lipton of Watchell Lipton (Starbuck 1993). Tischmann, as good as it claimed to be, did not live up to these requirements. Two results arose out of this state of affairs: one, it could not attract the large cases; and two, as a consequence of the first point it could not attract the associates who liked to work in litigation. And those it had were leaving—at least four did so during my period with the firm—for bigger firms.

This series of factors, namely, not enough work combined with too many partners versus associates (and not being able to take on too many more associates to correct the balance because the partners are not attracting enough clients to generate sufficient amounts of work) led to a form of stasis tending towards possible decline. This situation produced a series of emergency countermeasures. The main one was the merger with Bernstein, designed to expand the firm's client base. Tischmann hoped to do this off the backs of two senior partners in Bernstein, who were quite elderly and were presiding over a deteriorating firm that needed to be rescued. Tischmann rescued Bernstein, thereby hoping to save itself. Did it achieve salvation? Only partially. One of the partners died some time before the merger had been fully consummated, raising the possibility that his clients might go elsewhere.

The main drawback to the merger was the staffing or personnel problem. Instead of gaining an influx of clients and associates to service them, Tischmann acquired a crop of partners, mostly in the middle range tending towards the senior, and few associates. Their Bernstein mentors had in effect promised those associates who came in with the merger partnerships. As mentioned before, Tischmann's solution was to hold back the final decision for a year to give the Tischmann partnership time to observe and test the Bernstein associates. This delay exacerbated the ratio problem. Following the merger, six candidates were up for partner. In a firm of

80 lawyers, this meant nearly ten percent of the lawyers in the firm were about to be made partner in one sweep. (See Chapter 4.)

Recruiting was another problem that is increasing Tischmann's difficulties. Law firms traditionally spent enormous numbers of lawyers' hours and money on recruiting. There was the preparation of circulars describing the firm, the decision about which law schools to send them to, and most importantly, at which schools to visit to interview. Tischmann had for many years, as stated above, recruited from the University of Chicago and Northwestern University with a few from Harvard and Yale. And it had generally hired students who were on the law reviews. The firm prided itself on its intellectual prowess: it expected its lawyers to write and publish learned articles, which many did.

With the tremendous growth in the size of law firms, Tischmann could not compete in salaries or types of "sexy" work. Also, when Skadden opened an office in Chicago, it paid New York salaries to its associates—about $10,000 higher than standard Chicago rates—which worsened many firms' problems. Consequently, Tischmann no longer was able to attract the law review "stars" it had been used to recruiting. Instead it had to look at the second or third tier of law students from the usual schools, and look further afield at other law schools. Wisconsin-Madison and Minnesota law schools became part of the firm's recruitment game plan.

But perhaps the biggest shift was towards the local law schools in Chicago, such as Chicago-Kent, DePaul, and John Marshall, schools normally not considered at all. It is worth noting, though, that when Tischmann first took on a litigation partner, its choice was a graduate of Chicago-Kent. Tischmann was in a better position to recruit the law review students from such places than their typical ones.

The radical plan proposed by one senior partner, who had not met with any positive response from the partnership, was a possible solution. His idea was to avoid hiring recent graduates from law school, but instead to hire only "laterals," attorneys who had first worked elsewhere for a number of years. The standard procedure was prohibitively expensive and produced lamentably poor results (cf. Brandon 2011a). He argued that since the best graduates wanted to go to the largest firms for reasons of money and status, Tischmann should let them go because it could not compete. Most associates realizing that they would never make partner in a large firm because the odds were stacked against them, and knowing that two or three years spent at a large firm would look good on their resumes, would spent that amount of time in the large law firm, then look around for another situation often in a smaller firm.[57]

---

[57] This partner would never realize how far in the vanguard he actually was. It was not until the 2000s that law enterprises such as Axiom Law (www.axiomlaw.com) and

This is the point at which, this senior partner insisted, that Tischmann should try and recruit, since it is much easier to go from a larger firm to a smaller one than vice versa. The firm would thus be able to hire associates who, though somewhat expensive initially, would be good academically, already trained and profitable, and motivated to become a partner.

Also, as firms generally prefer to have an associate under observation for at least three years, this was a good time to enter the recruitment market. This was so far from the norm—the Cravath principle of training one's own and not taking in laterals was so ingrained—the partnership would not countenance it and the idea was rejected. And Tischmann was still left with the problem of how to obtain the best lawyers in a sellers' market.

If Tischmann were to succeed, it would probably have to merge with another firm. The merger with Bernstein was more of an acquisition for obtaining clients rather than a merger per se. This would not necessarily be an easy task, however. Law firms are quirky institutions where status and prestige are given on the basis of how good a rainmaker one is as opposed to how well one handles the law—the associates do that. When one is ostensibly a co-equal with one's partners, decision-making can be a time consuming process. For two firms of roughly equal size to come together and synchronize styles of work and governance is difficult. Tischmann still contains partners who think the firm is currently too big. They would have great difficulty in coping with a 200-lawyer firm where communications across departments and networks are extensive, and where people are assigned to specific departments with no or minimal contact and interaction with others in the firm.[58] But as I mentioned in Chapter 1, Tischmann eventually succumbed to a merger with a larger Chicago law firm in 2003—"One of 2003's Biggest Law Firm Mergers"— and in so doing gave up its name and its offices and assumed the identity of the other.

Law firms like Tischmann were beset by organizational difficulties hitherto unknown to the legal profession. To demonstrate this proposition, I turn here, to some extent, from the firm itself to the environment in which it conducts business. Before the advent of the mega-law firm, there was room in the legal industry for most forms of practice. Firms like Tischmann had a niche unoccupied by either large or small firms. Mega-

---

Lawyers on Demand adopted this precise policy. See especially http://www.lod.co.uk/index.cfm/join-us/1851 for how this system works in practice.

[58] For example, a colleague of mine who worked in one of the major Chicago law firms for several years never dealt with more than eight people, those in his department. He knew few others in the firm.

lawyering (Galanter 1983) and aggressive marketing by "legal clinics" such as Hyatt Legal Services and Jacoby and Meyers (Muris and McChesney 2006; Hornsby 2011)—a result sanctioned by the Supreme Court's pro-advertising decision in *Bates and O'Steen v. State Bar of Arizona*[59]—made competition for clients very intense. The one could offer virtually unlimited resources, at an admitted cost, the other could offer routine, standardized services at low cost. Firms in the range of 50 to 100 lawyers are in an untenable situation. Depending on both individual and corporate clients, they are in danger, if they remain a general practice firm, of losing their clients (and possible leading partners) to these other entities. General practice, medium-sized firms are thus effectively caught in a pincer movement.

There are fundamentally two answers to the question of what direction such firms can move in to avoid the pincers: Either the firm grows large, preferably quickly, or it diminishes in size by becoming a niche firm or "boutique". Whichever direction the firm goes, there are costs. One of the costs of enlarging the firm is loss of familiarity with its members. One of Tischmann's desirable characteristics, from the partners' perspectives has been its collegiality—a loose grouping of relatively unspecialized lawyers. A small firm can retain that gemeinschaft quality: a large firm cannot. A large firm, and the examples in Chapter 1 demonstrate this, is forced to take on a bureaucratic cast for organizational reasons (Faulconbridge and Muzio 2008). Rather than being a relationship of colleagues, the large firm becomes a gathering place for strangers. Lawyers in one department may never speak to those in another, except once a year at the firm dinner and dance. Small firms, if specialized, have the drawback of generally depending on referrals from other larger firms; a situation which lessens one's autonomy.

None of these strains, however, exist in a vacuum. The environment in which law firms do business has an enormous impact on the shape of the organization (Stinchcombe 1965; Aldrich 1979). Stinchcombe graphically portrays the dilemma facing organizations when he writes: "If there are ... populations in which the "liability newness" is exceptionally great, organizational innovation will tend to be carried out only when the alternatives are stark..." (1965: 148). Interestingly, the "liability of newness" may no longer be as great in the business community at large. Hirsch (1986: 801) reported "that the ten largest of 1983's 1500 mergers changed the lives of up to 220,000 employees...." Law firm mergers, too, have been a rising phenomenon. Firms like Finley, Kumble, Wagner, Heine, Underberg, Manley, Myerson and Casey were constantly searching for "sleeping

---

[59] 433 U.S. 350 (1977).

beauties" (i.e., vulnerable targets) to take over (Eisler 1990). Tischmann became a vulnerable target, and, according to the senior partner, resisted four overtures in the previous year.

Tischmann was at that point in size where, if it were to sustain itself as a general practice law firm, it would have to make a drastic change in its organization. It could not afford to sustain itself by incremental growth alone. The firm was subject to both internal and external forces. First, the firm had too many partners compared to associates. Second, Tischmann wanted to remain a general practice firm. Third, Tischmann existed in a business/profession that was growing rapidly in absolute numbers and was developing more and more larger institutions. The best response to these forces would be for Tischmann to grow to compete with the market and to correct its partner/associate ratio. But these changes would be linked with a change in internal organization. The quicker Tischmann grew, the greater the number of strangers within the organization and the more structured would be the internal organization of the firm—committees, departments—to cope with the decline in trust between members.

The reason the internal organization of the law firm changed with an increase in size and a rise in the number of law firms in the market, which in itself was a function of an increase in demand for legal services, was that it had to convert from a collegially organized institution to a more bureaucratically structured organization, one in search of profit and expansion. A collegially organized law firm is traditionally one in which the members came together to practice law and perhaps enter politics.

There was in law practice some sense of vocation, of applying knowledge to problems (Freidson 1986). Monetary reward was taken as a by-product of one's endeavors. In the present with law firms having to market themselves aggressively in the marketplace, the tolerance of the collegium is out of place. In its stead, the pursuit of profit is paramount. And the pursuit of profit requires rational accounting and management procedures, especially as an organization grows in size.

One problem not covered here is that of resource availability. The main resource for law firms is associates—of which there is a shortage for the elite bar (cf. Lazega 2001). One solution is for the elite bar to "lower" its standards and select recruits from "inferior" schools. To some extent that was already happening.[60]

---

[60] Another aspect of the relation of environment to structure not approached here in detail, but which arises in the literature (Hannan and Freeman 1977; and see 1984), is the type of competition that occurs between organizations. Hannan and Freeman suggest that organizations of equivalent size only compete with each other (1977: 945-46). I am suggesting that medium-sized firms have to compete with not only firms of similar size but also much larger law firms. While to speak of a shortage in the recession

The medium-sized firm is under threat in a tightly competitive market, and the solution is radical and brutal (see Aldrich and Auster 1986). It requires a rapid transition from gemeinschaft to gesellschaft if the firm is to survive. Departments replace collegiality, and bureaucracy points to the earnest desire for profit over professionalism, with authoritarianism presiding over collegiality. It is fair to say that stasis is impossible in the law world. The business of law is too competitive.

Finally, it was too much for Tischmann. In 2003 it merged into, or rather was taken over by, a much larger Chicago-based firm. The merger was led, with the assistance of a law firm consultant, by the key rainmaker who realized that Tischmann's survival depended on being national and international, which it could not achieve on its own. The rainmaker, who became the Chairman, tried a number of strategies. According to one Chicago newspaper:

> Initially [Tischmann] focused on trying to hook up with out-of-town firms looking to establish a bigger presence in Chicago. This way, the firm could have access to other practices and offices and still keep a measure of local independence. The firm talked to a number of firms, including Bryan Cave LLP of St. Louis.
>
> But [the Chairman] found that these firms had "a hard time articulating why they want to be in Chicago." In addition, he said he found that local offices of national firms tend to struggle in the early years as they build name recognition.

He widened the search and found a firm that was looking to expand its practice areas and gain new clients. Now Tischmann is part of big law.

---

might be thought strange, there is an over-supply of lawyers generally but a shortage of specific kinds.

PART TWO

LAWYER AND CLIENT

7

Doing Business: The Role of Office Lawyers

Introduction

My purpose in the next two chapters is to concentrate on the details of the interactions between lawyer and lawyer and lawyer and client. These interactions are displayed in a number of case studies that I develop at some length. Rather than presenting lawyers as types, I will draw them as real people engaged in tasks of moment that have consequences to themselves and those with whom they interact. But this is not *L.A. Law* or *Boston Legal* and so it is not sexy and exciting. Much of lawyers' work is routine and mundane, yet nonetheless has meaning and significance for those that do it and those that receive the benefits of it.

The focus of these chapters is what lawyers do for clients. There are two interpretations of this issue—theoretical and practical. The emphasis is on the former but will involve considerable discussion of the latter. If a lawyer says, "I'm a litigator," or "I do ERISA," or "I'm in structured finance," other lawyers will immediately recognize what and who they are. Outsiders—lay people—might on the whole find the terminology puzzling at times. But even with insiders there are degrees of "insiderness" and comprehension might not be uniform across all degrees. Heinz and Laumann (1982) argue that criminal defense lawyers would fail to understand the arcana of corporate lawyers' collateralized debt obligations and securitizations. And similarly, corporate lawyers would be confounded by the intricacies of death penalty appeals. At the general level, the problem poses an issue basic to much work on the legal profession, namely, *the problem of what lawyers do* (cf. Llewellyn and Hoebel 1941; Abel 1980; Abel and Lewis 1989; Mather 2003; Levin and Mather 2012).

It is curious that the noun *lawyer* lacks a verb that connotes a set of cognate activities to the same degree as other naming nouns. It is intuitively simple to understand painters painting, auditors auditing, nurses nursing and ministers ministering—the dictionaries have them all—but lawyers lawyering makes little semantic sense compared to the others. Indeed, the verb "to lawyer" is a neologism; both the *Oxford English Dictionary* and *Webster's Online Dictionary* carry no entries for the verb, but they do for the others above. We can take this a step further. Interestingly, we find the notion of *practice* enters as a descriptor of professionals' work, e.g., she practices law. The term denotes improvement through doing and the *OED* defines to practice as "do repeatedly as exercise to improve skill."

One solution to handle the lack of precise descriptors is to examine lawyers' actual work practices in a closely textured way (Maynard 1984; Heritage and Maynard 2006). However, we have few examples of this compared to studies undertaken in the sociology of medicine. There is one other wrinkle to the situation, which is that the authority of lawyers often depends on factors other than their direct legal knowledge. Their work as we shall see covers areas of advising that are more fitted to business than law. This also raises questions about what exactly it is that distinguishes lawyers from other professionals (Abbott 1988).

Ultimately, these theoretical concerns about professional work—what people do—are dependent on the nature of the interactions that form the infrastructure of the relationship between professional and client. Everett Hughes (1971: 304) framed it this way:

> The division of labor, in its turn, implies interaction; for it consists not in the sheer difference of one man's kind of work from that of another, but in the fact that the different tasks and accomplishments are parts of a whole whose product all, in some degree, contribute to. And wholes, in the human social realm as in the rest of the biological and the physical realm, have their essence in interaction. Work as social interaction is the central theme of sociological and social psychological study of work.

Donald Schon (1983) argues an analogous theme with his conventional model of professionals as technically rational problem solvers, which to him is insufficient for capturing the methods professionals use. Doing-in-action and knowledge-in-action are preferable as they rely on interactive methods. To understand professionals' work we must focus on the interactions in that work.

The approach I take in this book is that the central role corporate lawyers play is managing uncertainty for their clients as well as themselves. The concept of uncertainty management derives from Renée Fox's ethnographic work in medicine (1957, 1959, 2000; Fox and Swazey 1992). Fox describes two types of uncertainty: one is based on incomplete grasp of knowledge, and the second is based on the limits of current knowledge. From these she derives a third type, that which is caused by the inability of the actors to distinguish between the first two forms of uncertainty (1957: 208-9). Her presentation of the uncertainty variable arises in the context of doctor's training and the ways they begin to recognize and acknowledge its existence. Fox intertwines uncertainty into the training trajectory: "With the growth of [students'] knowledge and skill ... and the widening and deepening of his experience, a student's perspective on his own uncertainty changes" (ibid: 219).

Describing the student's awe at the amount of knowledge that must be absorbed early in the training, Fox says that by the student's third year a change in manner occurs. "He adopts a *manner* of certitude, for he has come to realize that it may be important for him to 'act like a savant' even when he does not actually feel sure" (ibid: 227). This manner is, however, short-lived because in the fourth year the student is given sole responsibility for patients; uncertainty intrudes sharply. One of Fox's student-subjects summarizes his feelings this way: "Experiences makes you less sure of yourself.... Instead of looking for the day when all the knowledge you need will be in your possession, you learn that such a day will never come" (ibid: 228). And so the doctors-to-be realize that feelings of uncertainty will never depart, but at least they are made aware of this phenomenon.

Like Fox's novices, would-be lawyers are introduced to the notions of uncertainty during their professional school training. Their texts are no longer comprehensive and inclusive, designed to facilitate the student's acquisition of knowledge step by step as most college texts do, but rather apparently random and chaotic collections of disjointed materials with little or no connective narrative (cf. D'Amato 1987; Schlegel 1989). This does not mean, however, that lawyers are necessarily fully imbued with the values of uncertainty in law school. Uncertainty is controlled, for the approach of law school is essentially theoretical, more concerned with appellate judicial decision making, than the situations students face after graduation when the real world of practice pitches them into the maw of uncertainty where the court is rarely invoked, and where solutions are not always found but often created. Indeed, the tension between the search for a "right answer" which seems implicit in such law teaching and the notions of indeterminacy which are easily inferred from the substance of the cases infuses much of the law school experience with a kind of ambivalence about uncertainty. One could argue that medicine, by virtue of its continuing ties to the hospital—during training and afterwards in practice—smoothes the entry of its students into practice. The training commingles theory and practice. Doctors never server the connection between their training institutions and their places of work because they are often the same. Law schools entirely lack this capacity: they are not functional equivalents of the hospital and they are not conspicuously successful in mixing elements of theory and practice (Stevens 1983). Although they raise the issues of uncertainty for their students, this is not a theme that recurs in the law school experience. It is the move into practice which prompts the thought that "experience makes you less certain of yourself."

The uncertainty of practice functions at more than one level. Each type of uncertainty is contingent on the situation. For my purposes there are three main types of uncertainty ranging in degree from high to low risk, plus a fourth kind that it is ancillary to the other three:

1. Where the lawyer is not handling law per se or tightly specified sets of facts. Instead, the situation is fluid, open and constantly changing. The lawyer must rely on experiential skills rather than "book learning." A typical example is a business negotiation.

2. Where a lawyer is ignorant of the law on the topic. Sometimes faking knowledge—"a snow job"—is necessary to reassure the client and to preserve the lawyer from exposure.

3. Where the lawyer needs to buy time in order to develop a satisfactory answer.

4. Where the lawyer finds himself in the vortex of the politics of the firm.

If the first two were visible to clients, they would embarrass the lawyer raising questions about what lawyers are supposed to be doing for their clients. How much uncertainty is experienced is a function of the status of the lawyer. It is potentially more embarrassing for a partner than a first-year associate to show ignorance. Telling clients about the third form of uncertainty is not entirely bad. It tells the client that the lawyer has concern for the client's welfare and justifies research and billing. Kagan and Rosen (1985: 404) describe one of the roles of the lawyer as "Insurer." Buying time is a valuable insurance policy. So, the first two types of uncertainty concern the state of the lawyer's ego and the third is focused on the client. The lawyer hopes to preserve harmony for herself and her community and not alarm the client.

The case studies presented here delve into typical transactions that lawyers do with and for clients. Within these studies I hope I will be able to show what kinds of tasks lawyers carry out for their clients and to display what role law plays in these tasks. I have broken down these tasks into two broad categories, namely, facilitative law and litigation, as they capture conceptually the two poles of what lawyers engage in—consensus and conflict.

Business lawyers, who will also be referred to as office lawyers, do considerably different work than do litigators. Although the two groups are found in the same law firm, they are quite distinct in both their form, so to speak, and their function.[61] Litigators essentially play a reactive role:

---

[61] The analogy with the respective roles of barristers and solicitors in the UK is helpful here.

a crisis occurs and someone is needed to remedy or to repair the damage, or to salvage something. Their role is that of *ex post facto* fixers. Office lawyers operate on an *ex ante* basis; their role is to plan things so that crises do not occur. They are essentially proactive. One could say a business lawyer has failed when a litigator is brought in. That is one of the reasons the Tischmann old guard used to ridicule litigators as second-class citizens. As one senior partner once said to a litigation associate from the University of Chicago law school: "What's a graduate of the University of Chicago doing in litigation?"

Business lawyers carry out a large range of tasks: arranging loan agreements with banks, engaging in international business, incorporating companies, floating securities' issues, negotiating the purchase of shopping malls. In this chapter I shall examine in some detail how some of these transactions are put together.

All these tasks can be boiled down to two: office lawyers essentially draft documents and negotiate (often about the documents they have just drafted).[62] The process is not entirely a matter of client walking into the office and saying, "Draft me a loan agreement." The drafting is not undertaken until the lawyers have a clear idea of what a client wants. At this stage it is likely that the lawyers will be involved in business discussions. For example, a client may need capital to expand his business. If he needs advice, then one of the possible groups of advisers a businessman may turn to is a corporate lawyer. Depending on the degree of expertise if the client and the degree of intimacy with the lawyer, a client may ask for advice on whether or not to borrow and how to do it or simply ask for the best means of raising money. Such questions are not entirely simple, however, as the means of raising money is closely related to the uses it will be put to.

In Tischmann great emphasis was placed on establishing strong ties with clients, which range from small to large companies, closely held and publicly held. The senior partner would have parties at this home for clients and some of the senior lawyers. Every year favored clients would be taken to the Chicago Bar Association's Christmas Spirits Show.[63] Some of the senior lawyers had almost avuncular relationships with their clients, such that clients would call for advice on all sorts of matters. (See Chapter 5 above for further discussion of this.) For example, one lawyer frequently gave advice on how to act in the stock market. A client called asking if he should sell his block of 24,000 shares in General Foods to Philip Morris

---

[62] Compare Flood and Sosa 2008 and Flood and Skordaki 2009, where different types of document construction are analyzed.

[63] The show, a musical, sells out each year and it was not an inexpensive outing.

during a takeover war, even though the price was still rising. The lawyer told him to sell now, at $118 per share, rather than wait for $120 "because the deal is going through and any increments [on the share price] would be small. If you sell now, you will only lose $4,000; cheap insurance for getting a good price." The client preferred his lawyer's advice to that of a stockbroker.

Office lawyers, though not exclusively, must be able to give advice quickly when asked, but they may sometimes say they will need to have some research done first. In one instance, a senior lawyer received a call from a longstanding client, the treasurer of a closely held business. The lawyer responded to the client's questions about the potential effects of the company's president taking early retirement as follows:

> Hi, Dave. Pete wants to retire in a month's time? Now he's currently president? And he has a deferred earnings plan. If you want him to stay on as director, you may have trouble with Social Security. They'll say you're paying him for services now. But now if he goes altogether and you take over as president, you're going to need a new director. You wouldn't be happy with just your mother, sister and you. There's Joe [a longtime company employee], but he might want extra money. He'd like the title though. He's been with you long enough.

The client then raised a different issue:

> Yeah, Dave, there's a possible change in the tax law which might affect the dividend credit. You may want to make a payment before the end of the year. Think about it.

The conversation then reverted back to the first issue:

> No, there's nothing to prevent you being both president and treasurer. The Act used to forbid the same person being president and secretary, but I'm not certain that's even true any more.

The lawyer finished the conversation with a promise to check on the question of his client holding more than one post.

Sometimes the issues are not so easy to resolve, but the lawyer does not want to refuse to speak or attempt to answer the client's question for fear the client will go elsewhere. A securities lawyer, named Jones, was called by a group of cattle feed investors from Texas. They had started an investment program in cattle in which they would first solicit investors and then purchase the cattle. They expected to purchase between one million and two million dollars' worth of cattle. The original cattle feed agreement, however, had been drawn up without a lawyer, so it was full of mistakes. On going to see a lawyer on an ancillary matter, the lawyer realized that all kinds of problems would ensure unless the feed investors obtained expert advice. The Texan lawyer knew of the securities lawyer at Tischmann because he had heard him speak at a securities conference.

Jones knew nothing about cattle feed investment programs, but was not going to admit it, so he said: "Let's assume, hypothetically, that I know nothing about this and you tell me all about it." The ploy worked and Jones discovered that there was sufficient overlap between cattle feed investment programs and capital equipment investment that he could make some intelligent extempore comments. The cattle feed investors were unable to recognize how or even why they had gone wrong. Jones explained that since the original agreement did not meet SEC requirements and the investors were not actively involved in the buying of the cattle—an expert did the buying—those running the program were at risk. They had balked at the possible cost of writing as complex a document as they thought they would have to produce to satisfy SEC requirements. Jones explained that the document need only run to 22 pages without exhibits. They should revise their document—he would do it for them—and submit the revisions to their investors and offer them the right of rescission.

The original investors were unsure whether to continue with their program now that they were in breach of the law. Jones told them to go ahead since, as they were already in violation, there was no reason why they should not continue. He could extract them, "with their asses", from any difficulty with the SEC; he had just handled a similar case with much worse facts and brought out the clients "intact." Jones said that doing this kind of retroactive repair work "was like seeing a box of lawnmower bits come into the office and being asked to put it back together again."

The ability to do these "snow jobs", so that clients will not recognize how something is being done on their behalf, is widely admired among lawyers as a desirable talent. The purpose is so that clients will never see or receive any intimation that their lawyer is fallible (Flood 1991). Of course this kind of veil cannot be held up all the time, but it can hide errors and gaps in knowledge much of the time. Doing snow jobs involves considerable interactional work for the lawyer.

In another situation, a client bank asked a corporate lawyer for help with a transaction they were conducting with an English bank involving a letter of guarantee. American banks do not issue these, relying instead on standby letters of credit. The corporate lawyer, a partner, knew nothing of letters of guarantee but wanted to hide his ignorance in this area from the bank, so he drafted two associates to research the issue and come up with a recognizable letter of guarantee which he could present to the bank officers. The international lawyers in the firm had been unable to supply any answers. One of the associates learned that American branches of English banks would, on notice of the issuance of a letter of guarantee, issue in its stead a standby letter of credit. The associate believed this would resolve the problem. The corporate lawyer would not accept this solution, demanding to be told what a letter of guarantee looked like.

After several hours of research, the associates located some cases that had parts of such letters in them and patched together a near facsimile of a letter of guarantee. After the partner had told the bank what a letter of guarantee was and that using an American branch of an English bank could circumvent it, the client bank decided to adopt the latter course. Thus the lawyer was able to extend his knowledge at the expense of his client and forestall any displays of ignorance.

This instance of a snow job exemplifies Goffman's (1959) distinction between front stage and backstage performances. For a snow job to work the two areas must be kept distinct; one must not be allowed to leak into the other. The lawyer's ignorance was never publicly displayed to the client, and was fended off by the claim of having to research the matter. Backstage, within the firm, ignorance is a private disability that is to be collectively overcome. Sometimes snow jobs require immediate improvisation without the respite of retreating backstage to find new props. The case of the lawyer counseling the Texan cattle feed investors is one. Here the lawyer had to construct a role virtually within the purview of the audience, his clients, developing that character as he revealed clues. He had no time to rehearse a script. Most lawyers avoid such roles because the ability to make mistakes is enormous.

I said at the beginning of this chapter that much of an office lawyer's work is drafting and negotiating documents. Document creation is both a quick and tedious process. The firm already has created and stored most documents, such as loan agreements. Tischmann, like many other firms, keeps a document file that contains an array of documents ready for "cannibalization." If the document required is not in the document file, someone will generally know of a file with a good model. Thus, the collective memory of the firm is important in the process of document creation.

Associates are usually given the responsibility for drafting documents (see Spangler 1986: 49-50). This is generally done by cutting and pasting an existing document to take account of their clients' particular needs. For example, one associate who spent much of his time drafting wills, some of them very complex, had a battery of ten in model form stored. They had originally been drafted by a senior partner to allow for different clients' levels of income and capital. Some of the wills were hundreds of pages long. The associate was expected only to plug in the details specific to his clients and not tinker with the structure of the document. He confided that "Irwin is very protective about his draft wills. I've tried to get him to change them sometimes because the language gets too baroque in places, but he wants them just the way he wrote them."

Example 1: Constructing a Loan Agreement

Sometimes the lawyer will simply modify an existing document rather than draft a new one. Loan agreements are a prime example. These are sometimes framed by the lending bank as preparation for negotiating a final form. The following example, described in some detail, shows how such a document is transformed from a unilaterally conceived agreement into a consensual one (cf. Flood and Sosa 2008). There are essentially two reasons for presenting this and the next examples in detail. The first is that they show in a finely-grained way what the very processes of lawyering are. The second is that approximately 18 percent of lawyers' time is taken up with talking face to face with others.[64] What I hope will emerge from this example is how the document is rendered into a final form in a very gradual way. The document's final form is as much a result of the interaction between the two senior lawyers—Peter Black and Marvin Broad—on either side of the transaction as it is a quest for the most profitable and efficient form. These two lawyers, both of whom have been in practice for many years, know each other well and it is their personalities that dominate. As they thrust and parry, we will see how a legal institution—a contract—is cut up, then eventually stitched together and given new life.

In this example, a large, closely held company (Company Ltd.) wanted to borrow $5,000,000 from a medium-sized bank (First Bank). The negotiations extended over three meetings: in the first two, the clients—the president, the senior vice-president, and the chief financial officer—were present; the final meeting was held between the lawyers without their clients. I should add that the clients had used Tischmann for at least ten years, and that the senior partner had also been the lawyer of the previous owners of the company. In one respect, he was almost a godfather to the present company, having been involved with the company longer than his clients had.

The senior partner in Tischmann (whose client this was) was annoyed by the complexity and wordiness of the document since, as he saw it, it was drafted by First Bank's lawyers. The loan agreement opened with a two paragraph statement on who the parties were and the amount to be borrowed. The statement was then followed by thirty-eight single-spaced pages of terms and conditions. Several pages of schedules were to follow the main document. According to the senior partner, the other main bank he had dealt with, Second Bank, used much shorter and simpler agreements, but he was unable to use Second Bank for this loan.

---

[64] See Chapter 4 for further details of how lawyers spend their time.

The First Meeting

The first meeting, held at Tischmann, was between First Bank's representatives, an accountant from the bank, three outside lawyers from a firm that traditionally handled First Bank's legal work, and two lawyers from Tischmann: the senior partner and a middle-level partner who frequently worked with the senior partner and the clients mentioned above on corporate matters. The two teams of lawyers knew each other well, having worked on similar matters before.

The cast is as follows:

Peter Black	First Bank outside senior counsel
Margaret Taupe	First Bank outside counsel
David Green	First Bank outside counsel
Brian Ochre	First Bank accountant
Clive Small	Company Ltd. President
Earl Long	Company Ltd. Senior vice-president
Frank Short	Company Ltd. Chief financial officer
Marvin Broad	Tischmann senior partner
Ray Narrow	Tischmann partner

The meeting started, in a low-key fashion, with a discussion about ownership of the company and similar provisions found in other banks' documents:

Marvin Broad   There a number of areas where the bank can exercise for any fault.

Brian Ochre   We take fifty percent of inventory.

Clive Small   You must remember these are perishable goods, not nuts and bolts.

Marvin Broad   There are listed a number of subsidiaries which are just names. I'm not trying to hit everything, but I ..

Peter Black   ...You're doing fine.

Marvin Broad   But there's a provision in here about owner-ship.[65]

Brian Ochre   We look for continuity.

Clive Small   Sure. If we sell the business...

Marvin Broad   ...We're not dealing...

Peter Black   ...with that.

Marvin Broad   This is not a one or two man business and when Second Bank dealt with this, this provision didn't exist.

Brian Ochre   Second Bank lends on people, we don't. Didn't they give you a document like this?

Clive Small   No.

Peter Black   OK, we'll give you a grace period. If only one goes, we do nothing. If both go, we'll give a ninety-day period.

Marvin Broad   It must be more than ninety days, say six months

Margaret Taupe   Too long. We must see the management who'd be dealing with us. Ninety days would be good.

Clive Small   Four months.

Peter Black   One hundred and twenty days—fine.

Marvin Broad   Fine.

In this discussion the lawyers, bank representative, and the client were concerned with the actions the bank might take if the clients were to sever their connections with Company Ltd. Clause 8.16 makes the company merely the sum of its owners, with no separate existence, despite the fact that the loan is to the company and not its owners, individually or collectively. This apparent version of reality has to be countered by the fact that the loan will be spent by the owners. In corporation law, a corporation is supposed to have a separate existence from those that constitute it (Henn and Alexander 1983). But the lending bank here is aware that such

---

[65] The provision in the document reads: "8.16. The Borrowers (i.e., the company) shall use their best efforts to prevent [Clive Small and Earl Long] in the aggregate from owning at any time less than eighty percent (80%) of the legal and beneficial interest of the voting common stock of [Company Ltd]. Borrowers shall use their best efforts to cause [Clive Small and Earl Long] to remain engaged in the active management of the Borrowers and Subsidiaries and to perform duties substantially similar to those presently performed."

a company depends considerably for its success on those who have the greatest interest in it—its owners. This is why First Bank insisted on Clause 8.16. Although First Bank's accountant, Brian Ochre, insisted the bank did not "lend on people"—as claimed by the senior partner, Marvin Broad, for Second Bank—First Bank in fact achieved the same end as Second Bank by tying the owners into the business to secure the success of the company and the loan.

It is interesting to note here how lawyers negotiate over units of time (Zerubavel 1979, 1999; Parkes and Thrift 1980; Thrift 1990). In the discussion of the grace period if Clause 8.16 were to be invoked, the lawyers would tend to speak in terms of number of days rather than any other unit of time. The initial period specified is 90 days, approximately three months, but months represent a poor unit of measure because they are irregular and can be measured in more than one way (e.g., calendar and lunar). Moreover, the only time a lawyer uses months is as an obvious negotiating ploy to extend the initial 90 day period: "It must be more than ninety days, say six months." Marvin Broad knows he will not receive his demand; all he is striving for is to set an upper limit. When the final resolution comes—suggested by Clive Small as four months—the lawyers convert it to the appropriate number of days, 120. This notion of time crops up again later in the meeting:

> Marvin Broad   Three point one,[66] Frank [Short] is in your province.
>
> Brian Ochre   We'd like to receive statements and payments by the tenth of the month.
>
> Frank Short   Ten business days or ten calendar days? If the first, we can do it.
>
> Brian Ochre   OK.

Sometimes time, or rather the potential for time, is important without it being measured in precise units. The following piece of talk about the presence or omission of notice to the borrowers in the event of default illustrates this.

> Marvin Broad   Legally, I have no problem until we get to nine point seven.[67] Even if we are in default, why shouldn't we have notice?

---

[66] Clause 3.1 has to do with periodic reports from the company to the bank describing the state of the business.

Peter Black   We don't want to get into questions of notice. You might challenge the propriety of the notice and so on.

Marvin Broad   Yes, but problems could be mitigated if notice is given.

Peter Black   The waiver...

Margaret Taupe   This is no problem because notice has to be given under certain sales, for example, UCC.[68] It's only recovering the collateral.

Marvin Broad   Well, I'd like to think about that.

Here there is no express discussion of the quantity of time. Instead, its marked absence in the document is an index that drastic action—repossession—is about to occur. The bank and its lawyers signified the importance of this waiver of notice clause by printing it in upper case characters. The company's lawyer is saying that the omission of notice will only exacerbate difficulties if they arise. With notice, a potentially inflammable situation can be rendered harmless and solvable. What Margaret Taupe offers by way of an alternative is the Uniform Commercial Code requirement that sales of certain items require notice, indicating that the company would therefore have notice of a sort. Ultimately, Marvin Broad puts the issue to the side. The meeting ended soon after this discussion.

Sometimes at these meetings the lawyers throw jibes at each other. As the senior partner was turning the pages of the document, the bank lawyer said, "Are you looking for a major one, Marvin?" To which the senior partner replied, "Yes". Both knew that the other was joking, despite the undertone of truth insofar as the senior partner was looking for contentious points (and found some, which come up later).

---

[67] Clause 9.7 reads: "*Waiver of Notice.* IN THE EVENT OF A DEFAULT, THE BORROWERS (PURSUANT TO AUTHORITY GRANTED BY THEIR BOARDS OF DIRECTORS) HEREBY WAIVE ALL RIGHTS TO NOTICE AND HEARING OF ANY KIND PRIOR TO THE EXERCISE BY THE LENDER OF ITS RIGHTS TO REPOSSESS THE COLLATERAL WITHOUT JUDICIAL PROCESS OR TO REPLEVY, ATTACH OR LEVY UPON THE COLLATERAL WARRANTY WITHOUT PRIOR NOTICE OR HEARING. THE BORROWERS ACKNOWLEDGE THAT THEY HAVE BEEN ADVISED BY COUNSEL OF THEIR CHOICE WITH RESPECT TO THIS TRANSACTION AND THIS AGREEMENT." That the clause is important is acknowledged by it being printed in capitals rather than lower case which is used in the rest of the document.

[68] Uniform Commercial Code.

The Second Meeting

At the second meeting, held approximately a month after the first, the participants (the same as before) discussed two central issues: trademarks and waiver of jury trial. One of Company Ltd.'s most valuable assets was its collection of trademarks, which had achieved national recognition. Because they identified the company in the public mind, they were of great importance to First Bank as well as Company Ltd. The meeting began with the following discussion:

Marvin Broad   Clive, you indicated you didn't like filing trademarks as collateral.

Clive Small   But if the business fails don't they get our trademarks?

Marvin Broad   They need an assignment if they want to sell it. The other way is to give a negative covenant that you won't sell it to anyone else.[69]

Clive Small   Yes, this company is worth more as an entity than its pieces.

Marvin Broad   I personally question the assignment of the trademarks.

Clive Small   But you're giving them the ability to cut out the trademarks. I would rather they sell the business.

Brian Ochre   But what do we do if we don't have them?

Marvin Broad   People do a trademark search and they find you have done a collateral assignment that might impugn your credibility.

Brian Ochre   How do we look to the inventory without the trademarks?

Margaret Taupe   You have the tangibles. We need a secured interest by having a filing in the Patent and Trademark Office.[70]

---

[69] *Black's Law Dictionary* (5th ed.): Negative covenant – A provision in an employment agreement or a contract of sale of a business which prohibits the employee or seller from competing in the same area or market.

[70] *Black's Law Dictionary* (5th ed.): Security interest – A form of interest in property which provides that the property may be sold on default in order to satisfy the obligation for which the security interest is given.

Marvin Broad   Once we're in default, yes, but what does it do to the reputation of the company?

Earl Long   Did it happen before?

Frank Short   No, I don't know what effect it would have.

Marvin Broad   For the bank it's a valuable asset.

Peter Black   It's *the* asset.

Earl Long   Would you do it if we're in default?

Peter Black/Brian Ochre (together)   It's an option.

Brian Ochre   To go back: to sell it in toto would realize more.

Marvin Broad   In bankruptcy, of course, the bank wouldn't have priority. It's up to the court.

Brian Ochre   If we're in there selling the real estate, et cetera, and the trustee in bankruptcy is selling of the trademarks, I don't see how we're better off. I don't like it.

Marvin Broad   Ray, let me see the previous agreement.

Marvin Broad   [To Brian Ochre] Did we discuss it before?

Clive Small   Why don't we put it aside and go on?

There is a tension here as to the fate of the trademarks. Without them the company is valueless: if another company were to acquire them, it would immediately gain the prestige, and potential market, of Company Ltd. Clive Small recognizes this when he says: "But you're giving them the ability to cut out the trademarks. I would rather they sell the business." The bank accountant and the bank lawyer are convinced that the only asset worth rescuing from a dying company would be its trademarks, hence their insistence on making a filing with the Patent and Trademark Office. The senior partner offers, though not very strongly, a countermeasure, that of giving a negative covenant—a legally binding undertaking not to something—not to sell the trademarks to any other entity or person except First Bank. He is concerned that others in the business world will draw the wrong inferences from First Bank's filing, which could damage or mar Company Ltd.'s reputation as a creditworthy business.

As important as the trademarks and their possible fates are, they are perceived as blocking the negotiation of the document. It is Clive Small, the client, who proposes leaving the issue to one side, thereby placing it in the category of something primarily for the lawyers to resolve. Marvin

Broad implicitly agrees when he says later, "I'm going to skip over a lot of things which don't involve the principals [clients] here."

Much of the talk at such meetings revolves around "language" as an abstract entity—a structure without apparent substance. That is, lawyers will routinely say, "We need some "language" here, without specifying what that "language" will be. To a large extent, when such a statement is made, the actors agree either explicitly or implicitly by not objecting; this also suggests that there is a tacit, uniform understanding about what the appropriate "language" is to be inserted even though it is not expressly articulated. The problem usually comes about when the associate whose task it is to do the drafting does not know what "language" to insert. For example, in the first meeting the following exchange took place:

> Marvin Broad   Can you give statements, Frank, on a timely basis, that is, a hundred and twenty days?
>
> Frank Short   Yes.
>
> Brian Ochre   From a mechanical point of view that doesn't give us much time on renewal.
>
> Peter Black   We can just add a sentence of some sort.

To the lawyer, most problems are soluble by inserting the correct "language" at the appropriate point in the document, that is, documents are fundamentally infinitely interpretable. Clients and nonlawyers do not always recognize this aspect of lawyers' work, that documents are scripts to be rewritten many times before the final version is approved. They see lawyers tinkering with documents couched in esoteric legalese as absorbed in arcane rituals. Sometimes, however, the invocation of "language" fails to repair the situation. Consider the following discussion:

> Ray Narrow   What about "lender's discretion"? [Ray Narrow is referring to Clause 3.2 *"Eligible Accounts,"* wherein it says: "Lender shall have the right in its sole discretion to determine if an Account is an Eligible Account...."]
>
> Marvin Broad   Isn't it supposed to be out?
>
> Margaret Taupe   No...
>
> Peter Black   No, if there is a situation where we disagree—for example, the Air Force not being a government agency—then someone has to make a decision.

Marvin Broad   With the language you've got here, the day after we start operating you could demand a lock box.[71] I have a
problem with your suggestion with "reasonable basis" for a lock
box. There are no standards.

Frank Short   Only a portion of our receipts go in the lock
box.

Brian Ochre   We're not asking you to change how you do
business.

Peter Black   We just want the right to have some funds in
a lock box.

Marvin Broad   Clive, how do you define what should go into
a lock box?

Clive Small   Our customers do it.

Brian Ochre   Clive, do you have a problem with this? We're
just reserving the right to protect our collateral. We expect each
other to act reasonably.

Marvin Broad   Let's put some language in about reasonable
basis, some exculpatory language.

Brian Ochre   We can always do business with another
company; you can go to another bank.

Clive Small   That's right.

Marvin Broad   That's what it comes down to.

Here there is a conflict between what the bank accountant considers
reasonable—that is, each party will act reasonably—and the desire by the
senior partner to write this into the document with "some exculpatory
language". He mistrusts the unanchored term "reasonable" floating
around the document ready to scuttle, perhaps, his clients' interests without warning; he wants to moor it to standards, though these too are unarticulated. And though Marvin Broad criticizes the term "reasonable" when
devoid of context, it does not prevent him, at a later point, asserting the
need for "reasonable" language himself: it is still linked, however, to the
word "exculpatory": "Let's put some language in about reasonable basis,
some exculpatory language". Words such as "reasonable" are extremely

---

[71] Marvin Broad is referring to Clause 3.7 which, among other things, says Lender has
the right to have all payments to Borrowers paid into a lock box account, which Borrowers would not be able to touch.

context sensitive. There is no a priori sense of what constitutes reasonable; only within a given set of circumstances can the word carry meaning. Marvin Broad's concerns focus on the imputation of blame in the event of a default. If he could persuade First Bank to accept exculpatory language, then First Bank would find itself with more obstacles to gaining access to Company Ltd.'s assets than if they had not accepted the exculpatory language. This, in claiming that no standards exist, Broad attempts to create new ones.

No one is disputing that some funds will have to go into a lock box, since some already had been placed there. What is being negotiated is how much and with what frequency. When the senior partner finally advocates inserting "exculpatory language" into the document, the bank accountant, Brian Ochre, reminds him, very strongly, that their relationship is not sacrosanct. First Bank is not involuntarily committed to lending to Company Ltd.; both can seek commitments elsewhere. What Ochre is implicitly saying is that, as co-members of an activity which all of them have engaged in before, Marvin Broad's demand for exculpatory language breaks the recursive mold which has been established over time (Boden 1987: 45). Thus, Broad's demand has to be countered with the threat of a harsh sanction—a twofold sanction since it would affect his relationship with his clients as well as with the bank.

The two sides finally come to some form of resolution when the senior partner brings up the issue of waiver of trial by jury. This provision is contained in Clause 10.8, which, like the waiver of notice provision was printed in uppercase letters.[72] In the following extract we see how the senior partner objects to this provision and ties it into the matter of the trademarks discussed above.

Marvin Broad   We don't want this waiver [of trial by jury] in the agreement.

Peter Black   Marvin, for this to operate, you would be in default. Then it's not the time to argue technicalities. If there's going to be a big fight, there'll be a fight. It's standard provision.

Marvin Broad   Waiving trial by jury is not standard.

Peter Black   It is.

---

[72] Clause 10.8 reads: "*Submission to Jurisdiction* ... AT THE OPTION OF THE LENDER, THE BORROWER WAIVE, TO THE EXTENT PERMITTED BY LAW, TRIAL BY JURY...."

Marvin Broad   It depends what side you're on as to whether you want a jury. In the agreement with Second Bank it wasn't there.

Peter Black   We don't have that agreement. You show us that mystical agreement and let's see what they did.

Brian Ochre   We've asked several times to see that agreement.

Marvin Broad   How many?

Brian Ochre   Several, and I suppose our sister bank must have some insecurity language in there.

Marvin Broad   No, I would never let my client agree to such language.

Brian Ochre/Peter Black [together]   Well, we think of it as standard.

Peter Black   We have to also resolve the trademark issue.

Marvin Broad   Two issues: trademarks and jury trial.

Brian Ochre   I don't see, Clive, what the problem is over the trademarks.

Marvin Broad   The problem could come up because trademark collateral assignments aren't that common. Someone might do a search because they want a mark. So how much damage, which I can't totally evaluate, might occur?

Clive Small   We'll give up the trademark for the jury trial.

Marvin Broad   No. They're not interchangeable like that.

Clive Small   Which is important? Is the jury trial important?

Marvin Broad   Not as important as the trademark. It's not a legal question, it's a business one.

Earl Long   We can give up the trademark.

Marvin Broad   That leaves us with the jury trial.

Clive Small   I think it's a quid pro quo.

Marvin Broad   If they're suing us for damages, we want that protection.

Brian Ochre   I need to talk to Peter about this.

Marvin Broad   Use my office.

Brian Ochre, Peter Black and Margaret Taupe leave the conference room. While they are out, the Tischmann lawyers chat among themselves and with their clients. At one point Clive Small says, "I don't mind giving up the trademark." The others return after about five minutes and Peter Black says, "We'll give you the jury trial waiver."

The final resolution is a trade of giving up the trademark collateral assignment in order to keep the right to a trial by jury. The senior partner considered this a successful outcome, as did his clients. Before the deal was cut, Marvin Broad attempted to invoke, as he had done previously, prior agreements with Second Bank, which he claimed contained no provisions waiving jury trial. Previously, he had been able to rely on it without question; at this stage, however, his bluff is called. The document is never produced, and, consequently, is no longer appealed to.

In order to avoid an impasse, the lawyers join the issues of trademarks and jury trial waiver. During this discussion, Marvin Broad has the handicap of his client, Clive Small, joining in and suggesting a trade off. The senior partner tries to close out his client, but the bank's representatives take the client's intervention as an opportunity to discuss matters among themselves, after which they agree to the trade. The bank accountant said, as the meeting was closing, that he would be glad when the discussions were finished so that the bank and Company Ltd., could "get down to business."

The relationship between lawyer and client was cordial in these meetings. Company Ltd. had been a client of the senior partner's before it came into the ownership of Clive Small and Earl Long. In fact, Marvin Broad was instrumental in bringing about the changeover and they had relied on his advice for many years. With this background, the senior partner was able to direct his clients, especially by taking control in meetings. He would sit in the center with the clients at his sides.

In First Bank's situation, by contrast, the bank accountant was in control; the lawyers provided help only as and when needed. (For purposes of this loan, the bank accountant was the client, although the individual with primary authority to act as "the client" is sometimes complex and difficult to ascertain precisely (Hazard 1978).)

The Third Meeting

The first two meetings had taken place at Tischmann's office. The third meeting, between the lawyers only, was held at the office of the bank's lawyers. This meeting was oriented to more detailed work than the other two. Much of the discussion concerned changing one or two words in a clause. Though this was the final meeting, not all the remaining issues were resolved. Some had to be taken back to the clients, especially to the bank. The following exchange exemplifies the very detailed changes that were made:

> Marvin Broad Do you have any comments, Ray?
>
> Ray Narrow At the top of page nine[73] it says, "The Borrowers promise to pay the amount <u>reflected as owing by them under their Loan Account...</u>" Take out the underlined phrase and put in "owed by them hereunder" as in the note.
>
> Marvin Broad Good point.
>
> Margaret Taupe OK

There is no great change in substance here. Rather the alteration is for the sake of form, so that the agreement and its accompanying note are consistent. And even when the problem is more complicated than that of consistency, most of these changes are accomplished amicably. For example:

> Marvin Broad On seven point eight,[74] we want to change the wording about ERISA.[75] ERISA is so slippery and elusive that you can find yourself liable under ERISA without knowing it. And we shouldn't be in default because of that. We closed a facility in San Diego and the Teamsters Union put in a demand for over a hundred thousand dollars. We eventually settled for thirty thousand, and it shouldn't have been done that way, but they thought they were acting properly.
>
> Margaret Taupe Can we put in "reasonably expected" before "material liability" in line five?
>
> Marvin Broad That's acceptable.

Here again the term "reasonable" is invoked, and here, too, the parties "know" what is meant by it. Of the issues could not be resolved and some had to be referred back to the clients, consider the following:

---

[73] Clause 2.4 "*Loan Accounts*".

[74] Clause 7.8 "*Pension Plans*" says, "The Borrowers shall and shall cause the Subsidiaries to (i) keep in full force and effect any and all Pension Plans which are presently in existence or may, from time to time, come into existence under ERISA, unless such Pension Plans can be terminated without [*reasonably expected*] *material liability* to the Borrowers...."

[75] ERISA stands for the Employee Retirement Income System Act. It is a statute containing extremely complex and stringent requirements for pension and retirement plans, and consequently has generated much work for lawyers.

Marvin Broad   On seven point ten,[76] I'm going to take a strong position on having this out. Just because the banking laws change doesn't mean we should have to indemnify the bank. In other First Bank agreements, and I've done a lot of them, one as recent as two or three weeks ago, they weren't in.

Margaret Taupe   Yes, but you have option of prepaying and we don't have reciprocal arrangements. This is to protect us.

Marvin Broad   Well, I want it out. It may be in the standard agreement, but it should come out.

Margaret Taupe   I'll talk to Brian Ochre about it.

Marvin Broad   Please do.

In the bank lawyer's view, this wide-ranging measure is a balance to Company Ltd.'s right to prepayment. By having the right to prepay, the company can save considerable amounts of interest payments (which is how the bank makes its profit). Because the senior partner also realized that it was a powerful instrument in the bank's hands, he refused to let it stand. Ultimately, the bank withdrew the provision from the agreement; it did not consider it worth jeopardizing the entire transaction for a single somewhat remote clause. The meeting ended shortly after this discussion, and the outstanding problems were resolved by telephone and letter. Interestingly, without the clients present, Marvin Broad no longer invokes the name of Second Bank as the arbiter of correct form, as he did in previous meetings. In fact, he does very much the opposite, and mentions First Bank. Instead of opposing First Bank with another's agreement, he brings them face to face with their own procedures. But Margaret Taupe avoids the issue by passing it to Brian Ochre, the bank's accountant.

---

[76] Clause 7.10 *"Supervening Illegality"*: "If, at any time or times hereafter, there shall become effective any amendment to, deletion from or revision, modification or any other change in any provision of any statute, or any rule, regulation or interpretation thereunder or any similar law or regulation, affecting the Lender's extension of credit described in this Agreement, the Borrowers shall, at the Lender's option, either (i) pay to the Lender the then outstanding balance of the Liabilities, and hold the Lender harmless from and against any and all obligations, fees, liabilities, losses, penalties, costs, expenses and damages, of every king and nature, imposed upon or incurred by the Lender by reason of Borrower's failure or inability to comply with the terms of this Agreement or any of the other Financing Agreements, or (ii) indemnify and hold the Lender harmless from and against any and all obligations, fees, liabilities, losses, penalties, costs, expenses and damages, of every kind and nature, imposed upon or incurred by the Lender by reason of such amendment, deletion, revision, modification, or other change." This is a strong provision holding the borrower liable for any change in the law that might affect the lender. Note also the great amount of redundancy in the provision—(ii) repeats (i) almost word for word—which is typical of such business agreements.

This example shows that legal documents are not immutable objects, but are open to change and reconstruction, as long as the basic structure is unimpaired. It further shows that lawyers engage in complex processes of practical reasoning (Lynch 1985). That is, the process of formulating a document recognizably acceptable to all the actors is an unfolding and contingent process that is not—as one might expect from a traditional reading of law as a "principled discipline"—merely an explication and application of some fundamental axioms.

Example 2: Selling a Shopping Mall

The second example involves the sale of a shopping mall. Like the first example it is a complex transaction requiring close attention to many disparate details that have to be attended to separately then be all brought to completion at the same time: the deal has to be able "to close" as a house sale closes. This kind of transaction, however, requires more people and takes much longer than a house sale.

The buying and selling of shopping malls are extremely complex events. In part this is because there are so many parties involved in the transaction—lawyers, accountants, bankers, insurance companies, government agencies, and developers. In one such acquisition of a mall, to the value of $43,500,000, the file comprised seventeen expandable folders and 116 sub-folders as listed in Figure 7.1. So, these are protracted, complicated deals entailing many man-hours from the parties and their associates. What is especially interesting about the following example is that although the development company is selling the shopping mall, it wants to keep control of it for a few years. Such an arrangement is unusual inasmuch as a transfer of property from one party to another generally entails the transfer of the property itself and the rights to do whatever the new owner wishes (subject to some covenants and easements etc.). So in this example some of the rights that would usually move to the purchaser are staying with the seller. The retention of these rights has a significant influence on the subsequent negotiations.

FIGURE 7.1

Summary Description of Acquisition of Mall Shopping Center File

Folder 1 –   Correspondence, Notes and Memoranda.
  0.5   Summary description of file
  1.0   Correspondence
  2.0   Correspondence: Associate I file
  3.0   Correspondence: Associate II file
  4.0   Notes and Memoranda: Partner I file
  5.0   Notes and Memoranda: Associate I file
  6.0   Notes and Memoranda: Associate II file

Folders 2a, 2b, and 2c – Contract Drafts.
  7.0   Contract drafts

Folder 3 –   Contracts and Supporting Documents
  8.0   Mall contract
  9.0   Seller II contract
  10   Bank contract
  11   Consulting agreement
  12   Draft amendments to Mall and Seller contracts
  13   Assignment and assumption of fee contract
  14   Contract exhibits
  15   Joint order escrow instructions

Folder 4 –   Surveys
  16   Old survey
  17   Various new surveys
  18   Final survey
  19   Tract legal
  20   Perimeter legal

Folder 5a –   Title and Loan Documents
  21   Title commitments
  22   Final title commitments
  23   Title policy
  24   Reinsurance
  25   Title documents

Folder 5b –   Title and Loan Documents
  26   Ground leases
  27   Partnership documents
  28   Loan documents
  29   Insurance company estoppel letter

Folder 6 –   Closing materials
  29.1   Closing memorandum

29.2	Closing agendas
29.3	March 1, 1985 letters to Seller I and Bank re closing
30	Authority documents
31	Minutes of Purchaser investment committee
32	Wire transfer instructions
33	Assignment and assumption of the ground leases
34	Absolute assignment and assumption of [tenant] leases
35	Bill of sale
36	Assignment of intangible property
37	Tenant I escrow
38	Letter from bankruptcy trustee's attorney re ex-tenant
39	Letter from purchaser to sellers re audit of 1985 rents
40	Promissory note from purchaser to Seller II
41	Deed of Trust
41.5	Release deeds
42	Indemnity agreement re taxes
43	Assignment and assumption of contracts and warranties
44	Letter of purchaser re percentage rent due Bank
45	Letter to Bank re percentage rent due Bank
46	Amendment to Seller II contract
47	Letter agreement re Tenant II ground lease
48	Authorization of release of Bank earnest money
49	Letter agreement re Bank deed
50	Bank exculpation certificate
51	Direction to transfer funds to Bank
52	Deed
53	Assignment and assumption of lessor's interest in [ground] leases
54	Disbursement instructions to Chicago Title
55	Letter to Chicago Title re status of title
56	Letter to tenants
57	Draft closing statements
58	Joint proration statement
59	Mall closing statement
60	Seller II closing statement
61	Bank closing statement
62	Bank settlement statement
63	Seller I closing statement

Folder 7 – Leases – major Tenants
64	Tenant I lease (movie theatre)
65	Tenant II lease (pharmacy/drug store)
66	Tenant III lease (supermarket)
67	Tenant IV lease (department store)
68	Tenant V lease (department store)
69	Tenant VI lease (department store)
70	Tenant VII lease (department store)

Folder 8a – Lease Memorandum and Leases 1-20
71	Memorandum re form leases
72	List of tenant leases
73	Tenant leases 1-20

Folder 8b – Leases 21-45
   74   Tenant leases 21-45

Folder 8c – Leases 46-62
   75   Tenant leases 46-62

Folder 8d – Leases 63-93
   76   Tenant leases 63-93

Folder 9 – Tenant Lease Summaries
   77   Tenant lease summaries

Folder 10 – Estoppel Letters and Various Lease materials
   78   Unexecuted estoppel letters
   79   Executed estoppel letters
   80   Estoppel letters of major tenants
   81   Estoppel letter and lease problems
   82   Seller I certificate re tenant IX percentage rent
   83   Seller I certificate re unexecuted estoppel letters
   84   Bank estoppel letter
   84.2   Merchants Association estoppel letter

Folder 11 – Duplicate and Expired Leases
   84.5   Duplicate and expired leases

Folder 12a – Miscellaneous
   85   Drafts of various documents
   86   Pennsylvania transfer tax statute
   86.5   Transfer tax issue
   87   Map of City of Pittsburgh
   88   Pennsylvania excise/franchise tax questions
   89   Letters from local counsel
   90   Mall Associates agreement of limited partnership
   91   Engineering report

Folder 12b – Miscellaneous
   92   Tax file
   93   Financial data
   94   CAM file
   95   Ex-tenant bankruptcy
   96   Jones-Bank contract
   97   Roof warranties
   97.5   Management agreement
   98   Closing book index

Strawberry Fields, a mall owned by a real estate company, Segal Partners, was sold to a large, national bank, Meganational Bank. It provides an interesting comparison to the previous example of the bank loan transaction because of the roles of the actors involved. The real estate company had developed the mall with guarantees from a large insurance company, Equity Insurance. Segal Partners expected to sell the mall for approximately $30 million, and retain management control. The deal had to be closed by the year's end in order to take advantage of certain changes in the tax laws.

Although the negotiations between the parties including the lawyers were close to fruition, two problems were outstanding. The first, relatively minor, was that Segal Partners would not allow its lawyers to copy the documents for Meganational and its lawyers because Segal Partners considered the cost too prohibitive.[77] As a result, Meganational and its lawyers would be seeing the latest draft of the final agreement for the first time at the meeting, which meant there could be no major hitches. The parties would be pressured to expedite matters in order to meet the projected closing date, which was in December.

The second problem concerned the real estate company's guarantee of fourteen million dollars with Equity Insurance, which appeared intractable. The guarantee was tied to specific profit projections that the property company had to meet within a certain time or else lose control of the mall. The issue was whether it could meet the projections, since having sold the mall to the bank, Segal Partners would have no control over how the guarantee was paid off. This particular problem had already consumed considerable amounts of Tischmann lawyers' time. The lawyer for Equity Insurance, the guarantor, was a stickler for detail: he demanded multiple copies of documents and was very slow in responding to letters and enquiries. He proved very frustrating for the other layers.

An additional tangential problem also slowing down the pace of the transaction was that the property company was balking at paying the insurance company's legal fees, even though this arrangement is considered the norm in commercial real estate business.

The meeting which is described here consisted of a Tischmann partner and associate, three representatives from the real estate company, two bankers and two lawyers acting for the bank who came from a 250 lawyer firm in Los Angeles. They are as follows:

---

[77] Why Segal Partners was being so miserly was a mystery to the lawyers. At most, the copying would have cost $250. An interesting sidelight here on the economics of photocopying is that during 1985, Tischmann made a net profit of $20,000 on photocopying.

Dick Parsons	Meganational banker
Roy Porter	Meganational banker
Hal Posner	Meganational outside counsel
Seymour Perry	Meganational outside counsel
Andrew Segal	Segal Partners senior partner
John Simmonds	Segal Partners associate
Bill Stanley	Segal Partners associate
Michael Shapiro	Tischmann partner
Paul Strauss	Tischmann associate

The Meeting: The First Part

In an attempt to produce an acceptable final draft of the sales agreement, the meeting was to be an all day affair. It started early in the day in a disjointed way:

Hal Posner	Who wants to get this thing off the ground?
Seymour Perry	Why don't we go through the purchase agreement?
Dick Parsons	Which copy are we using?
Michael Shapiro	I'm using the September 13 copy.
Dick Parsons	Well, I have the latest. Let's have some copies made.
Michael Shapiro	Should we be doing assignment of benefit interest?
Dick Parsons	Isn't there a statute?
Michael Shapiro	Next point: parcel three isn't part of the transaction.
Seymour Perry	That'll be part of a separate REA [Reciprocal Easement Agreement]
Michael Shapiro	About the recitals on 1(a), you're not buying the entire marketplace.
Dick Parsons	That's right.

Michael Shapiro   We get to see how much square footage there is at Strawberry Fields? We may be selling X plus agreements to build others, i.e., a cinema and Taco Bell. On Taco Bell, if they default and don't build, we won't put anything there.

John Simmonds   We're covered through a holdback.

Bill Stanley   We'd find someone else.

Michael Shapiro   The parking spaces number isn't correct. There's more to be done yet. Our site is actually constructed, but Alpine's [another developer] site isn't.

Bill Stanley   Size depends on how you measure it: inside, middle, or outside of the wall. When you're the landlord, it's outside; when you're the tenant, it's inside.

Although this was to be the crucial meeting to discuss major issues systematically, the participants meander into the discussion in a random, almost free-form, way with no indication of clear direction. Points are brought up and dismissed quite rapidly. For example, the "assignment of benefit interest" is dealt with and dismissed by the reply, "Isn't there a statute?" Other points started, dropped, and picked up again in a quasi-philosophical manner. When Michael Shapiro asks the question about the square footage at Strawberry Fields, no one replies until four exchanges later when the property company representative, Bill Stanley, discourses on how measurements are interpreted by different people. After a few more exchanges along these lines, the participants begin to go through the documents more systematically and tackle larger issues.

Andrew Segal   Next one, (e),[78] I have a big problem with. I don't give a damn what a guy's net worth is. Let me give you an example of a guy who got a Vie de France franchise. He did very well though he has limited net worth. Then on another development we wanted restaurants, so we went to him and told him we wanted him to run one. We'd finance, but he'd own it. A good tenant is best.

Roy Porter   Yes, that's venture capital.

Andrew Segal   If you're in real estate that's venture capital. If it's in then you're worried about it.

Roy Porter   I guess that's our only way of isolating it.

Andrew Segal   We get financial statements.

---

[78] This section required that certain examinations be taken of potential tenants' assets.

Hal Posner	When do we get to look at the tenants?
Andrew Segal	You want to approve every lease?
Seymour Perry	Is there another economic test we could use?
Roy Porter	Could we isolate it?

Andrew Segal   We're not gambling. We put a tenant in, he improves the place. The worst that can happen is that he's in and out in a year. You could make on turnover, lease it.

Roy Porter   That's not our tenant.

Andrew Segal   Why don't we isolate it? Under three thousand five hundred square feet we don't bother, over that you approve the lease.

Seymour Perry   We could have a security deposit.

Andrew Segal   Not being demanded any more.

Seymour Perry   Why not restrict it to a three-year lease with a three year option?

Andrew Segal   That's good.

Roy Porter   Andrew's right; it creates a bit of turnover.

Michael Shapiro   OK.

The two sides start the true substance of the meeting by arguing over who should examine prospective tenants.[79] Andrew Segal opens in a very aggressive manner by disparaging the bank's need to examine the financial creditworthiness of prospective tenants. He backs up his demand with a success story, which the bank representative immediately identifies as venture capital, that is, a high-risk investment. Segal then attempts to reinforce his story by saying his organization obtains financial statements. Here he is implying that he does not give away tenancies without scrutinizing prospective tenants, so the bank should not want to inspect every lease.

What the two sides are trying to determine is at what point the authority of the manager, Segal Partners, cedes to the owner, Meganational Bank. The arrangement is that whereas Meganational is buying the mall, Segal Partners will manage it for the bank. Segal Partners, because of, in part, the guarantee from Equity Insurance, want to extend their control

---

[79] See MacCullum (1967) for an interesting discussion of social control in the American shopping mall.

over the leasing arrangements as far as they can. For it is in the choice of tenant that the future of the mall lies. The bank is essentially arguing that conservatism should rule choices, with the implied possibility that the profits from such a tenant will be relatively low but secure. Segal Partners wants to pursue a riskier, more radical line by putting in less financially stable tenants, who nonetheless might generate large profits. This difference reflects the difference in organizational ethos between an established bank and a risk-taking property developer. An image that might bring this distinction to life is that of a stream, which can be crossed by a series of stepping-stones, placed irregularly. The bank is the stream with a constant flow of income and profits: the property lawyer is like a person who wishes to cross the stream and must jump from stone to stone never quite certain if the next jump will result in a landing on a stone or in the water. Each deal, then, is a jump made with hope. One of the bankers, Roy Porter, suggests "isolating the economic test" put forward by the bank lawyer, Seymour Perry, which Segal says should not be applied below 3,500 square feet. The bank's lawyers are unable to accept this initial suggestion and offer their alternatives of taking security deposits on anything more than a three-year lease with a three-year option.

The protagonist in this scene is the property company representative, Andrew Segal. The antagonists are the bankers and their lawyers. Interestingly, the Tischmann partner played a very small, passive role, that of summarizing and concluding the proceedings with the utterance, "OK." This is in a direct reversal of the bank loan meetings, where the Tischmann lawyer controlled the dialogue in a dynamic way. Here the bank's lawyers were vociferous in demanding rights for their clients, who were comparatively quiet. Part of the reason for the differences is found in the geographical situation. The property company people know the Mid-West well, since it is where they concentrate their investments. The bank, in contrast, disperses its investments throughout the country. It is reasonable, therefore, for the bank lawyers to speak to their clients (even though, in the property company's perception, they suffer from the "handicap" of being Californian). In the case of the bank loan, the lawyer was much older than his client and could lay claim to greater "worldly" experience. In this instance, the lawyer and his clients are approximately the same age. Consequently, there is a more precise division of labor. The lawyer attends to the details of the transaction and monitors the pace of the meeting. For example, as the following exchange shows, quibbles over language are the lawyer's province:

Michael Shapiro	"Seller shall ... consent" Let's add the word "substantial."
Hal Posner	We prefer the word "material."

> Michael Shapiro OK, I don't have a problem with "material." If necessary, we'll pick up the phone and ask them [the bankers].

If one consults a dictionary for the entries, substantial and material, one would discover that each is a definition for the other.[80] The clients, however, are concerned with the larger substantive issues.

The Meeting: The Second Part

One of these larger issues is that of trust, which is brought out in the following extract:

> Hal Posner We're still thinking about this. These partners are giving up their rights to review things.
>
> Andrew Segal They're not. They're putting their trust in us.
>
> Hal Posner For every one that succeeds, a few will bomb out.
>
> Andrew Segal No, doesn't happen. You've got to know the marketplace.

Here we see the counterpoint of "rights" versus "trust and knowledge of the marketplace." Segal is trading on the ignorance of the bank in this type of venture. The bank is not normally a party to real estate deals, so lacks the nous necessary to make an informed judgment. Their lawyers, aware of this, try to characterize the issue as one of rights and their abandonment. (Later in this chapter, I will analyze the matter of rights in more detail, since it is a concept central to law.) Segal is also placing his, and the market's integrity at stake. As we see in the next part of the meeting, his gambit failed to draw the bank's agreement.

> Hal Posner We want the space small—two thousand five hundred square feet.
>
> Andrew Segal OK, let's say three thousand and a three plus three.[81]
>
> Hal Posner OK.

---

[80] The *Oxford English Dictionary* (1933) defines the words, under "legal", as follows: "material: applied to evidence or facts which are of such significance as to be likely to influence the determination of a cause, to alter the character of an instrument; "substantial": belonging to or involving essential right, or the merits of a matter.

[81] Three year lease with an option to renew for a further three.

Roy Porter	Two thousand five hundred only applies to two tenants.
Hal Posner	I think two thousand five hundred is appropriate.
Andrew Segal	Let's just do three plus three.
Hal Posner	No, we want square footage too. We want to participate in the review process. It's reasonable.

Immediately abandoning rights and integrity, the participants enter a haggling match over what the minimum should be. They try different combinations of space and time, ending with Hal Posner claiming, "...It's reasonable." The theme of reasonableness is continued:

Andrew Segal	Yeah, reasonable. It's what the courts want it to be.
Hal Posner	It's different in California.
Andrew Segal	Yeah, it only takes ten years to get a building permit. Do you want to knock out the three plus three to three thousand?
Seymour Perry	Knock out the three and three and go to two thousand eight hundred.
Andrew Segal	I don't like it.
Bill Stanley	I don't like it either.

Segal is exasperated by Posner's invocation of reasonableness and his reply is a sarcastic one: "...It's what the courts want it to be." In conjunction with his comment about California, Segal is cynically making fun of the lawyers' obtuse use of language. At this stage the negotiations ate without direction. In order to salvage the deal, Segal proposes the opposite of Roy Porter's idea of isolating the economic test by suggesting that it be connected to something else:

Andrew Segal	Let's tie this to another issue. Let's get rid of the D and B [Dun and Bradstreet].[82] We have never required them anywhere in the organization. What do you need for marketing? Do you need a D and B to sell these?
Ray Porter	We've got other sources that are more reliable.

---

[82] A service designed to examine the creditworthiness of companies.

Michael Shapiro   You have to have financial statistics that show three times their net worth.

Bill Stanley   Uh huh.

Michael Shapiro   We end up with two thousand five hundred, no D and B, but financial stats. On to (f).

Andrew Segal   Sometimes we give free rent.

Hal Posner   Look, when it's more than three months free rent you come to us, though any concession will be agreed to if you pay for it.

Andrew Segal   OK.

Michael Shapiro   OK ..., (g).

Segal adroitly brings in another way of solving the problem of what the criteria should be for determining the worth of the eligibility of prospective tenants. Shapiro quickly grasps the opportunity proffered and formulates a summing up of an acceptable square footage and no credit check. Segal, unfortunately, spoils this victory by interjecting his comment about free rent, which he is forced to recant.

The differences in the division of labor—between Marvin Broad and Michael Shapiro—in two examples are also a function of the types of work being done. Commercial rest estate is more a matter of business and commerce than of law. Although corporate deals are also predominantly a matter of business, they involve a greater need for legal constructions, in part because they are subject to greater governmental regulation than real estate deals. The success of commercial real estate transactions is often as much a function of local political intrigue than anything else. When a partner was attempting to obtain industrial development revenue bonds for a client so that he could develop some property within the city, the main hurdle was whether a split Chicago city council would decide the issue before the year's end. If the council failed to agree on the issue or to meet in time, changes in federal tax laws would render the matter redundant. The partner had no means of predicting—or influencing—what the outcome would be.

The Meeting: The Third Part

The final issue discussed at the meeting was the problem of the insurance company's guarantee. Failure to pay off the guarantee would affect both parties, so both wanted to see it resolved. Notwithstanding the mutuality of interest, the discussion was not without tension.

Michael Shapiro   We have a problem with the insurance company where if we don't reach limit within fifteen months, we're on the guarantee for the full term of the loan—ten years.

Hal Posner   I hope you can change it with the insurance company. We've had one like this where we couldn't get rid of the management group. So if you're still on the guarantee, then it's because you're not doing a good job, but we'd want a new manager. We could let you approve a new manager.

Andrew Segal   We don't' like it. Our company is a good developer with a good reputation.

Hal Posner   Once you've been burned once, you're leery about doing it again.

Roy Porter   Is there some language we could use when if they don't' reach the limit in fifteen months, they'd pay a penalty?

Hal Posner   That doesn't do it.

Michael Shapiro   The two guarantees don't coordinate.

Andrew Segal   I have problems guaranteeing anything when we don't have ownership.

Roy Porter   What if our Meganational guarantee kicks off, but you're still on the insurance company one?

Michael Shapiro   That's it. It's what happens after we might lose management control.

Andrew Segal   The insurance company won't extend. They've been very inflexible. I went to them because they were supposed to be easy to deal with.

Michael Shapiro   Our concern is that in three years we deliver you a beautifully leased development and in two years you turn it into a piece of crap.

Hal Posner   But you have control.

Michael Shapiro   We won't, that's the trouble.

Hal Posner   But if we're owners, we should be able to throw you, as manager, out if you want us to exercise rights of ownership.

Andrew Segal   Yeah.

Hal Posner   If you want to exercise rights of ownership, then it's different. We'll do the best we can, but you want us to step up to your obligations.

Andrew Segal   It's not that we're doing a bad job because you have control. We wouldn't want to be around then. We've put ourselves in your hands.

Michael Shapiro   You'll use your best efforts to pay Equity's loan?

Hal Posner   Yeah.

Michael Shapiro   Andrew, you won't distribute any monies to your partners until the insurance company loan is paid. That helps.

Andrew Segal   My expectation is that the bank'll pick up the guarantee, as small as it is.

Michael Shapiro   The insurance company would have to agree to the substitution. But if they agree to not take any money out then it'll do.

Andrew Segal   Is there a risk?

Michael Shapiro   A small one.

John Simmonds   You're close to kicking off the insurance company loan anyhow. We have to find out how close we are to that number.

An Analysis of Rights

From the perspective of the interactions between the lawyers and clients, this section of the meeting is most interesting. The Tischmann lawyer participates more actively at this stage than he has before. His role here is to protect his client from the bank lawyer's disinclination to grant any leeway to the property company: "But if we're owners we should be able to throw you, as manager, out if you want us to exercise rights of ownership." The Tischmann partner is trying to deflect the idea that his client is responsible for the intransigency of the insurance company. As the property company representative says: "The insurance company won't extend, They've been very inflexible. I went to them because they were supposed to be easy to deal with." That the insurance company has acted unreasonably seems to be implicitly accepted by everyone at the meeting. When the Tischmann lawyer asks, "You'll use your best efforts to pay the insurance company loan?", the bank lawyer replies, "Yeah," even though he has been quite determined to underline the fact that the property company could be ousted as manager. The Tischmann partner follows this with a directive to his client about how none of his partners should withdraw any money from the project until the loan is paid. The bank group accepts this admission as correct behavior on the part of the property company representative.

Although the clients are active during this segment of the meeting, the central characters are the lawyers. And though none of the language employed actually addresses substantive legal issues, there is a strong analytical and jurisprudential subtext that may not be apparent to the other participants. What is being articulated is an argument over rights, duties and liabilities: the constituents of social relations. Hohfeld (1964: 36) classified legal relations according to a scheme of "opposites" and "correlatives". He set them out in pairs thus:

Jural Opposites	right	privilege	power	immunity
	no-right	duty	disability	liability
Jural Correlatives	right	privilege	power	immunity
	duty	no-right	liability	disability

Hohfeld's scheme was designed to attach a single meaning to each of the terms above to aid analysis of relations and avoid confusion caused by assigning multiple meanings to terms. On the surface the scheme is quite simple. The jural opposites denote the presence and absence of certain qualities: for example, if I have a right, I then have an affirmative claim against another. The other therefore possesses no-right, the opposite of right. The jural correlatives, however, denote the different aspects of a relationship. For example, if A lends B money, then A has the right to be repaid at some date and B owed the duty to repay A at some date. Thus the jural opposites are in the relation of "A or B" and the jural correlatives are in the relation of "A and B". What Hohfeld was attempting to do was unpack the overladen terms of right and duty and draw out from them the other meanings that are hidden in them, and therefore assign every term a precise and unambiguous meaning. Some, but not all, of these terms are useful in analyzing the last stretch of conversation over the consequences of not fulfilling the conditions of the insurance company's guarantee.

The essence of the bargain being struck is the real estate company's sale of a shopping mall that it built to a bank that will have ownership, but leave the day to day management in the hands of the real estate company. If the real estate company fulfills the terms of the insurance company's guarantee, there is no problem and the deal can be completed as described. If, however, it fails to fulfill those terms, then not only is the real estate company inextricably linked to the insurance company for ten years (see Michael Shapiro's first statement), but the bank, in the guise of its lawyers will take remedial action which will result in the real estate company losing its managerial rights over the mall. What the bank is acquiring then is, in Hohfeldian terms, a power. Thus:

> A change in a given legal relation may result (a) from some su-
> peradded fact or group of facts not under the volitional control
> of a human being (or human beings); or (2) from some super-
> added fact or group of facts which are under the volitional con-
> trol of one or more human beings. As regards the second class of
> cases, the person (or person) whose volitional control is para-
> mount may be said to have the (legal) power to effect the par-
> ticular change of legal relations that is involved in the problems.
> (Hohfeld 1964: 50-1)

A power allows a party to a transaction to alter the relationship of the parties to that transaction. In the transaction just described, the bank is acquiring the power to take away the real estate company's managerial control. So the bank does not merely have a right that it can affirm against the real estate company, but instead it has something quite different: the ability to alter the nexus of their relationship.

The correlative to a power is a liability. This is not necessarily nega-tive as the word might connote. Rather, Hohfeld was thinking of the po-tential to have one's status altered by the actions of another. For example, all potential management groups who might be interested in contracting to manage the mall are under a liability to have that power conferred on them at any time. What the real estate company and its lawyer are arguing for is a radically different interpretation of the situation. When the repre-sentative of the real estate company says, "...We've put ourselves in your hands," and his lawyer adds later, "You won't distribute any monies to your partners until the insurance company loan is paid. That helps." They are subtly asking to be accorded the status of having a privilege rather than a liability. And the correlative of a privilege is a no-right, and its opposite is a duty.

Privilege signifies a freedom from the right or claim of another. To possess a privilege, therefore, would place the property company above the dictates of the bank, and place the bank in the position of having a no-right. This is not the only satisfactory analysis using Hohfeld's classifica-tion, which explains what is taking place at this moment. Alternatively, we might say that the property company is seeking immunity from the bank's ability to change relations. The correlative of immunity is disability, which Hohfeld characterizes as "no-power" (1964: 60). Thus, by becoming im-mune to the banks' ability to take away managerial control from the prop-erty company, the property company renders the bank powerless. Ulti-mately, by the time the deal was closed, the situation was resolved such that the bank formally retained the power to take away the property com-pany's right to managerial control; nevertheless, there was an informal understanding that the property company would not be deprived of its management rights unless the situation became extremely deleterious to the bank.

Finally, to round off this example, what took place after the meeting had broken up was interesting in the context of what had been said at the meeting. An associate who had been working on the sale for the partner came into the room:

> Paul Strauss   I've worse news. Our third tenant from Straw-
> berry Fields has just walked, after six weeks. A franchise. I told
> [another associate] to start a suit, but he said he'll [the tenant]
> go bankrupt if we do.
>
> Michael Shapiro   How big?
>
> Paul Strauss   Two thousand feet.
>
> Michael Shapiro   A small tenant. It's going to show on the list
> [of defaults].
>
> Andrew Segal   I haven't told about the others.
>
> Michael Shapiro   You mean on the list. They're down. Andrew,
> we've just told them there are no faults, except [X and Y]. You
> gotta tell them, you gotta tell them.

This little extract raised the specter of the disingenuous client. The lawyer finds himself here party to a deception of which he is not aware, though he would eventually find out. The client was sufficiently confident that he could persuade Equity Insurance to change its agreement on the guarantee that, although there was considerable difficulty about paying off the loan in time, especially that now the occupancy rate of the mall was dropping, everything would be resolved in the end. The lawyers were not so sanguine, however, and badgered the client to tell the bank that it could expect problems. He knew that such a maneuver would only increase the risk of his company losing managerial control.

The lawyer here is powerless to do anything. All he can do is counsel the client on what he considers the best action to be, and hope the situation improves rather than deteriorates. As this was a valuable client to the firm, the client's wishes were usually granted. In this case, he did not want the bank to be told anything until he had spoken with the insurance company, which he did the next day. His negotiations were successful and the insurance company accepted the bank as substitute.

Legal Knowledge and Expertise

One aspect of the above analysis that has not been clearly rendered in the above examples is the role of legal knowledge and expertise in putting these transactions together. What should be made apparent now is the paucity of actual *legal* work involved. Yet lawyers are a pervasive force in most corporate transactions and have resisted incursions from other groups, such as accountants and bankers (Abbott 1986).

Ronald Gilson (1984) argued that lawyers are transaction cost engineers, not mere legal technicians. He tested his hypothesis by examining the elements of a corporate acquisition agreement. In so doing he found lawyers reduce information costs, among other things, to the participants and so increased the value of the transaction. They achieved this end by playing the role of "reputational intermediary" (Gilson 1984: 290). Thus the buyer and seller are guaranteed by the lawyers on both sides of the transaction that the "thing" they are acquiring is without hindrance and that it will be paid for. Furthermore, Gilson argued that lawyers are chosen to perform these tasks over others, such as accountants, because lawyers are able to structure the deal within whatever is the prevailing regulatory set of norms. But still, though lawyers may have a background knowledge of law of which they are aware and can call on, we do not explicitly see the application of any legal principles in the work (cf. Flood and Sosa 2008). Such occurs rarely, for example, when an associate may be called upon to do some legal research (but see Schon (1983) and above in Chapter 4). And I will argue in a later chapter that what is euphemistically called legal research and argumentation differs markedly from that found in any other discipline, especially the sciences.

8

Lawyers and Conflict

Introduction

Litigation is not facilitative; it is combative and adversarial. Litigators are concerned with trials and resolving disputes. Litigation, then, is the very antithesis of office lawyering. Tischmann started as, and continues as, a firm of primarily office lawyers. Within a short period of time, relative to how long the firm has been in existence, the litigation department at Tischmann has grown enormously, third only to corporate and real estate. The first litigation partner joined the firm in 1971. As mentioned previously, he was different from other lawyers in the firm in that he had been to a local law school rather than the University of Chicago or Northwestern University. The remainder of the litigation department, however, had graduated from the latter schools.

As I indicated in Chapter 1, litigation is not a continuous activity, as most office lawyering tends to be, but episodic. Litigation moves in fits and starts; a flurry of activity in writing and filing briefs, say, then nothing more for months. It is a process that requires a mind that can pick up and drop a subject without becoming frustrated (see Scheffer 2010). Some litigators become specialists—criminal lawyers are the most noticeable—though in Tischmann the litigators are generalists in that they will try any kind of case; that is, they must be able to try any case that is put their way. In one sense, they are, at best, specialists in procedure—form overrides substance.

Much has been written about the activity of litigation, both sensational and serious (see, e.g., Speiser 1980, Stewart 1983, and Brazil 1980). In this chapter I will concentrate on how lawyers deal with conflict between their clients and others at the stages prior to filing a lawsuit. One reason for taking this approach is that lawyers become bound by a maze of statutory rules about proper form at the moment of filing a suit. Before that point, however, lawyers are relatively unconstrained, bound, albeit often in name only, by their codes of ethics.

There is another aspect to this approach. Lawyers not only pursue suits for clients, but they also create the dispute for the client—they bring it into life. Cain's (1983) idea of lawyers as conceptive ideologists comes into play here. The client may know she has a problem but she may have no idea of whether anything can be done to make it work legally. The lawyer is therefore active in the "blaming and claiming" aspects of dispute processes (Felstiner et al 1980).

The great part of this chapter, then, is taken up with two case studies which demonstrate the wide varieties of cases that Tischmann litigators fought. (They also reflect, rather nicely, the distinctions Heinz and Laumann (1982) draw between the personal plight and corporate hemispheres.) The third example concerns an individual grappling with an adverse situation he faced at his place of business, an engineering school in a university. The fourth involves a conflict between a small business and a large corporation. The former points up dramatically how lawyers are able or not to manage situations where law is scant or nonexistent. How then do they make sense of their actions? They have to work with rules that are both within and without the legal system yet within its shadow (Mnookin and Kornhauser 1979). In the latter example a situation becomes starkly polarized when the lawyers enter the scene and it is pertinent to enquire whether lawyers are bound to have such effects—malign or benign—when they are brought in to resolve disputes and conflicts. The interplay of power and knowledge, then, is one of the key elements to emerge from these studies. First, I will present the stories and then analyze them afterwards.

Example 3: How the Problem Arose

The dramatis personae in this example are as follows:

Dr Sam Brass	the Tischmann client
Bill Steel	client's first lawyer; a partner
Ron Silver	client's second lawyer; a partner
Al Gold	an associate
David Maple	Mr Brass's departmental chairman
Mark Beech	engineering school general counsel
Pete Walnut	Mr Beech's associate
Mr Clay	chairman of appeal committee
Mr Plaster	counsel to appeal committee

The first case concerns a client who is an individual, an engineering professor in an engineering school. He both taught and practiced. The normal routine for members of his department was to receive a salary from the institution and any earnings from private practice were in large part given to the department. The client, Sam Brass, was primarily a practitioner rather than a theoretician and he had been teaching for about ten years. At the time he sought advice from the law firm, his department was changing its direction from practical work to research. Brass decided, because of the changing course of the department, he would seek more work in private practice where he could continue his applied function and reduce his participation in the department. Although Brass knew what he wanted to do, he was unsure how to achieve his goal. As a result, he approached a colleague for advice. The colleague had taught part-time in the department, but had not participated in the department for at least five years, and was a partner in the law firm.

At their first meeting, Bill Steel, the lawyer, suggested that Brass could best achieve his goal by following the line established by the first president of the school. This president had reasoned that the only method by which he could attract highly qualified faculty was to give them maximum freedom in structuring their professional lives. If such a person wanted to concentrate on private practice within the school, then the "price" for that freedom would be a commitment to teaching one or two classes a year. During the time the school had been in existence, many had subscribed to this method.

Steel, knowing of Brass's unhappiness in the department, advised him to set up an office in the professional building in preparation for further changes. When Brass had made his arrangements to share an office, which he did on an informal basis without informing the engineering school, he returned to Steel for advice on the next step. Steel, however, was involved in a trial, so he passed Brass to another lawyer in the firm. Ron Silver, Steel's surrogate, was also a litigator like Steel and had worked in government in the labor area.

Brass met with Ron Silver and explained that roughly two-thirds of the department held non-stipendiary positions: their incomes came from private practice. In Silver's view, the changeover from salaried to non-salaried could be handled fairly easily. All Brass needed to do was give 90 days' notice of his intention to withdraw his services. Silver drafted a letter for Brass to send to his chairman, which said, "...I am terminating my receipt of compensation and provision of services under my Faculty Effort Agreement.... However, I intend to contribute to the department and maintain my appointments...." Both Brass and Ron Silver regarded the letter as a prelude to negotiations with the departmental chairman.

The chairman, David Maple, did not treat the letter as such. He received it as a literal offer of resignation from Brass and so informed the administration of the school. Brass was aghast as he would be without a job in 90 days and had yet been unable to establish a private practice.

The lawyers thought it would be unwise for them to "surface" at this stage, preferring Brass to do his own negotiating with their assistance. Besides avoiding alienating the engineering community by appearing to "legalize" the affair prematurely, this would have the additional effect of keeping Brass's fees down. Brass's first step was to write to the dean and the president, informing them that he had not resigned and that he would be available for teaching. At the time Brass was sending off his letters, the chairman, Mr Maple, asked the school's house counsel to advise on next steps. During this period little happened.

The Difficulties of Negotiation

At the end of the 90 days, Brass wrote again to his chairman and the administration reiterating the point that he had not resigned. Simultaneously, he received a letter from Maple thanking him for his services and noting that he was no longer a member of the faculty. Brass was very distressed by the process, unable to plan his next move. Silver suggested that Brass invoke the appeal procedures laid down in the school's rules of governance. The rules in themselves raised their own problems because they had been drafted in an ad hoc way and did not present an entirely rational structure to work with, but they were all Brass and Silver had. In order to invoke the appeals procedure it was necessary to determine a particular route: the first problem was that the rules gave little guidance on how to determine tenure status. And Brass, himself, had never been told which position he occupied. Silver decided to start two lines of appeal to cover both possibilities. Letters were drafted by Silver, but Brass sent them on his own stationery. The lawyers had not yet "surfaced".

Maple, the chairman, passed on the request for an appeal to Mark Beech, the house counsel, who recommended that Maple reply saying no appeals were appropriate in cases of termination. The situation was an awkward one for Brass's lawyers, as they were unable to control any of the procedures, as they would have been able to in a "normal" legal forum. The school's stonewalling was an effective way of preventing anything from being done short of entering litigation, where discovery procedures would provide access to documents and witnesses.

Thought they had discussed it, neither the layers nor Brass wanted to start a lawsuit. Silver brought up the subject of a lawsuit by asking Brass how much he was prepared to spend on his case. Silver remarked, "You haven't spent much up to now, roughly 1,500 to 2,000 dollars."[83] To Silver, a corporate lawyer, this truly was not a significant sum; to Brass, in the context of academic salaries, it was. Brass said he would go as high as 5,000 dollars if the school did not try to remove him from his private practice. If the school attempted that move, he would seriously consider the cost of bringing a lawsuit. Steel later discussed this aspect of the case with Silver, advising against a lawsuit because Brass "hadn't a snowball's chance in hell of winning a case against the school."

Silver advised Brass that they were a long way from going to court and that their next maneuver should be to talk to Beech, the school counsel. Silver's reason for this strategy was to attempt to isolate the chairman as an irrational person by talking lawyer to lawyer with Beech. Brass felt extremely uneasy about this proposal. He was against the lawyers' "surfacing" because it might arouse even more institutional ire against him. Silver persuaded Brass to accept his idea, confident that two rational lawyers could resolve the problem practically.

Silver called Beech to set up the meeting at Beech's office; Beech said he was agreeable to talking. The meeting took place with Silver and his associate, Mr Gold, and Beech and his deputy, Peter Walnut; it started as follows:

> Beech   Tell me what you think we can do. [At this point Beech put his head down and began writing on a legal pad.]
>
> Silver   I've come to talk about the situation that's arisen with Mr Brass.
>
> Beech   What did you say?
>
> Silver   You heard me.
>
> Beech   Now look here ... if you're going to be rude we might as well stop this meeting now. You called this meeting and I expect you to conduct it properly. If you can't behave decently, it's pointless going on.

This outburst introduced a rather chilly atmosphere into the subsequent proceedings. But Silver continued with his account of Brass's problem—that he had not resigned and was being prevented from teaching by the chairman. Moreover Silver argued, Brass was a tenured employee (strictly, still undetermined) who could not be dismissed without cause. As Maple had used the word "terminate" in his letter to Brass, Brass believed he was within his rights to initiate appeal proceedings. Silver continued:

---

[83] The lawyers' hourly rates ranged from about $100 an hour to just over $150 an hour.

Silver   Really, it's quite simple: all Brass wants to do is what two-thirds of his department have already done. What's more, the department gets his teaching services for free.

Walnut   You expect us to believe that Brass is just like Albert Schweitzer? No one does that.

Silver   But that's how the department functions.

Beech   Except Brass decided to do this on his own account. The department is the one who decides these matters. It's all very clear.

Gold   Oh, come on.... That's not how an academic department works. It's not like a law firm with partners telling associates what to do. Academics are supposed to act collegially, more like equals. And, in any case, Brass discussed this with Maple, or at least tried to.

Ideally, Silver hoped to treat the situation as one where an incorrect decision had been taken elsewhere in the school. Beech refused to be persuaded that anything was remiss: assistant professors, by virtue of their lowly station, were not capable of making authoritative decisions; they were subservient beings. Walnut compounded this idea by reading Brass's actions as quasi-saintly and irrational, not those of a rational utility-maximizing individual.

Beech continued with the fact that Brass had refused to teach a graduate practicum when asked. Silver denied that Brass had ever refused *any* teaching obligation; indeed, it was the intransigence of Maple that prevented Brass from teaching all that he wanted, and that Brass was undertaking some teaching nevertheless. Beech said he would investigate, but his understanding of the entire issue was that all necessary steps had been taken and Brass would be leaving. Gold tried to rephrase the concluding remarks of the meeting:

Gold   Look, if Brass has been teaching his class, and it is our understanding he has and still is, there is no satisfactory reason to continue treating him as someone who has resigned. Can't we revert to the status quo then?

The following day Silver and Gold wrote to Beech summarizing the meeting. They concentrated on two points, namely, that Brass was trying to teach and that if found to be teaching there would be a rescission of his termination. Beech replied twice: by letter and by telephone. His letter accused Silver of mischaracterizing the meeting, acting irresponsibly, and not acting in the best interests of his client. In his telephone call, taken by Gold, Beech said:

Beech   I want you to know I resent your letter very much. I don't like the way you do business; I don't like your firm; I don't like Silver; but I want you to know that despite all, I like you. You behaved properly in this. Silver has been wasting time on sideshows. That is not the best way to act for your client.

Gold   I think that's unfair, but I'll pass on your comments to Silver.

Beech   And I also want you to know Brass's situation is his own fault. He resigned; he acted unilaterally and Maple didn't like it.

Gold   Can't we get the principals together to talk?

Beech   What's done is done. And I've told Maple, I think we're at the last ditch point before litigation.

When Brass next met with Silver and Gold, the situation had worsened:

Gold   Beech has told me that they're likely to put you out of your office in the professional building. I don't know when, but they could try it anytime.

Brass   If they do that, they'll destroy my livelihood. It's not so bad losing the faculty position, but I depend on my practice.

Gold   You might have to reconsider your situation in terms of going to court.

Brass   If they do that, I'll probably have to.

Later Silver was telling Steel of the most recent developments, Steel advised Silver to tell Brass that the costs of going to court to seek a declaration to force the school to follow its own procedures would be prohibitive. And to engage the school in a full-scale battle would be out of the question. If that was the only possibility, Brass might as well quit. Silver, then had the task of bolstering Brass's failing confidence:

Silver   Don't get depressed; one way of another we'll get them to listen to you.

Brass   Yeah, but everything they do stops us. I feel like everyone's against me and it's my fault everything has gone wrong. I never expected anything like this.

Silver   It's not your fault. They're the crazy ones; that's why it's difficult to get through to them.

Brass, himself, suggested that he try and meet with the dean of the school on an informal basis. On arriving at the dean's office, Brass found

Beech, the house counsel, waiting with the dean. And Beech refused to leave for most of the meeting. To Brass, Beech's presence signaled a sell-out by the dean and confirmed his growing paranoia that the school intended to demolish him. Silver did, however, draft a letter to the lawyers' disciplinary commission reporting Beech's unethical behavior, for a lawyer is bound by the Code and, in most states, the American Bar Association Model Rules of Professional Conduct not to communicate with another party when the lawyer knows that person is represented by another lawyer.[84]

The school followed up with a demand that Brass vacate the office he shared in the professional building. One of the real estate lawyers, a close colleague of Silver's, read the lease and agreed with the school—they could make Brass leave because he had no direct leasing arrangement with the school. Nor was Brass's office partner prepared to help; he was frightened.

How the Stalemate was Broken

During this particular period—one of great frustration for lawyers and client alike—a friend of Brass's discovered the name of a possible appeals' committee chairman, Mr Clay. Silver wrote to him asking for an appeal. Clay called Silver, uncertain of whom he was talking to:

Clay Hello, this is Clay.... Who am I talking to?

Silver We represent Brass in his dispute with the school. Have you heard about it?

Clay No.

Silver The issue is quite simple. Brass was trying to become an unpaid member of the faculty like the two-thirds that already are...

---

[84] See DR 7-104, Communicating With One Of Adverse Interest, *ABA Code of Professional Responsibility*, 1969: "During the course of his representation of a client a lawyer shall not: (1) Communicate or cause another to communicate on the subject of the representation with a party he knows to be represented by a lawyer in that matter unless he has the prior consent of the lawyer representing such other party or is authorized by law to do so."

More recently (and now in effect in nearly all states), Rule 4.2, Communication With Person Represented By Counsel, *ABA Model Rules of Professional Conduct*, 1983, provides: "In representing a client, a lawyer shall not communicate about the subject of the representation with a party the lawyer knows to be represented by another lawyer in the matter, unless the lawyer has the consent of the other lawyer or is authorized by law to do so."

> Clay   That's enough. I don't really want to talk to lawyers about it. Tell Brass to call me as soon as he can for an appointment. It sounds like a problem for my committee. I view my role as an advocate for the faculty, so I would like to look into this.

That Clay did not want to talk to lawyers gave no concern to Silver; he was pleased the stalemate was broken. Brass met with Clay and was told to submit a formal complaint to initiate proceedings. The main benefit to Brass was that the intervention of Clay's committee meant that all moves against Brass by the school—for example, the demand to vacate the professional building—were stayed until the committee had deliberated. And Clay had said that the committee could not sit for at least four months, which would mean the first hearing would be in July. Silver pointed out the advantages of his delay to Brass: it would give him valuable time to build up his private practice and establish contacts outside the institution. Also at this point, Steel told Silver to give Brass a bill for fees: "Always give the client a bill when you've done something well for them."

For practical purposes, Clay made Brass and Maple the parties to the dispute. This forced the house counsel into the role of Maple's lawyers. Moreover, as the dispute appeared to contain complex issues and had aroused considerable interest among the faculty, Clay decided to employ an outside lawyer as counsel to the committee. He chose a litigator, Mr Plaster, from a small, but highly esteemed, downtown firm, a firm that had once done some drafting of the rules of governance for the school. Neither Silver nor Beech objected to him.

Clay's first task, with Plaster's help, was to define the issue or issues to be put before the committee. Clay, to Brass's and Silver's chagrin, concentrated on the topic of resignation. To Silver this was far too delimiting; he wanted to introduce issues of competency to run departments, policy determination, and possible squandering of funds. Silver asked Brass several times if he could "dig up any dirt" against Maple, so as to apply suasion. Not only did Brass feel reluctant to do this; he could never work out how to achieve it, nor would anyone, he was convinced, agree to testify against Maple.

Clay asked the parties to submit briefs on the effect of resignation or change of status within a engineering school. Beech employed a large downtown law firm to write the school's brief, and Silver wrote his largely as a rebuttal of the school's. Silver had difficulties obtaining an associate for this task at first; he started to use one who had experience only in real estate. By the time Silver was able to assign a more knowledgeable associate to the job, there was little time left to complete the project. Ultimately, both sides found little law on the topic. Silver was still arguing for a broader interpretation of the problem. He called Plaster for assistance, who assured him that the role of the briefs was only advisory, not dispositive, and that the committee would be impossible to restrain if it wanted to examine other issues.

Silver told Brass to start assembling any documents he would be relying on—letters, memos, summaries—and also to think about his opening statement, which would be most important. Brass outlined a chronology of events for Silver as well as drafting his statement. Both Gold and Silver reviewed the statement and refashioned it so that it appeared "more lawyerly," that is, excluded what they considered extraneous information and was more tightly argued. Silver also suggested Brass employ witnesses to attest to his performance in the department.

The Hearings

The first hearing took place approximately 11 months from the time Brass submitted his letter stating his intention to change status. There were 16 members of the school in attendance, as well as the parties and their lawyers, and a court reporter. Although the committee chairman permitted the lawyers to attend, he would not allow them to speak for their clients, only advise them. Both the parties addressed the committee when the chairman opened the proceedings and then the committee members posed their questions to the parties. Despite his desire to keep the issues in narrow focus, the questions from the committee members ranged over many areas. During the questioning, Brass answered no questions without being prompted or briefed by Silver who sat at his side; Maple answered most of his questions without prompting. For Brass, it was as though his lawyer was doing most of the talking (there were long gaps between questions and answers). Given the randomness of the questioning, it was difficult for Brass (or rather Silver) to build a coherent, logically constructed case. The meeting was adjourned after three hours and held over for almost a month.[85]

Brass was extremely despondent after the meeting, feeling that both his presentation was inadequate and that the questioners were against him. Silver also felt Brass's presentation was poor, and was something to be corrected for next time.

At the second hearing, Brass tried to answer the points raised at the first as well as develop his theme of conciliation. Due to time scheduling, the hearing had to recess just at the moment the committee was to consider its decision. Again, the committee was not able to sit for a month. During this period, Silver pushed Brass to seek alternative arrangements

---

[85] The room being occupied by the committee was only available for a few hours, which restricted the duration of the meeting.

elsewhere—in another school or in private practice—and counseled him not to expect victory.

After the Hearings

The committee finally decided against Brass. The committee considered the chair's rights superior to those of others. But it nonetheless censured the chairman for being uncooperative. Although it had wanted this point included in its letter to Brass, Beech, the house counsel, would not permit such a comment to appear in the letter. He anticipated a lawsuit as a result of its inclusion.

Brass reported to Silver that he was both tremendously relieved and disappointed at the result. He noted that there was considerable support for his case among faculty. Consequently, Silver advised Brass to appeal to the next level of internal appeal. Silver submitted a petition, which was accepted. Over this next stage, he and Brass were able to exercise no control. The appeal council decided on the basis of the transcript and documents. The appeal council took three months to arrive at their decision, which affirmed that of the committee.

By this time, Silver was spending much of his time with Brass reassuring him that there was nothing wrong with him and that the institution was at fault. Steel also suggested to Silver that it was time the case was wrapped up. It was becoming very expensive and Steel and Silver were taking the case on a virtual pro bono basis.[86] Brass, too, was tired of the matter. It had consumed 15 months of his life. When he came to the law office to discuss whether he should appeal again (there was one layer of appeal remaining), he admitted that many colleagues were losing sympathy with his cause, even though, he pointed out, there were at least six "procedural" defects in the appeal council's reasoning. Silver joked that one of his previous clients had ended up going to law school as a result of his dispute.

Silver said that there was probably little more he could do. He proposed that Brass calculate the amount of time he needed to make alternative arrangements (he has by this time found a private practice group to join) and ask a senior colleague to negotiate with the president of the school for a readjustment period during which he could consolidate his position.

---

[86] At this stage Brass had run up fees of roughly $10,000, and the school had spent almost $25,000 for Maple.

Example 4: How the Problem Arose

In this example the cast is as follows:

John Brown	the Tischmann client
Paul White	client's first lawyer; a partner
Jonas Grey	client's second lawyer; a partner
Donald Cream	client's third lawyer; a partner
Daniel Wimsey	salesman for A & B Inc
Bob Holmes	vice-president for sales for A & B Inc
Stephen Sayers	president of A & B Inc
Jim Christie	general counsel of A & B Inc
Kent Spillane	senior partner in A & B Inc's outside counsel and director of A & B

The present example concerns a dispute that arose between the chief executive officer of a closely held chain of retail stores, John Brown, and a national, publicly held supply corporation, A & B Inc. For several years Brown had dealt with one salesman from A & B, Daniel Wimsey. Wimsey was at liberty to transfer supplies from store to store as and when inventories fell low. Brown's retail stores transacted in the order of $300,000 to $500,000 worth of business a month with A & B. One day Brown discovered Wimsey taking a valuable case of machine parts from a stockroom. Initially, he thought nothing of it. Then Wimsey started to account for his action. Wimsey claimed another of the retail stores in the chain was short. Brown checked and he found no shortage. To confirm his suspicions, he asked some other retail storeowners who dealt with Wimsey if they had noticed anything out of the ordinary. Although these others shared his suspicions, Brown could offer no firm proof of any illegal action.

Brown reported his findings to Bob Holmes, the vice-president for sales for A & B. A & B carried out its own investigation following which Wimsey's employment at A & B ended. Holmes claimed that Wimsey had resigned; he was not fired. Wimsey subsequently retained his own lawyer, from a large downtown firm, to represent him. A & B made no offer of compensation to Brown.

Brown then sought help from a corporate lawyer in the law firm who had once been on the other side of a deal Brown was involved in; he had been very impressed with the lawyer's performance. (See Chapter 5 for a discussion of attracting clients from the other sides of deals.) The corporate lawyer, Paul White, was unused to handling conflicts; he had never been involved in litigation. And since the case, at first impression, would involve some negotiation within an adversarial context, White asked Brown to let him bring in a litigator to assist. White said he preferred "putting deals together" and that he was "diffident and I need someone for the skirmishing." Before the meeting with the client, White asked an associate to find cases which would support Brown's claim. The associate found only two, and though they were decided in remote out-of-state jurisdictions. White had little choice but to accept them as the best-case authority available. Not that he wished to use them in the negotiations; if possible, White preferred to hold the cases in reserve if the situation ever appeared to escalate into a lawsuit. What the cases symbolized was that White had some justification in law for the claims he was about to make.

At his first meeting with White and Jonas Grey, the litigator, Brown explained that he suspected Wimsey of a great amount of theft from his retail stores and those of others. But he could not put a figure on the amount. Moreover, as A & B had done nothing except to remove Wimsey, Brown had withheld just over a month's payments owing to them—roughly $300,000—and ceased buying his supplies from them.

White's initial reaction was that Brown had "no leg to stand on" because he had no solid proof of his assertions and any claim made would have to be done with "chutzpah." He also thought Brown was doing the correct thing by withholding payment to A & B: "If they don't like it, they can always sue us." Which, of course, would have meant more work for the firm, something of which White was fully aware. Brown was aggressive in his conversations with White and Grey; he wanted "justice." And they acceded to his request. Both realized Brown was a potential "repeat player" client.[87] White then wrote to A & B asking for a meeting to discuss the issues, which was agreed. He was disappointed, however, that Brown expressly wished to be present at the meeting. White much preferred to work out of sight of clients: he felt lawyers together without clients could work much more expeditiously. He fantasized about it this way:

> If clients weren't there, the meeting would go something like this:
>
> First Lawyer   What are we going to do to sort this mess? We both know you haven't got a legal leg to stand on, but we've been in business for years now and we should keep

---

[87] In contrast to Brown as "repeat player", Brass, however, was considered a "one shot player". (See, for this distinction and terminology, Galanter 1974.)

on. So I'll tell you what I'll do. As we trust each other and I know you would like 150,000 dollars and you owe us 200,000 dollars, I will make you an offer of between 85,000 and 100,000 dollars, only if you go to your people and have them accept it. If they won't, then I haven't made it.

Second Lawyer   OK.

This conversation, then, epitomized—and idealized—the facilitative role of lawyers reconciling differences smoothly and comfortably as co-equals in a common cause, not as combatants in a fight to death.

The First Meeting

The meeting was held at A & B's headquarters. There were three law-yers present: White and Grey, Brown's counsel, and Jim Christie, A & B's general counsel. Also present were the parties: Brown; Stephen Sayers, president of A & B, and Bob Holmes, vice-president for sales of A & B. It was obvious from the ways the people present acted towards one another that some knew each other well and others not at all. Brown, Sayers and Holmes greeted each other effusively, and while these greetings were taking place the lawyers just stood to one side waiting and eyeing each other with some suspicion. When the lawyers, White and Grey, and Chris-tie were introduced to each other, they were reserved and formal, in con-trast to how Brown and the others were chatting among themselves. The reserve was indicative of how the lawyers felt about the discussions to come: large amounts of money were at stake and so the problem was not one to be solved by a slap on the back between friends. And when the parties sat at the table to start the negotiations, the clients sat next to each other, but the lawyers placed themselves on opposite sides of the table. White opened the meeting in this way:

Paul White   Brown hired me because I'm a wonderful lawyer and he likes the work I did for him on a corporate matter. Brown has ten retail stores, and one day he found Wimsey of A & B taking a case of machine parts from a stockroom. Now this had been going on for some time.

Jim Christie   You know that?

Paul White   Yes, and we want to keep relations good. That's our introduction; you take it from there.

Brown told of the kind of open access Wimsey had to his stockrooms and how he might have been doing the same to other retail storeowners. Then he asked:

> John Brown   Did you find out where Wimsey was putting the stuff? He was running an A & B warehouse in his garage. He told me all this. He was also involved in hot TVs.
>
> Jonas Grey   Is this a bonded carrier?
>
> Jim Christie   Yes, but this investigation didn't prove anything, but if it had you won't need an insurance company.
>
> Jonas Grey   Your insurance carrier has been put on notice?
>
> Jim Christie   Yes. Also Wimsey's lawyer had Wimsey take a polygraph test and he passed.
>
> Jonas Grey   We know what kind of evidence that is, but we have a problem to solve.
>
> Jim Christie   Do you have a solution? You've made accusations that must be true.
>
> Jonas Grey   That's legal. We're here to find a solution.
>
> Jim Christie   Our concern is to keep the relationship going. If you think we're responsible economically.... Do you have a dollar term?

These particular stretches of talk show the differences between the approaches of the client, the corporate lawyer, and the litigator. The client is working with the assumption that what he knows is self-evidently true and that questions about proof are irrelevant. Implicit in Brown's stance is that he is a very attractive customer for A & B and therefore he can afford to be aggressive. White's opening bid is friendly and wry, with a strong sense of narrative. Grey, however, is matter of fact and elicits the first specific response from Christie in their discussion of whether A & B was a bonded carrier—that is, was A & B covered by insurance for Wimsey's wrongdoings—which Christie attempts to push to the side as not central to the main issue: keeping a good relationship with Brown. One other interesting contrast which emerges from the talk between Grey and Christie is the way that finding a practical solution is opposed to producing a legal result: "That's legal. We're here to find a solution."

After this discussion, Christie asked if Brown had any idea of the scope of his alleged loss. Brown said that he needed to run some tests to determine actual loss. Although he reiterated his desire to maintain business relations, A & B, on the other hand, wanted payment for the goods they had sold to Brown.

John Brown   I like A & B.

Bob Holmes   We like your business too John. But there's the other business of the overdue account of 250,000 dollars.

Jonas Grey   We'll put it in escrow for you.

Jim Christie   Why not pay us? We'll be here; we're not going to run away; we're good for the money. If we owe, we'll pay.

Paul White   If we put it in escrow, we're good for the money too.

Jim Christie   Why would you want to do that?

Jonas Grey   It gives us leverage.

Jim Christie   That's going to put us on the defensive. What value do you get except leverage?

Paul White   We're not looking for an antagonistic position.

Jonas Grey   Let's not be naïve about this.

In the first part of this piece of talk there is some jockeying as to what should be done about the payment Brown owes A & B. A & B believe they have made some concession by agreeing to listen to Brown and to be prepared to examine any proof he might muster to demonstrate the extent of his loss. As long as the reasons for paying nor putting the money in escrow were unarticulated, the discussion continued; but at the moment Christie demanded a reason from Grey, the potential for deep antagonism is displayed.

The meeting ended soon afterwards. Both the Tischmann lawyers and Brown were satisfied with the outcome. They had established a strong bargaining point and were prepared to risk A & B suing them. Brown said he would calculate his losses and let White know as soon as he could; then they could arrange another meeting with A & B. Also at this time, Brown started buying his supplies from A & B again, paying each bill as it came due. White and Grey also told Brown that they thought Stephen Sayers, the president of A & B, would not allow Christie to prevent any settlement favorable to Brown because he would want to keep him as a customer. They both thought Christie was a "jerk" who had no conception of what the true realities of business were like. He was too much like a lawyer.

The Second Meeting

Two weeks later, Brown returned to the law firm with his estimate of his losses, which he calculated to be approximately $400,000 (and he still had not paid the month's unpaid bill). White and Grey quizzed him on the reliability of his inferences. Brown calculated his losses on a before and after basis from when Wimsey finished working for A & B. He supplied no supporting data, however, and the lawyers wondered if the lack of data meant he kept more than one set of books. But that was not a question they felt able to ask, nor did they want to; Brown had given them their instructions and their ammunition, so now it was their burden to make the best use of it if they could. Grey drafted a demand letter for $400,000. He showed it to Brown before it was sent who approved it. No reply to this letter was received before the second meeting. Brown had also been making further inquiries about Wimsey's activities among retail storeowners. He learned that A & B was making an examination of Wimsey's "thefts" (though they would not admit them as such publicly). Both White and Grey were convinced that A & B would capitulate fairly quickly, although at a lower figure, because A & B valued Brown's business too highly to lose it permanently. Eventually, a second meeting was arranged with A & B. Brown and his lawyers were convinced the only major topic for discussion would be the amount A & B would offer in compensation to Brown. One minor topic that had rattled Brown was that A & B had recently given him a negative credit reference, which seemed to run counter to their assurances of wanting to continue in business with him. It is interesting to note here that much of the talk that occurred between Brown and his lawyers was "pep talk". Both lawyers and client continually buoyed each other up: they were certain A & B would talk settlement terms. Only when they were out earshot of Brown did the lawyers express any reservations about the case to each other.

Christie, A & B's house counsel, was for the most part the only representative of A & B. Brown again accompanied Grey and White. This meeting became stormy on occasion; in fact, Christie set this tone in his opening statements:

> Jim Christie   There are two items I'd like to cover. First, how your numbers were arrived at; and second, I need some kind of protection for A & B in the event of either John Brown's or his companies' bankruptcies. We want to protect our position.

> Paul White   I think I heard it. We expect this negotiation to go on for some time. Jim is saying he wants some protection.

> Jim Christie   From the legal point of view, it is a debt beyond the normal length.

John Brown   Your officers demand a financial statement from me? I'm highly insulted!

Jim Christie   It wasn't meant to be insulting; it has to be said.

Jonas Grey   That's not really the essence of our meeting.

Jim Christie   Why not put some money in escrow?

John Brown   A & B wasn't concerned about disasters when you had a thief working for you!

Jonas Grey   We'll have to discuss this with John out of your presence.

The opening of this meeting was completely contrary to what Brown's lawyers had been expecting as Grey's statement about essence indicated. Brown was still convinced that proof per se was redundant to the basis of his claim. He firmly believed that his position was morally secure. But at the same time, a shift from their previous position was beginning to emerge, since Christie had adopted the idea of Brown's money being put into escrow. Grey and White were essentially unprepared for this. Grey realized that Brown was becoming overheated and Christie's statement, following Grey's last, showed he was also aware of that. He deflected attention from what would have been a cul-de-sac in the negotiation by saying, "How did you arrive at the figure?"

Christie and the others then continued to discuss the competing methodologies for measuring Brown's loss, which Christie was still wary of acknowledging:

Jonas Grey   You have given no reason to doubt John's methodology.

Jim Christie   John, you're suing us in effect for 400,000 dollars.

John Brown   He was caught with those items.

Jim Christie   False: I don't want to get into that.

John Brown   I have two witnesses. That's one instance. He had access to ten retail stores. I came to a conclusion that's very, very reasonable. If you want to wait longer, you can.

Jim Christie   There are too many intervening factors. It can't all be one cause.

Here, even though Christie had tried to avoid the issue of Brown's personal integrity, Brown would not let it lie. Again, they discussed methodologies with Christie laying out in detail how he would like the analysis to be carried out. He wanted Brown to use the criteria of "efficiency, product mix, and items from other suppliers," rather than Brown's comparison of purchases and sales over a short period. In effect Christie was asking for an accounting that Brown wanted to avoid. The two sides eventually agreed that accountants should calculate the extent of the losses. As Christie announced: "We're not ducking the issue: at 400,000 dollars the calculations must be right." Finally Christie returned to his original claim for protection against Brown's possible bankruptcy:

Jim Christie	And what about point one [the potential bankruptcy]?
Jonas Grey	We'll discuss this with John and get back to you.
Jim Christie	Not good enough.

Paul White   It would be wise to get this thing over with. I share your desire for fuller documentation, but we can't go into extraordinary risk because you think John might go into bankruptcy after say four months.

Jim Christie   The way to resolve the review.... The money is now in the bank account. So put the money in a block account;[88] keep the interest and who wins, gets the interest ultimately. You can check with your bankruptcy people.

Paul White	It's not going to happen.

John Brown   What would've happened if I'd gone bankrupt because of your thief? What would I have done?

Jim Christie	Sued us.
John Brown	Why was I given a negative credit reference?
Jim Christie	Hopefully, it was accurate and true, I can't comment.
Jonas Grey	Look into that.

Jim Christie   If we don't resolve point one, A & B can't wait for your accountant to get ready.

John Brown	Then we should find another way.

---

[88] *Black's Law Dictionary* (5th ed.): Block account – Governmental restrictions on a bank account; usually with reference to transfers to foreign countries.

Jim Christie	One way to handle this is to avoid a three or four month tail.
John Brown	There *is* no risk.
Jonas Grey	Jim, have you discussed this [bankruptcy protection idea] with your principals?
Jim Christie	Yes, but no one has any doubts of the viability of his business.
Jonas Grey	So, it's your idea. So, you're not acting on your principal's actions.
Paul White	Jonas...
Jonas Grey	How about fourteen days [to review the losses]?
Jim Christie	Not good enough.
Paul White	This is getting hot. We will discuss it. We will advise you in due course. If you don't like it, you can do what you want.

Brown had expected A & B to produce positive settlement figures, instead they impugned his integrity. Nevertheless, Christie's demand for a rational accounting was not unreasonable. And Brown, and his lawyers, while agreeing in principle, lay down obstacles to the venture, such as, the difficulty of his accountant finding the time (this was just before April, the end of the tax year) to carry out the project. To Christie, stretching out the current dispute for another three or four months was not to be contemplated. Underlying his argument was the implicit threat of bringing suit against Brown. Brown expected the thought of the delay would push A & B into settling rather than demanding better figures, and included in his thinking was the denial of the previous offer to put his money owing into escrow.

White was appalled at the way the meeting had progressed. He was convinced that the "businessman's approach" should have been the dominant modus operandi; instead, he found himself in a distinctly adversarial mode. To Grey, this was perfectly normal. He had expected nothing more; he already considered Christie a "bastard." When they returned to the office after the meeting, White told Brown that he

shouldn't put the money in escrow because A & B would just stonewall for months. You should wait a couple of days to see if Sayers [the president] or Holmes [the vice-president for sales] calls you and then say you were insulted by Christie's opening gambit and that these damn lawyers are jockeying about with positions when all you want to do is settle the matter.

Brown liked the idea and said he, himself, would call Sayers if no call came through in a few days.

To assuage his doubts, White talked to another litigator in the firm, one more senior than Grey, about the case. Donald Cream, the senior lawyer, reassured White that the situation was not out of control and that he and Grey should continue as they had. Grey, however, was piqued at Cream's incursion into the case, and accepted no justification or excuse from White for his lack of "faith" in his abilities. Moreover, Cream's name was now added to the file as senior litigator. In terms of office politics, Cream benefited from being involved because it increased his influence generally in the litigation department. Brown was never involved in these discussions; although he was told that Cream had been asked for an opinion, Brown always considered White "his lawyer"; all others were ancillary.

Soon after the second meeting, Brown had a discussion with Sayers at Sayers's instigation, but it proved abortive. One of the reasons for its failure was that Sayers was accompanied by Christie, without either Brown or his lawyers being forewarned.[89] Brown felt undue pressure was being put on him, though both Grey and White believed he was more than capable of standing up to it. Sayers offered a "minuscule" and "derisory" amount of $20,000, and he and Christie invited Brown to join A & B in suing Wimsey. Sayers also claimed that A & B had no responsibility for Wimsey's actions and recovery would have to be from Wimsey. Brown refused to accept this interpretation of events, and also stopped purchasing his supplies from A & B again.

Within a few days of this discussion, and without notice, A & B filed suit, using outside counsel, against Brown and his companies for accounts outstanding. White was shocked. Cream and Grey accepted the complaint matter-of-factly. And Brown was neither surprised nor perturbed: he still believed A & B would give him what he was asking.

A few days after receiving the complaint, White met Kent Spillane, who was both a senior partner in A & B's outside law firm and a director of A & B, and reported his conversation with Spillane by memorandum to Cream and Grey in this manner:

> [Without] premeditation I seized the opportunity of a by-chance, noon hour, street corner encounter with Kent Spillane to say to

---

[89] See note 84, above, for provisions of the Rules of Professional Conduct and Code of Professional Responsibility, on the prohibition of lawyers approaching others' clients without first consulting the others' lawyers.

him that a company of which he was a director had just surprised me by filing a suit against a client of mine.

In the following brief conversation, I identified the parties, and said that the matter had seemed to me very clearly one that should have been settled on a sensible basis between two responsible business organizations, that I supposed that the reason I was mentioning the matter (probably out of turn) was that I had been so startled by the immediacy with which the conversation between Christie and Grey had turned hostile and inability to do anything about that development; and, also because the suit had been filed at a time when we thought the discussions were to continue on the basis of information we were proceeding to gather and that I regretted this further exacerbation of the situation.

Spillane understood without my telling him that I want him to make his own judgment, and he said he would look into the matter.

Both Cream and Grey considered White's attempt at mediation in this manner futile, and nothing did result. For them the case had moved onto another plane, that of litigation, and could not be rescued by wishful thinking.

What Lawyers Do

In this section I shall examine the interactions in, and the implications of, the cases above. One main feature I want to draw out of these cases is that they are, in a sense, in the shadow of the law, not tied to any particular legal institution at that particular time. That is, although they both involve lawyers, neither involves a legal forum such as a court and, consequently, they are open-textured in that they could take many forms, whereas in a court, the norms and processes would be prescribed by a set of external rules (cf. Atkinson and Drew 1979). Macaulay (1963), for example, presents a revealing and pertinent quotation from one of his lawyer-subjects on the layperson's view of what constitutes a legal "thing":

> Often businessmen do not feel they have "a contract"—rather they have "an order". They speak of "cancelling the order" rather than "breaching our contract". When I began practice I referred to order cancellations as breaches of contract, but my clients objected since they do not think of cancellation as wrong. Most clients, in heavy industry at least, believe that there is a right to cancel as part of the buyer-seller relationship. There is a widespread attitude that one can back out of any deal within some very vague limits. Lawyers are often surprised by this attitude. (1963: 61)

The cases do, however, take place within the potential for litigation. Marc Galanter (1984) has coined the term "litigotiation" for the single process of disputing. Following Mnookin and Kornhauser (1979), Galanter refers to the process as one where the courts bestow bargaining endowments on the parties to the dispute. In other words:

> Bargaining chips derive from the substantive entitlements conferred by legal rules and from the procedural rules that enable these entitlements to be vindicated. But rules are only part of the endowment conferred by the law—the delay, cost, and uncertainty of eliciting a favorable determination also confer bargaining counters on the disputants. Everything that might affect outcome counts—all the outcome for the party, not just that encompassed by the rules. The ability to impose delay, costs, risk, embarrassment, publicity comes into play along with the rules. (Galanter 1984: 269)

Power: Individual versus Corporate

These are cases, then, where the clients perceived they needed help and, for their practical purposes, lawyers were the appropriate persons to provide that help. But I do not mean to suggest they were necessarily the best providers of help. These were situations that had arisen in which the assistance of an intermediary or broker could perhaps generate a solution or specify the conditions under which one could be brought about (Boissevain 1974). It was not that lawyers qua lawyers were the essential ingredient, but that lawyers possessed, or again, were perceived to possess, some skills that could be usefully employed in resolving problems.

In Sam Brass's case, there were other plausible intermediaries that he could have employed: colleagues, a member of another department, or perhaps an administrator. And one could speculate the effect these persons would have had on the development of the case. As members of the institution, would they have been better equipped to interpret the institutional codes and etiquette that necessarily articulate the institution?

Luhmann (1979) once noted that power was based upon the ability to control channels of communication. And it is valid to raise the question in this context whether the lawyers ever had the opportunity to control such channels or even exploit them.

One fact, that both client and lawyers here are "professional people," should not be ignored. One could hypothesize a symmetrical power relationship between two professionals. Dr Brass did not possess legal knowledge but he did possess knowledge of the ways institutions functioned, except when they indulged in, to him, Kafkaesque games. The lawyers were not in the simple position of the ideal-typical "personal-plight" law-

153

yer who, in Cain's terms (1983), is able to take on the problem, translate it and resolve it in a straightforward way. They had to receive constant flows of information in order to make judgments.

This dependency on information streams forces the lawyer-client relationship out of the ideal-typical mold of lawyer controlling client into a relationship where routine matters have to be shared. But to what extent? Though they were both professionals, Brass's perception of his world as a rational place had received a severe dent, which made it difficult for him to rely on and trust his own judgment. Thus, at a deeper level, the lawyers held the balance of power and could strongly influence their client.

Although professionals as a class share certain common features, such as a body of knowledge, a degree of autonomy, and so forth, we cannot necessarily infer that inter-professional relationships are consistently harmonious and that lawyers would prefer to transact business with doctors or engineers rather than entrepreneurs. This is evidently not true. The following extract from an interview with a tax attorney might be more representative of the true color of lawyer and other professional relations:

> Interviewer (I):   How astute are [professionals] in the area of tax?
>
> Respondent (R):   You're talking about...?
>
> I: The physicians, the dentists, the engineers...
>
> R: Well, they tend to look to each other for guidance. That's a Catch-22 because they're notoriously bad business people and they make decisions rather emotionally, and it tends to be a bandwagon effect. Sometimes that works advantageously for practice because if you have a good working relationship with one physician you'll find them flocking to your door. But I think their decision making process is not the most efficient or best informed.
>
> I: Is that true more so for them than for your other closely held corporations?
>
> R: Yes. The typical businessman is forced daily to make tough business choices; the typical physician isn't. The source of his livelihood is unrelated to business decisions.
>
> I: Do you find their financial arrangements in general...
>
> R: ...Generally poor—I mean there are exceptions of course, but if you ask me to generalize, I would say as contrasted with many other groups my experience has been that they, more often than not, default in planning.
>
> I: Basically because of their training?

R: Well, you know, you can attribute it to a lot of other different factors. I think there is a serious ego impediment. I think there is a kind of bad complex that they have to overcome or they have to content themselves to thinking that maybe they don't know everything about everything. Maybe that's OK. As I try to explain it to them, they do what they do, and I do what I do, and that's why we need each other. But you're dealing with sometimes insecure people, defensive, who knows. I can't play psychologist about it, but I think the point is well established that they are not great in that area.[90]

Conversely, in John Brown's case, it is, I would argue, both reasonable and plausible that Brown would choose a lawyer above another kind of intermediary. Brown had already had preliminary dealings with A & B and their general counsel was involved. Also, the potential for litigation as an outcome was that much greater than in Brass's case, for the simple reason that the sum concerned was considerable, around $350,000 on both sides. Though measurable, Brass's livelihood was not so easily calculated as Brown's loss. Brown required agents who could prepare for the contingencies of a lawsuit. To use Evan's phrase, lawyers are necessary "culture carriers" in this context, more so than another, for example, an accountant, would be (Evan 1963; also Weider 1974).

In this example, the "first chair" lawyer, Paul White, and the client, Brown, essentially perceived themselves as businessmen sorting out a relatively straightforward venture that has gone awry, but which is capable of easy repair. Client and lawyer face each other as equals: they are men of business. A certain irony is inescapable when Brass qua client is compared to Brown qua client. Brass's status should, perhaps, have been sufficient to place him on an equal footing with his lawyers—as professionals qua professionals—but was not. Circumstances dictated otherwise. Brown, who is a successful entrepreneur with no professional qualifications or attainments, can converse freely and forcefully with his lawyer. Part of the reason for this discrepancy in style had to do with the personal characteristics of the two clients. Brass was used to an academic environment based on the intellectual pursuit of knowledge and rationality. Crisis and catastrophe, in its current form for him, were markedly abnormal members of his world. For Brown, in business, crises of a sort were quite standard and were to be coped with. Their relationships with their lawyers reflects this difference in approach and style, the lawyers being more used to the latter than the former. That is, the world of business made more sense than a world driven by something other than profit.

---

[90] I am grateful to Mary L. Coyne of the American Bar Foundation Taxpayer Compliance Project for bringing the above extract to my notice.

Glaser (1972), writing about the building of his house, encountered one particular problem which was that of the subcontractors disappearing from time to time: constancy was not the norm. He termed the phenomenon "elsewhereism." It occurs in lawyering also. At the beginning of Brass's case Steel delegated his role to Silver. Steel was a senior partner and could so parcel out his cases in that fashion—and, of course, this is often the norm for corporate law practice—but even more telling is that Steel preferred cases involving large amounts of money which had a strong likelihood of going to court. Neither of these features was apparent in Brass's case.

From time to time, Steel would ask Silver how the matter was progressing and suggest submitting a bill. Financially, Brass was in difficulty. His private practice had not yet taken off, yet he was building up large bills with his lawyers. This, of course, made him vulnerable to "elsewhereism," and consequently curtailed his right to self-determination. In one respect his lawyers had ceased to be agents and instead were independent contractors.

In Brown's case the opposite obtained. White had hopes of Brown becoming a "repeat payer"—which he eventually did—bringing a constant stream of business into the firm with him as billing partner. As billing partner, i.e., the attorney who is responsible for the client, one increases one's claim on the points that determine the size of one's draw when the partners decide how to share the profits. Brown possessed the ability to take his legal business elsewhere. To his, and the corporate, way of thinking, law firms, and perhaps lawyers, were essentially fungible and his lawyers recognized it. Consequently, Brown never suffered from "elsewhereism." Brown, too, was able to reinforce this view of himself by paying his legal fees when asked. From this perspective, Brown's lawyers were very much agents, not independent contractors (see Kritzer 1984).

This question of the nature of the relationship between lawyer and client also raises the problem of autonomy. The idea of autonomy is often cited as central to explicating the concept of profession (Freidson 1972). Heinz and Laumann (1982) essentially split the legal profession according to the degree of autonomy lawyers exerted: corporate lawyers exercising little, personal plight lawyers possessing great autonomy. My own observations tend towards the view that autonomy is not a crucial factor in corporate lawyers' thinking, either consciously or unconsciously. Corporate lawyers have the same goals as corporate clients: there is no or little divergence. Each is able to influence the relationship: the lawyer exerts control through suggesting and devising the strategies to be used; the client controls by increasing or decreasing the flow of money that maintains the lawyer's activity. Or, as Heinz rather pithily said, "I think that most corporate lawyers are enthusiastic about being in bed with their clients" (Heinz 1985: 496).

The Heinz and Laumann two hemispheres thesis, predicated on Johnson's typology of occupational control, is in need of tuning. Adopting this typology, Heinz and Laumann argue that corporate lawyers captive to their corporate clients are *not* professional in the true sense of collegial professionalism, that is, controlling the social distance between professional and client, but are in a patronage relationship in which all the power lies in the hands of the client. The personal sector lawyer is, however, not so constrained. It is true that Heinz and Laumann's picture of the structure of the Chicago bar depicts this kind of arrangement, but the picture of lawyers in action does not completely agree. For corporate lawyers and their clients, the terms power, control and autonomy, though admittedly analyst's terms, are not entirely meaningful. As Heinz pointed out, the two are quite happy in bed together. Corporate lawyers are not concerned with *who* calls the shots, but only *how* the shots are called (cf. Heinz 1983: 892). But again, this requires further research in the nature of the lawyer-client relationship.

From this perspective, Heinz and Laumann omitted some questions about corporate lawyers. They missed, for example, the importance of the diagnostic relationship in the professional-client dyad, which is central to all forms of lawyering (Johnson 1972: 57-58). The businessman might know to some degree what his problem is, but he will often lack the knowledge and expertise to solve it within a legal context. And even where the client is in-house counsel, he might not understand the full ramifications of the problem before him. This is the province of the lawyer. We would not, therefore, expect corporate lawyers and clients to argue over goals, but over only how to achieve them together (see Gilson 1984).

But the problem is not all theirs. Johnson's theory of professionalism presupposes an element of conflict between professional and client. Case study II illustrates a situation where no conflict arises and there is no social distance to fight over. Thus, the theory lacks the potential to explain consensual situations. This is not a case, for example, where the responsibility for this lacuna can be abdicated by interposing the mediative form of resolution of the social distance between professional and client: that is, giving the responsibility to a third party such as the state (Johnson 1972: 75-86). No third party intervenes here. To succeed in explaining the professions, we will need a more embracing theory than Johnson's.

It is quite evident in the two case studies presented that each falls on either side of the divide drawn by Lukes in his conception of power, that is, an exercise of power is a function of whether a conflict of interests exists between the parties (Lukes 1974: 32). There is no perceivable conflict of interests between Brown and his lawyers. Brown has power inasmuch as he can take his business elsewhere, but he is at the same time subject to the authoritative views of his counsel; they, not he, are the ones skilled in negotiation. And this lack of conflict is further demonstrated inasmuch as White considers himself a kindred spirit with Brown—they are both businessmen. Brass is subject to manipulation because he has no "clout"; instead, he is dependent on his lawyers for his livelihood. He is in no position to make the kind of demands made by Brown. Whereas Brown sets his own agenda, by himself or in conjunction with his lawyers, Brass has no control over his. What then does this all mean for the concept and role of the fiduciary?

Knowledge and Rationality

From the perspective of being able to interpret the local knowledge of an institution, the lawyers serving Brass were failures (Geertz 1983). Their initial approach was too legalistic, even though the original discussion between Brass and Steel was about Brass's goals and how the institution could be exploited in his favor. This might have been avoided, as Steel had been intimately acquainted with the institution at one time.

Fundamentally, Steel was not very interested in Brass's problem, and consequently abdicated responsibility and failed to share his knowledge. In this way, he acted exactly like one of Glaser's subcontractors who avoids committing himself to a job by intense "elsewhereism." Given that level of knowledge, the letter that was drafted for Brass failed to take account of the informal mode of implementation of the policy on private practice. That is, although the first president of the school expected his faculty to engage in private practice, no explicit policy was articulated on the ways in which faculty would enter private practice from salaried positions. It was usually facilitated between faculty member and chair. The language of the letter instead introduced formal features; the central one being Brass's "termination of services."

Occasionally, Brass would speak of the local idiosyncrasies of the institution, and more occasionally still, the lawyers asked him for information about them, but their approach was basically one of containing the enemy camp. And to Brass this was not a completely alien view; he now thought of his own institution as the enemy, not his community. He was nervous about "taking on" the school. His nervousness increased when the school took his offer to terminate literally. At the same time, his reliance on his lawyers increased.

The more the institution reacted to Brass, the less he was able to evaluate his own feelings and actions, and the more he became dependent upon a third party to take responsibility for his future. As the school had not reacted according to Brass's expectations of type, his powers of self-evaluation and autonomy were diminishing.[91]

Moreover, there was a hiatus in the activity of the lawyers during the 90-day period of the engineer's notice. Absent some action on the part of the school, the lawyers felt they could achieve nothing for their client. Only when the school accepted and acted upon Brass's "termination"—in essence a legal step—were the lawyers able to act. Or, perhaps, they merely failed to act, although able, during this period. The lawyers required legal triggers, such as the termination, which is brute fact, to do their work. Their perception was the reverse. They considered their actions—their advice and refusal to "surface" as open representatives—means of preventing the situation from becoming legalized.

The plaintiffs' lawyers in each case were convinced that the most efficacious way to resolve the disputes was for the lawyers on each side of the matter to meet and discuss the issues. In Brass's case, this maneuver necessitated the lawyers' "surfacing" as the representatives of Brass. The lawyers, Silver and Steel, believed a lawsuit against the school was a hopeless proposition. But Silver thought two lawyers could settle the matter *rationally*. Silver's idea was based on his perception that the administration was incompetent to cope with disputes in a rational manner. Lawyers, however, by virtue of their training, could be rational. This belief is paralleled in Brown's dispute with A & B, where White's fantasized anecdote about two lawyers' settlement talk contains the same belief in lawyers' rationality.

Silver's meeting with Beech, the school's counsel, was a disaster. The two lawyers indulged in struggle as to who should control the proceedings and thereby intensified the dispute. Their dispute was not connected substantively to the other, but in both matters they established courses that seemed to lead inexorably to chaos. Neither Silver nor Beech was able to find a common discourse that would permit rational intercourse. Invoking comparisons with Albert Schweitzer and the structure of law firms only

---

[91] See Katz (1984) for a discussion of the nature of autonomy. Katz defines the term as "the capacities of persons to exercise the right to self-determination" (1984: 105). Of course the parameters of autonomy and freedom are variable and often context dependent. See Heritage (1985: 1): "[A]ction is *context shaped*.... Conversational actions are *context renewing*." There is also a telling exchange on the "context of autonomy" in Joe Orton's play, *Loot* (1967), in which Inspector Truscott is searching a house for the proceeds of a bank robbery when the doorbell rings:

FAY   Would you excuse me, Inspector?

TRUSCOTT   You're at liberty to answer your own doorbell, miss.
That is how we tell whether or not we live in a free country.

served to polarize their perspectives on the problem.[92] In effect, the lawyers set up a sideshow that ran parallel to the engineer's dispute, but the one was fueled by the other. Their letters to and criticisms of each other following the meeting merely exacerbated the hostility between them.

White, in Brown's matter, fantasized about the ideal negotiation between lawyers. It would be rational, untrammeled by pettiness or spite, but the actual interaction did not follow the pattern of the ideal. Even if one introduces the clients' presence as the wild card, the direct interaction between the lawyers was closed, guarded and hostile. Most of their time was spent jockeying for a position, rather than trying to resolve the dispute. This was especially so between Christie and Grey; only White was really concerned about maintaining good business relations, as were the businessmen. Although there were substantial outstanding sums at stake, they were able to continue doing business. But at the second meeting between the parties, even that fragile thread had broken. Christie's attack on Brown's financial integrity caused the meeting to decline into a series of personal insults. There was a strong suspicion that Christie had his own agenda that diverged from his principals', which was proven for Brown's lawyers when A & B filed suit.

In both case studies there were strong displays of knowing-in-action; neither demonstrates the rigors of technical rationality, nor could they be expected to, as these were not manipulable experiments (cf. Lindblom 1959; Lindblom and Cohen 1979). From the perspective of knowing-in-action, we can see that lawyers essentially make forays into the dark; the application of legal knowledge (knowledge-in-books) is virtually ineffective in such situations. Only knowledge-in-action works to guide lawyers through the unknown territory of problems and contingency. It is the contingent nature of lawyers' work that is striking; a series of ad hoc steps in response to whatever action has been taken by the other side.

Alongside the question of autonomy in the nature of lawyer-client relationship is the problem of knowledge. In neither case was any high degree of legal knowledge required. But that does not signify that lawyers are not relying on the experience they have garnered in their years of practice. What legal research was needed, however, was carried out by junior associates. And perhaps this is indicative of the inverse structure of knowledge in corporate law: those who are most junior and most inexperienced are the ones most versed in the law. What it also might indicate about the practice of law as distinct from the development of theory in law is that the practice of law is essentially based on experience as gained

---

[92] Cf. Griffiths (1985), who argues that lawyers on the whole prevent polarization of disputes, i.e., activity that "increases the zero-sum quality of the conflict." Instead, lawyers promote mutually acceptable settlements, at least in divorce cases.

through a master-apprentice craft system where knowledge-in-books is only of peripheral use.

I put this forward as a gross generalization although it fits within the finder, minder, grinder model. That is, the more senior a lawyer becomes in the hierarchy of the firm, the more that lawyer's time is spent on direct interaction with the clients and less with the minutiae of the law. What Brown's lawyers provided was knowledge of ways of negotiating business. Brass's lawyers were less successful in dealing with the school institution; business tactics were not appropriate for the environment. They moved incrementally through a series of ad hoc steps. In Brass's case, the lawyers were hampered by a lack of information. The school divulged little. In Brown's case, A & B did not play by the expected "rules". As much as lawyers would like to set agendas, and frequently negotiations are just that—Silver and Beech's argument over whose conduct was correct when they first met is a case in point—lawyers have to be content with merely tinkering with the course of a rudderless boat.

The language of the discussions between lawyers presupposes no great theoretical knowledge base. In both case studies there were attempts to locate cases on point, but the cases were never made the foci of the disputes. And at no other stage in the proceedings were formal knowledge schemes introduced, except when Silver and Gold and Beech and Walnut were asked to submit briefs by Stone to argue the legal aspects of tenure and its relationship to termination of appointment. One of the difficulties the lawyers faced with this task, as brought out in the example, was that the rules of governance were drafted in such a way as to avoid tackling the issue of tenure. The case law that existed dealt with clear tenure disputes where the rules were explicit.

For Silver and Gold, the briefs were always considered a sideshow to the main event. The briefs concentrated on an issue, which though germane, Silver and Gold did not want to address before the appeal committee, since they had maintained all along that Brass's tenure was already (although doubtfully) established. For Brass and his lawyers, theoretical knowledge was an antagonist in his struggle; for the other side, it was a welcome reinforcement. Perhaps Schon came close to the point when he wrote:

> Although the reflective practitioner should be credentialed and technically competent, his claim to authority is substantially based on his ability to manifest his special knowledge in his interactions with his clients. He does not ask the client to have blind faith in a "black box," but to remain open to the evidence of the practitioner's competence as it emerges. For this relationship to work, however, serious impediments must be overcome. Both client and professional bring to their encounter a body of understandings which they can only very partially communicate to one

another and much of which they cannot describe to themselves. Hence the process of communication which is supposed to lead a fuller grasp of one another's meanings and, on the client's part, to an acceptance of the manifest evidence of the professional's authority can only begin with nonunderstanding and non-acceptance—but with a willing suspension of disbelief. (1983: 296)

Outside Lawyers and In-house Counsel

Another feature of these case studies that should be noted is that the firm lawyers dealt with in-house counsel. There is conventional wisdom that in-house lawyers suffer a status strain because they are not in the mold of independent, professional practitioners. Instead, they are employed and serve only a single client (Donnell 1978; Spangler 1986; Rosen 2010).[93] Despite the fact that outside lawyers and in-house counsel must, by necessity, co-exist, the battle lines between the two have long been drawn. McKinney quotes the chairman of Shell Oil as saying in 1916:

> Lawyers are not business people; however large a lawyer's experience may be, in the conduct of business he is absolutely useless ... he is not a creative genius, he is able to give his opinion if a case is laid before him.... [T]o ask his opinion as to what you should or should not do is the worst possible way of conducting business. (McKinney 1986)

The firm lawyers made a point of noting to each other that their opposite numbers were in-house counsel. Jim Christie of A & B was accorded more respect (though grudgingly), as he also occupied the position of vice-president within the company: Beech, however, was just the director of legal affairs of the engineering school. And when one of the lawyers tapped his gossip network, he found that Beech was generally held in low esteem ("he's a little shit") and was engaged in a fruitless dispute with the president of the school over the control of the school's legal work: the president frequently spoke to outside counsel without informing Beech's office. Moreover, Walnut, Beech's associate, went to great lengths to explain to Silver and Gold that he was distantly related to Silver and had recently moved from a law firm to the school, but taught part-time at a local law school. Silver belittled both Beech and Walnut. And Beech was hostile to Silver's firm. As far as these case studies go, it is difficult to indicate to

---

[93] Given recent developments in the legal profession, especially the tendency for corporations to expand their own in-house legal departments, Donnell's study is somewhat out of date. Spangler sees the development of the salaried sector in the legal profession as symptomatic of a general move towards proletarianization.

what extent these differences affected the situation, though it is clear they did so.

In the second meeting in Brown's case there was a reference to whether Christie was acting on his own beliefs or those of the company. They are discussing the possibility of Brown going out of business:

Jim Christie   If we don't resolve point one [Brown's poten-tial for bankruptcy], A & B can't wait for your accountant to get ready.

John Brown   Then we should find another way.

John Christie   One way to handle this is to avoid a three or four month tail.

John Brown   There *is* no risk.

Jonas Grey   Have you discussed this with your principals?

Jim Christie   Yes, but no one has any doubts of the viability of his business.

Jonas Grey   So, it's your idea, So, you're not acting on your principals' action.

Paul White   Jonas...

Grey's response was that of one who has caught another cheating in some fashion. The prevailing view here was that Christie ought to be nothing but a mouthpiece. If he were an independent lawyer, he could be granted autonomy. White, who was more conversant with the business world of deals, tried to warn Grey off this track and would have been prepared to grant Christie some freedom of action. One reason Brown's lawyers put forward for Christie's intransigence was the then recent takeo-ver of A & B by another corporation. White and Grey believed Christie was trying to protect his own position within the new company by clearing up the outstanding debts as quickly as possible, which may not have been the best way of resolving the difficulty between A & B and Brown.

House counsel occupy ambiguous positions in some ways (Rostain 2008). At one moment in time they represent the institution and poten-tially all those in it; at another they might represent only a fraction. As a result, they have to modulate their behavior according to the context. Such situational flexibility can only induce degrees of role strain. In both cases, the institutions' lawyers contacted the firm's clients without informing the firm. Beech attended a meeting between Brass and the dean; and Christie attended a meeting between the president of A & B and Brown. Neither Beech nor Christie considered their behavior unethical or improper. Both

Brass's and Brown's lawyers were furious and imputed these lapses to the fact of being in-house counsel.

The relations between the outside lawyers and the in-house counsel in these case studies correspond, at least in part, to Schon's "Model I" theory of action (1983: 226-27; Argyris and Schon 1974, 1978). Schon contrasted Model I behavior with Model II. The latter demanded that the participants strived to create conditions that would provide mutually beneficial results. Model I opposed this. An actor behaving according to Model I will bring the following values to the interaction:

- Achieve the task, as I define it.
- In win/lose interactions with others, try to win and avoid losing.
- Avoid negative feelings, such as anger or resentment.
- Be rational, in the sense of "Keep cool, be persuasive, use rational argument. (Schon 1983: 226)

With these values in mind, the actor will try to control tasks unilaterally and be very defensive. Both sides in the case studies tried to control the tasks unilaterally; neither was determined to share values and attempt to reach a consensus. Initially, the firm lawyers strove for consensus (Model II), but were rebuffed on each attempt by the in-house counsel. Their behavior had the effect of pushing the firm lawyers into Model I values of "achieve the task, as I define it."

Model I behavior might be endemic to lawyers. For example, the plaudits rendered to a mergers and acquisitions lawyer for wrecking a deposition, considered a good piece of lawyering, is a telling case in point (Jervey 1986). That lawyer's sole concern during a teleconferenced deposition was to interrupt and to interject with requests for repetitions of answers putatively unheard so that the deposition document would be useless in court because it could not be read as a coherent rendering of what should have been an orderly question and answer session. Instead, it would be a travesty of a proper deposition and the other side would be compelled to spend further valuable resources trying to repeat the deposition. The distinction between Model I and Model II types is a phenomenon that needs more field research.

The differences between the two case studies may be summarized as follows:

FIGURE 8.1

Examples 3 and 4 Compared

BRASS	BROWN
Individual	Corporate
One-shot player	Repeat player
Low autonomy	High autonomy
Subject to influence	Less subject to influence
Subject to elsewhereism	Not subject to elsewhereism
Client and lawyer ignorant of appropriate procedures	Concurrence of views between lawyers and clients
Mistakes not generally rectifiable because of lack of funds	Mistakes generally rectifiable because of greater resources

9

The Future of Corporate Law Practice

In 1986 the American Bar Association Commission on Professionalism produced a document entitled *"...In the Spirit of Public Service." A Blueprint for the Rekindling of Lawyer Professionalism*. It represented, in many ways, the swansong of the legal "profession", recognizing that professionalism was an elastic concept (Daicoff 1997). The legal profession has always had two faces: the public and the private. Most research has concentrated on the former. This study is focused more on the private. The professional face of lawyers talks about service and high ethical standards; the private face emphasizes efficiency, marketing and profits.

The ABA Commission accepted this dichotomy, but, unlike myself, it believed the public face could be made over to replace the private. This is truly a forlorn hope. Law firms, especially corporate ones, are part of a larger financial community, international in scope, which believe in the tenets of competition, which is not always fair competition. And the market has taught lawyers that, if they are to survive as an independent part of this community, they must adopt its mores.

Through the case studies in Chapters 7 and 8, I attempted to show how lawyers actually do their work and how it fosters and perpetuates business mores. But there is no guarantee that they can maintain a monopoly over law interpretation; it appears to be taking up less and less of their time while business takes up more. If, then, lawyers are spending more time on business matters than law, what is to prevent other groups from invading lawyers' territory? The UK through the Legal Services Act 2007 has opened the door to other professionals with the Alternative Business Structures. With some American law firms running economic consulting businesses, there is in place a quasi-multidisciplinary partnership. Maybe it will probably not be too far into the future before we see conglomerates composed of such entities as investment banks, law firms, accounting firms, and insurance companies. However hopeful one may be about this, the key state that would have to invoke these changes has set itself firmly against them. New York has adopted the Younger Report recommendations on nonlawyer ownership and it is speculated that it could be up to a decade before the matter is on the agenda again.[94]

It is unlikely that New York will be able to stem the tide. Change in the legal services market has gone global. It is an integral part of GATS negotiations and bilateral treaties between the US and different countries such as Australia and Korea (Terry 2004, 2010). Even within the European Union change in legal services is being forced as means of revitalizing the economies of debtor countries. Greece, Ireland, Italy, and Portugal have all agreed to changes in the legal profession, courts and legal services as part of their rescue packages from the International Monetary Fund, EU, and European Central Bank. Legal services are a crucial part of the way economies function and they have to be viewed within a global context (Flood 2012b). (The 2007 Act and the US position on nonlawyer investment are discussed in more detail in the next chapter.)

Corporate law practice is facing more than the global threat. The recession has forced many firms to reconsider their business plans, not always successfully as the example of Dewey & LeBoef illustrated when it went bankrupt (Lattman 2012). Dewey went the way of Finley Kumble by overreaching its debt levels in order to fund lateral hires. This goes to a central problem of modern law practice: it is still a short-term model of organization. With the obsession for PEP (profits per equity partner) as the measure of success or failure, there are few incentives to build long-term structures in law as in other business fields (Heinz 2009). The problem will be exacerbated as the US law school crisis deepens (Tamanaha 2012) and law firms continue to retrench and shrink equity partnerships (Galanter and Henderson 2008).

Yet law firms continue to grow in size. Why? Both Burk and McGowan (2011) and Wald (2012) place more emphasis on reputational capital and controlling costs. Firms expand because they want more business and clients demand more. Wald's story of Brownstein Hyatt Farber Schreck LLP is one of client-driven organic growth which later becomes "smart strategic growth". There is nothing inevitable about the tournament to partnership as an engine of law firm growth nor about the predicted death of big law. Law firms, instead, have become more strategic about the direction they will take. Will they remain full-service? Become a litigation boutique? Or some other variety? As Burk and McGowan put it, corporate firms are big but brittle—their predictions about futures can go awry.

---

[94] New York has come out against external ownership of law firms, as detailed in Chapter 10. See, for example, New York State Bar Association, "Report of the Task Force on the Future of the Legal Profession," February 2011; New York State Bar Association, "Report of the Task Force on Nonlawyer Ownership," November 3, 2012.

Two more factors need to be taken into account here: the rise of technology and the increasing power of in house counsel. Technology is leading to more work being outsourced to its cheapest labor (Susskind 2010). As legal work is increasingly standardized and commoditized, it is capable of being done by computer and/or paralegal. More legal work will be disaggregated and more will require less expertise. Combining this with the law school crisis could produce a volatile mix in the future as the nature of legal work changes.

Law firms as outside counsel to companies have long enjoyed positions of authority and power, almost unassailable. Nowadays in house counsel have moved into the prime position as those who procure legal services and expect value for money. They are the gatekeepers (Lipson et al 2012).[95] Will law firms become more collaborative? In many respects they already have. We see this in part with the constant flow of law firm partners into positions of general counsel.

Another reason for this movement from professionalism to business is found in the tension between law as a learned profession and a practice. One expects a learned profession to adhere to scholarly norms, but law has a fundamentally different notion of what these norms are. In the sciences, for example, proof is dependent on there being sufficient evidence for one particular explanation holding sway over another (Kuhn 1970; Lynch 1985; Barnes 1985). Such explanations or theories are subject to the canons of scientific method. Law, too, once classified itself as a science—in 1870 when Langdell became dean of Harvard Law School (Gordon 1983; Chase 1985). But despite its purported scientism, and though some have tried (e.g., Kelsen 1945), the legal profession has never subscribed to the scientific method. This reluctance towards the standardization of knowledge in law is reflected in the resistance law firm lawyers have to bureaucratization despite their business outlook. Lawyers' "organic" knowledge seems to repel systematization and hence external control (Brivot 2011).

This failure of the scientific method is clearest in the practice of law. A litigation partner summed it up concisely:

> I don't believe in the rule of law. It's all a random system. I will dig anywhere to find a case that says what I want. I'll go anywhere in the English speaking world. I once used a case from New South Wales. I was at a seminar where two lawyers were trying to reconcile two lines of RICO cases.[96] And I pointed out

---

[95] See generally the *Wisconsin Law Review* Symposium, "The Changing Role and Nature of In-House Counsel," Vol. 2012, No. 2.

[96] Racketeer Influenced and Corrupt Organizations Act, 18 U.S.C. §§ 1961-1968 (1970).

to them that you couldn't do it because one set of judges like the statute and will expand it, but the other set doesn't like it and always wants to constrain it.

Thus, in law, single cases can be of sufficient authority to persuade a decision maker that one view ought to prevail over another. And here, I suggest, is the nub of the matter, the intersection of the positive and the normative. Law contains both of these elements, although obviously more of the latter than the former. In order to identify law as a learned, scholarly profession, its members have to argue that the normative elements, though in flux, are constrained by the positive framework. In this study, I have tried to demonstrate that the practice of law is not fully constrained by legal principles and is largely composed of moments of indexical construction and interpretation.

I believe I have only begun to tease out some of strands that can be intertwined to make sense of what happens within a particular set of professional practices. Both structural and interactional elements are necessary for a better understanding of what takes place. In this respect, the sociology of law has much to learn from the sociology of medicine, work, and occupations.

Borrowing from these fields will allow us to demythologize the privileged position of the legal profession.

10

Afterword

In this chapter I reflect and expand on the likely changes occurring in the legal world and those that are yet to come. The corporate law firm's future is entering a new phase, one that will take time to work through. In 2007 England and Wales passed the Legal Services Act, a statute that re-regulates the legal services market and permits new nonlawyer forms of ownership of legal services providers including law firms (Flood 2012a, 2012c). For American lawyers the most contentious part of the legislation was to permit nonlawyers to participate in the ownership of law firms and share fees.[97] The Model Rule of Professional Conduct, Rule 5.4, however, prohibits fee sharing or partnership with nonlawyers (Gottschalk 2012). Despite arguments for change to the rule by the Kutak Commission in 1983, lawyers and states have rejected moves in this direction (Cornell Law School 2001). The Legal Services Act 2007 has prompted a new wave of controversy and discussion because of the increasing international environment of legal practice with US firms in London and UK firms in New York. How are the differences to be reconciled? One option for Americans is to use a form of derivative ownership of law firms as proposed by MacEwen et al (2008), but it remains merely an academic possibility.

In late 2011 and early 2012 the New York State Bar Association's (NYSBA) Committee on Professional Ethics was questioned by two lawyers about sharing fees with nonlawyers.[98] The first enquiry came from a Washington DC lawyer on whether he could share fees with a nonlawyer who would assist in a class action brought in New York. The lawyer was also admitted in New York, hence the question. In answer the NYSBA committee said in Opinion 889 that the District of Columbia partnership did not have its predominant effect in New York even though the work would generate occasional fees from New York litigation. Therefore the DC rules would apply. The second question came in 2012 regarding a New York lawyer who wanted to associate with an English law firm that had

---

[97] The Washington, DC bar has a more liberal attitude towards multidisciplinary practices that involve nonlawyers. But for most US lawyers in DC the provision is unworkable because other states in which they are invariably licensed will not permit such arrangements (Luppino 2004; Hadfield 2008; Paton 2010).

[98] New York is by far the most important and influential state with respect to the legal profession because it contains the largest number of big law firms and the greatest number of foreign law firms.

nonlawyers in supervisory and ownership positions. As part of the firm, New York lawyers would form a New York office to represent New York clients but without sharing confidences with English lawyers (cf. Dzienkowski and Peroni 2008). In Opinion 911 the NYSBA committee held that the predominant effect would be in New York and therefore New York rules should apply so preventing the association.

Concurrent with these Opinions the American Bar Association's (ABA) Ethics 20/20 Commission was considering parallel situations in order to discuss changes to the Model Rules of Professional Conduct. The ABA 20/20 Commission also rejected nonlawyer ownership by deciding not to propose changes to the rules. And, furthermore, in early 2012 the NYSBA established a task force (the Younger commission) to examine the issue of nonlawyer ownership of law firms (NYSBA 2012).[99] Despite taking evidence from a wide variety of witnesses, including English and Australian regulators, the task force resolutely set its face against change in the rules. This has left the large corporate law firms in New York (and by extension elsewhere) in a most difficult and awkward position. If international competitors start taking advantage of external investment or even floating on the stock markets, how will New York law firms compete with them? The New York City Bar Association, which represents the larger firms, established an International Legal Practice Committee chaired by an eminent international lawyer from Baker & McKenzie with a remit to challenge the NYSBA position. It considers it has a tough uphill climb against the backwoodsmen (small firm lawyers) who constitute the majority of the NYSBA membership. Indeed it was suggested that the NYSBA might not revisit the issue for ten years or more.

To reiterate a point I made earlier, there are two major sets of state law in the world that dominate transnational legal work, namely New York State law and English law. Unlike the US government, the UK government actively promotes its legal system, courts, legal profession, and openness to foreign business that wishes to use English law and its courts (Flood 1996; Flood and Muzio 2012). The British Commercial Court, with its expert commercial judges, has begun, for example, to hear a series of Russian oligarch cases in which neither party has any direct link with the UK except a wish to use English lawyers and judges (Cranston 2007; Buckley 2011; Christie 2012). Organizations such as CityUK, the Managing Partners Forum, and the Law Society frequently participate along with

---

[99] Stephen P. Younger is a partner with Patterson Belknap Webb & Tyler in New York City. (See http://www.pbwt.com/younger_stephen_bio/) While Patterson Belknap is a major corporate law firm, it only has one office in New York. Besides having chaired this task force, Younger is a past president of the NYSBA. I interviewed Mr Younger and other members during late 2012 as well as some who gave evidence to the task force.

senior partners of law firms in foreign trade trips with government ministers. Government takes an active role in lobbying foreign governments such as India to open up their legal trade to competition.

UK law firms are strategically positioning themselves globally. Norton Rose Fulbright, for instance, is pursuing an expansionist strategy to convert itself into one of the largest law firms in the world. It has merged with firms in Germany, Australia, the US, South Africa and two in Canada, and developed new practice areas like Islamic finance (Freedman 2013).[100] Norton Rose Fulbright is indicative of the initiatives being promoted among law firms that seek to be in the top 25 firms in the world. It demonstrates two tendencies in law firms which at present occur more in UK firms than US firms, but they could be the catalysts for change in the thinking of the American bar.

The first of these is the shift from P² to MPB (Hinings et al 1999: 132). P² is the prototypical form of partnership—collegial, democratic, with peer control and little by the way of formal governance systems. Tischmann fits this model with a slight skew to wise elders having a preponderance of power over the other partners but not to an abusive level. The Cravath system typifies the P² model in its classic sense. P² also represents a classic era of law firm practice and governance, one very much associated with the 20th century. While autonomy was a key feature of the classic model, subordination has come to typify the 21st century law practice.

With few exceptions law firms have moved towards MPB away from P². MPB, the Managed Professional Business (Hinings et al 1999: 133), denotes a radically different structure that highlights centralized control, financialization, marketing, more specialization, with more rules (Greenwood 2007). Norton Rose Fulbright exemplifies this *dirigiste* approach to law firm governance where the central decision makers have directed the firm's expansion (Freedman 2013). Similarly, DLA Piper, a law firm with over 3,700 lawyers (*Lawyer* 2013), began its life as a provincial law firm in the north of England. Its entrepreneurial leaders, e.g. Sir Nigel Knowles, took it on a grand excursion to becoming one of the world's biggest law firms. It achieved this by merging initially with two US firms, Gray Cary Ware & Freidenrich in San Diego and Piper Rudnick of Chicago in 2005. The firm then took over parts of the defunct Coudert Brothers and the former Ernst & Young legal team, and has continued with this strategy (DLA Piper 2013). The consequence of this drive to continuous growth is the lack of organic development we find in the Cravath-type firm. Because the firm is composed of random elements brought together with different

---

[100] Norton Rose Fulbright, though not the largest law firm in the world, has over 3,800 lawyers in 52 offices in all continents. See http://www.nortonrosefulbright.com/about-us/global-offices/.

cultures and values, the leaders of DLA Piper have to impose their control over the firm. It ceases to be a partnership in the P^2 sense and becomes akin to a corporation with hierarchy and centralized control; in other words it is an MPB. The new law factory is then created (Faulconbridge and Muzio 2009; Muzio and Faulconbridge 2009). One feature of the law factory is the way it attempts to institutionalize clients across the firm, uncoupling them from rainmakers and diffusing their business throughout the firm. It harkens back to Julius Henry Cohen's question in 1916: *The Law—Business or Professional?* (Cohen 1924; Sayre 1926; Levine 2005).

The second tendency within UK law firms is to innovate along the lines provided for in the Legal Services Act 2007 (LSA). One of the eight regulatory objectives of the LSA is "promoting competition in the provision of services" (Legal Services Board n.d.: 9). The Legal Services Board (n.d.: 10) explains the objective thus:

> 35. A rigorous and robustly competitive market will encourage legal service providers to respond to consumer demand by providing new and innovative services and mechanisms for delivery and access. This will lead to the provision of 'better' information about legal services, greater choice and access. A successful market will be one where clients are empowered to make informed choices about quality, access and value between a plurality of legal service providers.

The competitive market is being augmented by the adoption of external investment and new organizational structures called "Alternative Business Structures" (ABS).[101] The advantage of ABS is that they can take in external investment and have nonlawyer ownership: they can even float on the stock markets.[102] The nearest analogue to the ABS is the MDP (multidisciplinary practice), but essentially it is broader. Supermarkets, banks, insurance companies and more can adopt the ABS form to deliver legal services.

Since the inception of ABS in 2012 close to 200 have been formed. And so far suppliers whose services can be commoditized are the ones who have taken the step. Corporate law firms, with occasional exceptions, have steered away from ABS territory.[103] Corporate and large law firms have

---

[101] See Solicitors Regulation Authority website on Alternative Business Structures at http://www.sra.org.uk/abs/.

[102] The first law firm to engage in an Initial Public Offering was Slater & Gordon, a personal injury firm in Australia. The flotation in 2007 was a success and since then Slater & Gordon has bought law firms in Australia and in 2012 bought its first law firm in the UK which it changed into an ABS (Cannon 1999; Slater & Gordon n.d.).

[103] Irwin Mitchell, a medium-large law firm, has received ABS licenses (Lawyer 2012). DLA Piper has used ABS for satellite businesses such as LawVest (http://www.lawvest.co.uk/downloads/LawVest-FAQs.pdf).

shied away from external investment because they fear it could damage their appearance of professionalism. Yet, these firms are in discussion with finance houses about seeking external sources of investment or even becoming public companies.[104]

The only significant study on this topic is one by Peel Hunt, a British broking house, which issued a briefing note, "Legal Services: To IPO or Not To IPO" (Peel Hunt 2011). Taking as its starting point the Legal Services Act 2007, Peel Hunt imagines alternatives to partnership with private equity as the most realistic option for law firms because it reduces exposure. But it considers flotation on the stock market as a distinct possibility for partners since flotation would crystallize "a better value for their equity", grant them access to capital, and ease problems of partner transition (Peel Hunt 2011: 10). On the downside there would be a radical change in organizational culture, public companies are very exposed, the press would constantly monitor them for bad news, and the journey to flotation would be fraught (Peel Hunt 2011: 12). For financiers the difficulty is valuing such a nebulous entity as a partnership where profits are routinely distributed year by year and goodwill is divided into personal and firm goodwill requiring substantial discounts to overcome its intangible nature (Peel Hunt 2011: 18). Peel Hunt uses Allen & Overy's published LLP financial statements to illustrate how a valuation could be achieved and then converted into a publicly quoted entity. With a profit of £1 million per full equity partner, a partner to staff ratio of 1:13,[105] and low capital contributions, the remuneration structure for partners would be reformed to give each partner a salary of £250,000 a year and "50% of the remaining profit paid to partners with the balance reported as earnings" (Peel Hunt 2011: 21). The equity of each partner would be worth in the region of £4 million. One effect would be to increase the financial transparency of law firms and thereby create renewed interest in legal careers. Without the burden of partnership tracks, lawyers could envisage careers with different structures with the rewards of real instead of illusory equity, equity which could be traded and enlarged.[106]

---

[104] I have conducted a number of interviews with lawyers and financiers on this topic from 2011 onwards. They are convinced it will happen; the only remaining question is when. Without being able to state categorically on this, I suspect we are dealing with an age cohort issue. When the present cohort of senior lawyers retires, the juniors will be more receptive to external investment.

[105] Note this is partner to *staff* ratio which includes secretaries, paralegals, and others, and is not restricted to associates only.

[106] For a contrary view, see Brandon (2011b) who believes the "anarchic" structure of law firms renders them too unpredictable for investors who will find their risk assessment too extreme for comfort.

If we combine this with efforts to develop online services for clients (e.g. Linklaters Blue Flag), accommodate clients' wishes to purchase lower-value services (e.g. Berwin Leighton Paisner's Lawyers On Demand), and promote increased use of outsourced legal services (e.g. Allen & Overy's outsource operation in Belfast), UK law firms would have created the potential to outstrip their US counterparts in the global legal great game. None of this involves value judgments about the ethos of partnership over corporate structures, but rather it is a reflection of the way corporate legal services are changing under pressure from the needs of corporate counsel, globalization and more mundane economic pressures.

The NYSBA Younger report on nonlawyer ownership of law firms now sounds more like a refusal to recognize the world has changed. It is coupled with an implicit desire that the world will see the "error of its ways and so return to the fold". This is improbable and unrealistic. Australia permits incorporated legal practices. As noted in Chapter 9, the "Troika" of the European Union Commission, the European Central Bank, and the IMFhave imposed analogous changes on Eurozone debtor countries, Eire, Greece, and Portugal (Iberian Lawyer 2013). The GATS talks and now bilateral treaty discussions include legal services in their portfolios without regarding legal services as especially distinct from other services (Terry 2010). Indeed the language of services provision equates professional services horizontally instead of sectorally. This places all professional services, whether hairdressing or legal, in the same category subject to the same strictures on competition and consumer wants.

The ABA is now facing challenges on this ground. During the ABA's attempts to draft a Model Definition of the Practice of Law it received a full comment from the U.S. Federal Trade Commission (FTC) (2002) that warned the ABA that its Model Definition was lacking in several respects. By restricting the delivery of legal services only to lawyers it could restrict access to justice for consumers since many services could easily be delivered by nonlawyers or online. Not only was this anticompetitive, it flew in the face of the way commerce in services was developing. There was no reason why accountants, realtors, bankers and others so skilled should not be able to provide legal advice and legal information. Indeed, it was in the public interest to permit lay provision of legal advice. The FTC invoked the New Jersey Supreme Court, which concluded:

> Not every such intrusion by lay persons into legal matters disserves the public: this Court does not wear public interest blinders when passing on unauthorized practice of law questions. We have often found, despite the clear involvement of the prac-

tice of law, that nonlawyers may participate in these activities, basing our decisions on the public interest.[107]

In the world of the 21st century, the Younger report can only be likened to King Canute's apocryphal story of attempting to command the tide to cease rising: of course it didn't. It will be interesting to see how long it takes for the US legal profession to change its collective mind.

---

[107] In re Opinion No. 26, 654 A.2d at 1352.

REFERENCES

Abel, Richard L. 1985. "Comparative Sociology of the legal Profession: An Exploratory Essay." *American Bar Foundation Research Journal* No. 1: 1-79.

Abel, Richard L. 1988. *The Legal Profession in England and Wales*. Oxford: Blackwell.

Abel, Richard L. 2003. *English Lawyers between Market and State*. Oxford: Oxford University Press.

Abel, Richard L. and Philip S. Lewis. 1989. "Putting Law Back into the Sociology of Lawyers." In *Lawyers in Society: Comparative Theories,* R.L. Abel and P.S. Lewis (eds.), Berkeley: University of California Press.

Abel-Smith, Brian and Robert Stevens. 1967. *Lawyers and the Courts: A Sociological Study of the English Legal System, 1750–1965*. Cambridge, Ma: Harvard University Press.

Abbott, Andrew. 1986. "Jurisdictional Conflicts: A New Approach to the Development of the Legal Profession." *American Bar Foundation Research Journal* No. 2: 187-224.

Abbott, Andrew. 1988. *The System of Professions: An Essay on the Division of Expert Labor*. Chicago: University of Chicago Press.

Aldrich, Howard E. 1979. *Organizations and Environments*. Englewood Cliffs, NJ: Prentice-Hall.

Aldrich, Howard E. and Ellen R. Auster. 1986. "Even Dwarfs Started Small: Liabilities of Age and Size and Their Strategic Implications." *Research in Organizational Behavior* 8: 165-198.

ABF. 2004. *Lawyer Statistical Report*. Chicago: American Bar Foundation.

Aggarwal, Alok. 2011. "Legal Process Outsourcing." *Evaluserve Article,* May. http://www.country-index.com/articles/article_123.pdf.

AmLaw 200. 2010. *2010 AmLaw 200*. http:// www.firstproinc.com/forms/ 2010%20AM%20Law%20200.xls.

Argyris, Chris, and Donald A. Schon. 1974. *Theory in Practice: Increasing Professional Effectiveness*. San Francisco: Jossey-Bass.

Argyris, Chris and Donald A. Schon. 1978. *Organizational Learning: A Theory of Action Perspective*. Reading, Ma: Addison-Wesley.

Atkinson, J. Maxwell and Paul Drew. 1979. *Order in Court: The Organisation of Verbal Interaction in Judicial Settings*. London: Macmillan.

Auchincloss, Louis. 1956. *The Great World and Timothy Colt*. Boston: Houghton Mifflin.

Auerbach, Jerold S. 1976. *Unequal Justice: Lawyers and Social Change in Modern America*. New York: Oxford University Press.

179

Ax, Joseph and Sakthi Prasad. 2012. "Dewey Files for Chapter 11 in Record Law Firm Collapse." *Reuters.* http://www.reuters.com/article/2012/05/29/us-deweyandlebouef-bankruptcy-idUSBRE84S01R20120529.

Barnes, Barry. 1985. *About Science.* Oxford: Basil Blackwell.

Bauman, Jon R. 1999. *Pioneering a Global Vision: The Story of Baker & McKenzie.* Chicago: Harcourt Professional Education Group.

Becker, Howard S. 1970. "The Nature of a Profession." In *Sociological Work: Method and Substance.* London: Allen Lane, The Penguin Press.

Berlant, Jeffrey Lionel. 1975. *Profession and Monopoly: A Study of Medicine in the United States and Great Britain.* Berkeley: University of California Press.

Bernstein, Lisa. 1995. "The Silicon Valley Lawyer as Transaction Cost Engineer." *Oregon Law Review* 74: 239-256.

Blaustein, Albert P. and Charles O. Porter, with Charles T. Duncan. 1954. *The American Lawyer: A Summary of the Survey of the Legal Profession.* Chicago: University of Chicago Press.

Blumberg, Abraham S. 1967. "The Practice of Law as a Confidence Game: Organizational Co-optation of a Profession." *Law and Society Review* 1: 15-39.

Boissevain, Jeremy. 1974. *Friends of Friends: Networks, Manipulators and Coalitions.* Oxford: Basil Blackwell.

Bosk, Charles L. 1979. *Forgive and Remember: Managing Medical Failure.* Chicago: University of Chicago Press.

Bourn, Judy E. 1986. "How Businesses Find Lawyers: A Study of Organizational Information Gathering." PhD diss., Northwestern University.

Brandon, Mark. 2011a. *Lateral Partner Hiring and Integration for Law Firms.* London: Ark Group.

Brandon, Mark. 2011b. "Would You Buy Shares in a Law Firm?" *Motive,* March 29, 2011. http://www.motivelegal.com/index.php/2011/03/would-you-buy-shares-in-a-law-firm/.

Brazil, Wayne D. 1980. "Views from the Front Lines: Observations by Chicago Lawyers about the System of Civil Discovery." *American Bar Foundation Research Journal* No. 4: 217-251.

Brivot, Marion. 2011. "Controls of Knowledge Production, Sharing and Use in Bureaucratized Professional Service Firms." *Organization Studies* 32: 489-508.

Brooks, Robert A. 2011. *Cheaper by the Hour: Temporary Lawyers and the Deprofessionalization of Law.* Philadelphia: Temple University Press.

Brown, Andrew D. and Michael A. Lewis. 2011. "Identities, Discipline and Routines." *Organization Studies* 32: 871-895.

Buckley, Neil. 2011. "Russians in London: Super-Rich in Court." *Financial Times,* October 7, 2011. http://www.ft.com/cms/s/0/6c2ee702-f0d5-11e0-aec8-00144feab49a.html#axzz2ZFG5NGBd.

Burk, Bernard A. and David McGowan. 2011. "Big but Brittle: Economic Perspectives on the Future of the Law Firm in the New Economy." *Columbia Business Law Review* 2011: 1-117.

Bystydzienski, Jill M. 1979. "The Status of Public School Teachers in America: An Unfulfilled Quest for Professionalism." PhD diss., SUNY-Albany.

Cain, Maureen. 1983. "The General Practice Lawyer and the Client: Towards a Radical Conception." In *The Sociology of the Professions: Lawyers, Doctors and Others* 106-130, R. Dingwall and P. Lewis (eds.), New York: St. Martin's Press.

Cain, Maureen. 1985. "L'Analyse des Professionels du Droit: Reflexions Theoretiques et Methodologiques." *Annales de Vaucresson* No. 23: 137-156.

Cannon, Michael. 1999. *That Disreputable Firm: The Inside Story of Slater & Gordon.* South Carlton, VIC: Melbourne University Press.

Caplan, Lincoln. 1994. *Skadden: Power, Money, and the Rise of a Legal Empire.* New York: Farrar, Straus and Giroux.

Carlin, Jerome E. 1962, 2011. *Lawyers on Their Own: The Solo Practitioner in an Urban Setting.* New Brunswick, NJ: Rutgers University Press; New Orleans: Quid Pro.

Carlin, Jerome E. 1966. *Lawyers' Ethics: A Survey of the New York City Bar.* New York: Russell Sage Foundation.

Carr-Saunders, A.M. and P.A. Wilson. 1933. *The Professions.* Oxford: Oxford University Press.

Chambliss, Elizabeth and David B. Wilkins. 2002. "The Emerging Role of Ethics Advisors, General Counsel, and Other Compliance Specialists in Large Law Firms." *Arizona Law Review* 44: 559-592.

Chase, Anthony. 1985. "American Legal Education since 1885: The Case of the Missing Modern." *New York Law School Law Review* 30: 519-542.

Christie, David. 2012. "Magnates for Law: Oligarchs in London." *Law Society Gazette,* September 13, 2012. http://www.lawgazette.co.uk/features/magnates-law-oligarchs-london.

Cicourel, Aaron V. 1975. "Discourse and Text: Cognitive and Linguistic Processes in Studies of Social Structure." *Versus: Quaderni di Studi Semiotici* Sept/Dec: 33-84.

Clark, Robert C. 1992. "Why So Many Lawyers? Are They Good or Bad?" *Fordham Law Review* 61: 275-302.

Cohen, Julius Henry. 1924. *The Law—Business or Profession?* (Rev. ed.), New York: G.A. Jennings Company.

Cornell Law School. 2001. "ABA Model Rules of Professional Conduct (Pre-2002) History." http://www.law.cornell.edu/ethics/aba/2001/history.htm.

Cranston, Ross. 2007. "Complex Litigation: The Commercial Court." *Civil Justice Quarterly* 26: 190-207.

Curran, Barbara A. with Katherine J. Rosich, Clara N. Carson and Mark C. Puccetti. 1985. *The Lawyer Statistical Report: A Statistical Profile of the U.S. Legal Profession in the 1980s.* Chicago: American Bar Foundation.

Curran, Barbara A. with Katherine J. Rosich, Clara N. Carson and Mark C. Puccetti. 1986. *Supplement to The Lawyer Statistical Report: The U.S. Legal Profession in 1985.* Chicago: American Bar Foundation.

Daicoff, Susan. 1997. "Lawyer, Know Thyself: A Review of Empirical Research on Attorney Attributes Bearing on Professionalism." *American University Law Review* 46: 1337-1427.

D'Amato, Anthony. 1987. "The Decline and Fall of Law Teaching in the Age of Student Consumerism." *Journal of Legal Education* 37: 461-508.

Danet, Brenda, Kenneth B. Hoffman and Nicole C. Kermish. 1980. "Obstacles to the Study of Lawyer-Client Interaction: The Biography of a Failure." *Law and Society Review* 14: 905-922.

Davis, Anthony E. 2009. "Professional Responsibility: The Future of Lawyer Regulation." *New York Law Journal* 3, September 14.

DeStefano, Michele. 2012. "Nonlawyers Influencing Lawyers: Too Many Cooks in the Kitchen or Stone Soup?" *Fordham Law Review* 80: 2791-2846.

Dezalay, Yves and Bryant G. Garth. 1996. *Dealing in Virtue: International Commercial Arbitration and the Construction of a Transnational Legal Order.* Chicago: University of Chicago Press.

Dias, C.J., Robin Luckham, Dennis O. Lynch and J.C.N. Paul. 1981. *Lawyers in the Third World: Comparative and Developmental Perspectives.* Uppsala: Scandinavian Institute of African Studies; New York: International Center for Law in Development.

Dinovitzer, Ronit. 2004. *After the JD: First Results of a National Study of Legal Careers.* Chicago: The NALP Foundation for Law Career Research and Education and the American Bar Foundation.

Dinovitzer, Ronit. 2006. "Social Capital and Constraints on Legal Careers." *Law and Society Review* 40: 445-480.

DLA Piper. 2013. "About Us > Our History." http://www.dlapiper.com/global/about/ourhistory/.

Donnell, John D. 1970. *The Corporate Counsel: A Role Study.* Bloomington, IN: Bureau of Business Research, Graduate School of Business, Indiana University.

Douglas, Jack D. 1976. *Investigative Social Research: Individualized and Team Research.* Beverly Hills, CA: Sage.

Dzienkowski, John S. and Robert J. Peroni. 2008. "Conflicts of Interest in Lawyer Referral Arrangements with Nonlawyer Professionals." *Georgetown Journal of Legal Ethics* 21: 197-236.

Eisler, Kim Isaac. 1990. *Shark Tank: Greed, Politics, and the Collapse of Finley Kumble, One of America's Largest Law Firms.* New York: Thomas Dunne.

Ellis, Dorsey and James E. Meeks. 1977. *Trial of an Anti-Trust Case.* Chicago: American Bar Association.

Empson, Laura. 2013. "Who's in Charge? Exploring Leadership Dynamics in Professional Service Firms." Cass Business School, June 2013.

Evan, William. 1963. "Comment [on Macaulay (1963)]." *American Sociological Review* 28: 67-69.

Faulconbridge, James R. and Daniel Muzio. 2008. "Organizational Professionalism in Globalizing Law Firms." *Work, Employment and Society* 22: 7-25.

Faulconbridge, James R. and Daniel Muzio. 2009. "The Financialization of Large Law Firms: Situated Discourses and Practices of Reorganization." *Journal of Economic Geography* 9: 641-661.

Federal Bar Council. 1984. "The Changing Nature of the Practice of Law." Bench and Bar Conference Proceedings, Dorado, Puerto Rico.

Federal Trade Commission. 2002. "Comments on the American Bar Association's Proposed Model Definition of the Practice of Law." http://www.ftc.gov/opa/2002/12/lettertoaba.shtm.

Felstiner, William L.F., Richard L. Abel and Austin Sarat. 1980. "The Emergence and Transformation of Disputes: Naming, Blaming, Claiming...." *Law and Society Review* 15: 631-654.

Finkelman, Paul. 1984. "Review Essay: Alexander Hamilton, Esq.: Founding Father as Lawyer." *American Bar Foundation Research Journal* No. 1: 229-252.

Fisher, Sue and Alexandra Dundas Todd. 1983. *The Social Organization of Doctor-Patient Communication*. Washington, DC: Center for Applied Linguistics.

Flood, John. 1983. *Barristers' Clerks: The Law's Middlemen*. Manchester: Manchester University Press.

Flood, John. 1985. *The Legal Profession in the United States*. Chicago: American Bar Foundation.

Flood, John. 1991. "Doing Business: The Management of Uncertainty in Lawyers' Work." *Law and Society Review* 25: 41-71.

Flood, John. 1996. "Megalawyering in the Global Order: The Cultural, Social and Economic Transformation of Global Legal Practice." *International Journal of the Legal Profession* 3: 169-214.

Flood, John. 2005. "Socio-Legal Ethnography." In *Theory and Method in Socio-Legal Research* 33-48, R. Banakar & M. Travers (eds.), Oxford: Hart Publishing.

Flood, John. 2007. "Lawyers as Sanctifiers of Value Creation." *Indiana Journal of Global Legal Studies* 14: 35-66.

Flood, John. 2009. "Ambiguous Allegiances in the Lawyer-Client Relationship: The Case of Bankers and Lawyers." http://ssrn.com/abstract=962725.

Flood, John. 2012a. "The Re-Organization and Re-Professionalization of Large Law Firms in the 21st Century: From Patriarchy to Democracy." *Journal of the Legal Profession* 36: 415-439.

Flood, John. 2012b. "When the 'Troika' Comes to the Rescue." *Iberian Lawyer,* July 9, http://www.iberianlawyer.com/panorama/3622-when-the-troika-comes-to-the-rescue.

Flood, John. 2012c. "Will There Be Fallout from Clementi? The Repercussions for the Legal Profession After the Legal Services Act 2007." *Michigan State Law Review* 2012: 537-565.

Flood, John and Daniel Muzio. 2012. "Entrepreneurship, Managerialism and Professionalism: The Case of the Legal Profession in England and Wales." In *Handbook of Research on Entrepreneurship in Professional Services* 369-386, M. Reihlen and A. Werr (eds.), Cheltenham: Edward Elgar.

Flood, John and E. Skordaki. 2009. "Structuring Transactions: The Case of Real Estate Finance." In *Contractual Certainty in International Trade: Empirical Studies and Theoretical Debates on Institutional Support for Global Economic Exchanges* 157-171, V. Gessner (ed.), Oxford: Hart Publishing.

Flood, John and Fabian Sosa. 2008. "Lawyers, Law Firms and the Stabilization of Transnational Business." *Northwestern Journal of International Law & Business* 28: 489-525

Foster, James C. 1986. *The Ideology of Apolitical Politics: The Elite Lawyers' Response to the Legitimation Crisis in American Capitalism: 1870-1920.* Milwood, NY: Associated Faculty Press.

Fox, Renée C. 1957. "Training for Uncertainty." In *The Student-Physician: Introductory Studies in the Sociology of Medical Education,* R. Merton et al (eds.), Cambridge, Ma: Harvard University Press.

Fox, Renée C. 1959. *Experiment Perilous: Physicians and Patients Facing the Unknown.* Glencoe, IL: Free Press.

Fox, Renée C. 2000. "Medical Uncertainty Revisited." In *The Handbook of Social Studies in in Health and Medicine,* G. Albrecht, R. Fitzpatrick and S. Scrimshaw (eds.), London: Sage.

Fox, Renée C. and Judith P. Swazey. 1992. *Spare Parts: Organ Replacement in American Society.* New York: Oxford University Press.

Francis, Andrew. 2011. *At the Edge of Law: Emergent and Divergent Models of Legal Professionalism.* Farnham: Ashgate.

Freedman, Joshua. 2013. "Norton Rose's Martocracy." *Lawyer,* July 8, 2013. http://www.thelawyer.com/firms/law-firms-international/norton-roses-martocracy/3006834.article?cmpdate=Not+so+Norton+Rosy&cmpid=dnews_1300483503&cmptype=newsletter&email=true.

Freidson, Eliot. 1972. *Profession of Medicine: A Study of the Sociology of Applied Knowledge.* New York: Dodd, Mead.

Freidson, Eliot. 1986. *Professional Powers: A Study of the Institutionalization of Formal Knowledge.* Chicago: University of Chicago Press.

Furlong, Jordan. 2012. "The Dying Cult of the Corner Partner." *Law21.ca.* http://www.law21.ca/2012/06/29/the-dying-cult-of-the-corner-partner/.

Galanter, Marc. 1974. "Why the 'Haves' Have Come Out Ahead: Speculations on the Limits of Legal Change." *Law and Society Review* 9: 95-160.

Galanter, Marc. 1984. "World of Deals: Using Negotiation To Teach About Legal Process." *Journal of Legal Education* 34: 268-276.

Galanter, Marc. 1983a. "Reading the Landscapes of Disputes: What We Know and Don't Know (and Think We Know) about Our Allegedly Contentious and Litigious Society." *UCLA Law Review* 31: 4-71.

Galanter, Marc. 1983b. "Mega-Law and Mega-Lawyering in the Contemporary United States." In *The Sociology of the Professions: Lawyers, Doctors and Others* 152-176, R. Dingwall and P. Lewis (eds.), New York: St. Martin's Press.

Galanter, Marc and William D. Henderson. 2008. "The Elastic Tournament: A Second Transformation of the Big Law Firm." *Stanford Law Review* 60: 102-164.

Galanter, Marc and Thomas Palay. 1992. *Tournament of Lawyers: The Transformation of the Big Law Firm.* Chicago: University of Chicago Press.

Garfinkel, Harold. 1967. *Studies in Ethnomethodology.* Englewood Cliffs, NJ: Prentice-Hall.

Garrison, Lloyd. K. 1935. "A Survey of the Wisconsin Bar." *Wisconsin Law Review* 10: 131-169.

Garth, Bryant G. and Joanne Martin. 1993. "Law Schools and the Construction of Competence." *Journal of Legal Education* 43: 469-509.

Geertz, Clifford. 1983. *Local Knowledge: Further Essays in Interpretative Anthropology*. New York: Basic Books.

Giddens, Anthony. 1984. *The Constitution of Society: Outline of the Theory of Structuration*. Cambridge: Polity Press.

Gilson, Ronald J. 1984. "Value Creation by Business Lawyers: Legal Skills and Asset Pricing." *Yale Law Journal* 94: 239-313.

Glaser, Barney G. 1972. *Experts Versus Laymen: A Study of the Patsy and the Subcontractor*. Mill Valley, CA: The Sociology Press.

Glaser, Barney G. and Anselm L. Strauss. 1967. *The Discovery of Grounded Theory: Strategies for Qualitative Research*. Chicago: Aldine Publishing Co.

Goffman, Erving, 1959, *The Presentation of Self in Everyday Life*. Harmondsworth Penguin.

Gordon, Robert W. 1983. "Legal Thought and Legal Practice in the Age of American Enterprise, 1987-1920." In *Professions and Professional Ideologies in America*, G. Gieson (ed.), Chapel Hill: University of North Carolina Press.

Gordon, Robert W. 1984. "Review: The Devil and Daniel Webster." *Yale Law Journal* 94: 445-460.

Gordon, Robert W. 2002. "The Legal Profession." In *Looking Back at Law's Century*, A. Sarat, B. Garth and R. Kagan (eds.), Ithica, NY: Cornell University Press.

Gottschalk, Jon. 2012. "Defining Fiduciary Duties in a Majority Nonlawyer-Owned Law Firm: How Allowing Nonlawyer Owners Could Impact State Requirements of Director Fiduciary Duties." http://ssrn.com/abstract=2047733.

Greenwood, Royston. 2007. "Your Ethics: Redefining Professionalism? The Impact of Management Change." In *Managing the Modern Law Firm: New Challenges, New Perspectives* 186-195, L. Empson (ed.), Oxford: Oxford University Press.

Griffiths, John. 1985. "Some Preliminary Notes on Polarization by Lawyers". Unpublished paper presented at ABF London Symposium.

Griffiths, John. 1986. "What Do Dutch Lawyers Actually Do in Divorce Cases?" *Law and Society Review* 20: 135-75.

Hadfield, Gillian K. 2008. "Legal Barriers to Innovation: The Growing Economic Cost of Professional Control Over Corporate Legal Markets." *Stanford Law Review* 60: 101-144.

Halliday, Terence C. 1983. "Critique: Professions, Class and Capitalism." *European Journal of Sociology* 24: 321-346.

Halliday, Terence C. 1986. "Six Score Years and Ten: Demographic Transitions in the Legal Profession, 1850-1980." *Law and Society Review* 20: 53-78.

Hannan, Michael T. and John Freeman. 1977. "The Population Ecology of Organizations." *American Journal of Sociology* 82: 929-964.

Hannan, Michael T. and John Freeman. 1984 "Structural Inertia and Organizational Change." *American Sociological Review* 49: 149-164.

Harbaugh, Joseph and H. Graham McDonald. 1977. *Task Analysis of the Criminal Justice Attorney: Implications for the Use of Paralegals*. Media, PA: The Pennsylvania Governor's Justice Commission Southeast Regional Planning Council.

Hazard, Geoffrey C. 1965. "Reflections on Four Studies of the Legal Profession." *Social Problems (Law and Society Supplement)* 13: 46-54.

Hazard, Geoffrey C. 1978. *Ethics in the Practice of Law*. New Haven: Yale University Press.

Hellman, Lawrence K. 1991. "The Effects of Law Office Work on the Formation of Law Students' Professional Values: Observation, Explanation, Optimization." *Georgetown Journal of Legal Ethics* 4: 537-617.

Henn, Harry G. and John R. Alexander. 1983. *Laws of Corporations and Other Business Enterprises* (3rd ed.), St. Paul, MN: West Publishing Co.

Heintz, Bruce D. and Nancy Markham-Bugbee. 1986. *Two-Tier Partnerships and Other Alternatives: Five Approaches*. Chicago: American Bar Association.

Heinz, John P. 1983. "The Power of Lawyers." *Georgia Law Review* 17: 891-911.

Heinz, John P. 1985. "Ethics and the Megafirm, III." *Loyola University Law Journal* 16: 496-501.

Heinz, John P. 2009. "When Law Firms Fail." *Suffolk University Law Review* 43: 1-12.

Heinz, John P. and Edward O. Laumann. 1982. *Chicago Lawyers: The Social Structure of the Bar*. New York: Russell Sage Foundation; Chicago: American Bar Foundation.

Heinz, John P., Robert L. Nelson, Rebecca L. Sandefur and Edward O. Laumann. 2005. *Urban Lawyers: The New Social Structure of the Bar*. Chicago: University of Chicago Press.

Heritage, John C. 1985. "Recent Developments in Conversation Analysis." *Sociolinguistics* 15: 1-18.

Heritage, John C. and Douglas W. Maynard (eds.). 2006. *Communication in Medical Care: Interaction between Primary Care Physicians and Patients*. Cambridge: Cambridge University Press.

Heumann, Milton. 1978. *Plea Bargaining: The Experience of Prosecutors, Judges, and Defense Attorneys*. Chicago: University of Chicago Press.

Hinings, C.R., Royston Greenwood and David Cooper. 1999. "The Dynamics of Change in Large Accounting Firms." In *Restructuring the Professional Organization: Accounting, Health Care and Law* 131-153, D. Brock, M. Powell and C.R. Hinings (eds.), London: Routledge.

Hirsch, Paul M. 1986. "From Ambushes to Golden Parachutes: Corporate Takeovers as an Instance of Cultural Framing and Institutional Integration." *American Journal of Sociology* 91: 800-873.

Hohfeld, Wesley Newcomb. 1964. *Fundamental Legal Conceptions as Applied in Judicial Reasoning*. New Haven: Yale University Press.

Holme, Howard K. 1969. "Paralegals and Sublegals: Aids to the Legal Profession." *Denver Law Journal* 46: 392-436.

Hornsby, William. 2011. "Challenging the Academy to a Dual (Perspective): The Need to Embrace Lawyering for Personal Legal Services." *Maryland Law Review* 70: 420-439.

Hosticka, Carl J. 1979. "We Don't Care About What Happened, We Only Care About What Is Going To Happen: Lawyer-Client Negotiations of Reality." *Social Problems* 26: 599-610.

Hughes, Everett C. 1958. *Men and Their Work*. Glencoe, IL: The Free Press.

Iberian Lawyer. 2013. "The Sting in the Troika's Tail." *Iberian Lawyer*. http://www.iberianlawyer.com/index.php/home/market-view/news-focus/3939-the-sting-in-the-troika-s-tail.

Jarvie, Ian C. 1984. *Rationality and Relativism: In Search of a Philosophy and History of Anthropology*. London: Routledge and Kegan Paul.

Jervey, Gay. 1986. "Dennis, the M & A Menace" *American Lawyer*, July/August: 27-76.

Johnson, John M. 1975. *Doing Field Research*. New York: The Free Press.

Johnson, Terence J. 1972. *Professions and Power*. London: Macmillan.

Johnstone, Quintin and Dan Hopson, Jr. 1967. *Lawyers and Their Work: An Analysis of the Legal Profession in the United States and England*. Indianapolis: Bobbs-Merrill.

Johnstone, Quintin and John Flood. 1982. "Paralegals in English and American Law Offices." *Windsor Yearbook of Access to Justice* 2: 152-190.

Johnstone, Quintin and Martin Wenglinsky. 1985. *Paralegals: Progress and Prospects of a Satellite Occupation*. Westport, CT: Greenwood Press.

Kagan, Robert A. and Robert Eli Rosen. 1985. "On the Social Significance of Large Law Firm Practice." *Stanford Law Review* 37: 399-443.

Kanter, Arnold B. 1983. *Kanter on Hiring: A Lawyer's Guide to Lawyer Hiring*. Chicago: Lawletters Inc.

Katz, Jack. 1982. *Poor People's Lawyers in Transition*. New Brunswick, NJ: Rutgers University Press.

Katz, Jack. 1985. "Caste, Class, and Counsel for the Poor." *American Bar Foundation Research Journal* No. 2: 251-291.

Katz, Jay. 1984. *The Silent World of Doctor and Patient*. New York: The Free Press.

Kelsen, Hans. 1945. *General Theory of Law and State*. Cambridge, Ma: Harvard University Press.

Kingston, Paul William and Lionel S. Lewis (eds.). 1990. *The High-Status Track: Studies of Elite Schools and Stratification*. Albany, NY: State University of New York Press.

Krishnan, Jayanth. K. 2007. "Outsourcing and the Globalizing Legal Profession." *William and Mary Law Review* 48: 2189-2246.

Kritzer, Herbert M. 1984. "The Dimensions of Lawyer-Client Relations: Notes Toward a Theory and a Field Study" (Research Note). *American Bar Foundation Research Journal* No. 2:409-25.

Kuhn, Thomas S. 1970. *The Structure of Scientific Revolutions*. (2nd ed.), Chicago: University of Chicago Press.

Larson, Margali S. 1977. *The Rise of Professionalism: A Sociological Analysis*. Berkeley, CA: University of California Press.

Latour, Bruno. 2010. *The making of Law: An Ethnography of the Conseil D'Etat*. Cambridge: Polity Press.

Lattman, Peter. 2012. "Dewey & LeBoeuf Files for Bankruptcy." *DealBook New York Times*, May 28, http://dealbook.nytimes.com/2012/05/28/dewey-leboeuf-files-for-bankruptcy/.

Lawyer. 2012. "Irwin Mitchell Finally Gets Keys to ABS Warchest." *Lawyer,* August 20, 2012. http://www.thelawyer.com/irwin-mitchell-finally-gets-keys-to-abs-warchest/1013952.article.

Lawyer. 2013. "DLA Piper." *Lawyer,* July 17, 2013. http://www.thelawyer.com/dla-piper/414865.supplierproducts#crumbtrail.

Lazega, Emmanuel. 2001. *The Collegial Phenomenon: The Social Mechanisms of Cooperation Among Peers in a Corporate Law Partnership.* Oxford: Oxford University Press.

Leach, Edmund Ronald, 1976. *Culture and Communication: The Logic by which Symbols are Connected.* Cambridge: Cambridge University Press.

Legal Services Board. n.d. "The Regulatory Objectives: Legal Services Act 2007." http://www.legalservicesboard.org.uk/news_publications/publications/pdf/regulatory_objectives.pdf.

Levi, Edward H. 1949. *An Introduction to Legal Reasoning.* Chicago: University of Chicago Press.

Levin, Leslie C. and Lynn Mather (eds.). 2012. *Lawyers in Practice: Ethical Decision Making in Context.* Chicago: University of Chicago Press.

Levine, Samuel J. 2005. "Rediscovering Julius Henry Cohen and the Origins of the Business/Profession Dichotomy: A Study in the Discourse of Early Twentieth Century Legal Professionalism." *American Journal of Legal History* 47: 1-34.

Lindblom, Charles E. 1959. "The Science of Muddling Through." *Public Administration Review* 19: 79-88.

Lindblom, Charles E. and David K. Cohen. 1979. *Usable Knowledge: Social Science and Social Problem Solving.* New Haven: Yale University Press.

Lipson, Jonathan C., Beth Engel, and Jami Crespo. 2012. "Who's in the House? The Changing Nature and Role of In-House and General Counsel." *Wisconsin Law Review* 2012: 237-250.

Liu, Sida. 2010. "Lessons for the Survivors." *Jotwell,* July 22, 2010. http://legalpro.jotwell .com/ lessons-for-the-survivors/.

Llewellyn, Karl N. and Edward A. Hoebel. 1941. *The Cheyenne Way: Conflict and Case Law in Primitive Jurisprudence.* Buffalo, NY: Hein Publishing.

Luhmann, Niklas. 1975. "The Legal Profession: Comments on the Situation in the Federal Republic of Germany." In *Lawyers in Their Social Setting,* D. N. MacCormick (ed.), Edinburgh: W Green.

Luhmann, Niklas. 1979. *Trust and Power: Two Works.* New York: Wiley.

Lukes, Steven. 1974. *Power: A Radical View.* London: Macmillan.

Luppino, Anthony J. 2004. "Multidisciplinary Business Planning Firms: Expanding the Regulatory Tent Without Creating a Circus." *Seton Hall Law Review* 35: 109-191.

Lynch, Michael. 1985. *Art and Artifact in Laboratory Science: A Study of Shop Work and Shop Talk in a Research Laboratory.* London: Routledge and Kegan Paul.

Macaulay, Stewart. 1963. "Non-Contractual Relations in Business: A Preliminary Study." *American Sociological Review* 28: 55-67.

Macaulay, Stewart. 1979. "Lawyers and Consumer Protection Laws." *Law and Society Review* 14: 115-171.

Macaulay, Stewart. 1984. "Lawyer-Client Interaction: Who Cares and How Do We Find Out What We Want to Know?" Working Paper, Disputes Processing Research Program, University of Wisconsin Law School.

MacCullum, Spencer. 1967. "Dispute Settlement in an American Supermarket: A Preliminary View" In *Law and Warfare: Studies in the Anthropology of Conflict*. P. Bohannon (ed.), Garden City, NY: The Natural History Press.

MacEwen, Bruce, Milton C. Regan and Larry Ribstein. 2008. "Law Firms, Ethics, and Equity Capital." *Georgetown Journal of Legal Ethics* 21: 61-94.

Mann, Kenneth. 1985. *Defending White-Collar Crime: A Portrait of Attorneys at Work*. New Haven: Yale University Press.

Marcus, George E. 1980. "Law in the Development of Dynastic Families Among American Business Elites: The Domestication of Capital and the Capitalization of Family." *Law and Society Review* 14: 859-904.

Martin, Joanne 1987. "Corporate Law Department Trends and the Effect of the Current Bar Admission System: A Survey of Corporate Counsel." Chicago: American Bar Foundation.

Marx, Karl. 1976. "The German Ideology." *Collected Works: Volume V*. London: Lawrence and Wishart.

Mather, Lynn. 2003. "What Do Clients Want? What Do Lawyers Do?" *Emory Law Journal* 52: 1065-1086.

Mather, Lynn, Craig A. McEwen and Richard J. Maiman. 2001. *Divorce Lawyers at Work: Varieties of Professionalism in Practice*. New York: Oxford University Press.

Maynard, Douglas W. 1984. *Inside Plea Bargaining: The Language of Negotiation*. New York: Plenum Press.

McKinney, Luther C. 1986. "Corporate Clients Want Outside Lawyers To Be More Than Technicians." In *Corporate Clients and Their Lawyers: A Colloquy*. J. Henning and J. Hamby (eds.), Chicago: Lawletters Inc.

Mnookin, Robert H. and Lewis Kornhauser. 1979. "Bargaining in the Shadow of the Law: The Case of Divorce" *Yale Law Journal* 88: 950-997.

Muris, Timothy J. and Fred McChesney. 2006. "Advertising and the Price of Quality of Legal Services: The Case for Legal Clinics." *Law & Social Inquiry* 4: 179-207.

Muzio, Daniel and James R. Faulconbridge. 2009. "Financialization by Proxy: The Case of Large City Law Firms." Working Paper No. 3. Centre for Employment Relations Innovation and Change, Leeds University Business School. http://lubswww. leeds.ac.uk/fileadmin/user_upload/Publications/Muzio_Faulconbridge_WP3_01.pdf.

Nelson, Robert L. 1981. "Practice and Privilege: Social Change and the Structure of Large Law Firms." *American Bar Foundation Research Journal* No.1: 95-140.

Nelson, Robert L. 1983. "Practice and Privilege: The Social Organization of Large Law Firms." Ph. D. diss., Northwestern University.

Nelson, Robert L. 1988. *Partners with Power: The Social Transformation of the Large Law Firm*. Berkeley: University of California Press.

NYSBA. 2012. "Report of the Task Force on Nonlawyer Ownership." November 17, 2012. http://www.nysba.org/AM/Template.cfm?Section=Home&ContentID=123065& template=/CM/ContentDisplay.cfm.

Okamoto, Karl S. 1995. "Reputation and the Value of Lawyers." *Oregon Law Review* 74: 15-56.

Orton, Joe. 1967. "Loot." In *The Complete Plays*. Introduced by John Lahr, London: Eyre Methuen.

Osiel, Mark J. 1990. "Lawyers as Monopolists, Aristocrats, and Entrepreneurs." *Harvard Law Review* 103: 2009-2066.

Parkes, Don and Nigel Thrift. 1980. *Times, Spaces, and Places: A Chronogeographic Perspective*. New York: Wiley.

Parsons, Talcott. 1954. "A Sociologist Looks at the Legal Profession." In *Essays in Sociological Theory*. (Rev. ed.), New York: The Free Press.

Parsons, Talcott. 1968. "Professions." In *International Encyclopedia of the Social Sciences*. New York: Macmillan and The Free Press.

Pashigian, B. Peter. 1977. "The Market for Lawyers: The Determination of the Demand for and Supply of Lawyers." *Journal of Law and Economics* 20: 53-85.

Pashigian, B. Peter. 1978. "The Number and Earnings of Lawyers: Some Recent Findings." *American Bar Foundations Research Journal* No. 1: 51-82.

Paton, Paul D. 2010. "Multidisciplinary Practice Redux: Globalization, Core Values, and Reviving the MDP Debate in America." *Fordham Law Review* 78: 2193-2244.

Postle, Denis. 1980. *Catastrophe Theory*. London: Fontana Paperbacks.

Pound, Roscoe. 1953. *The Lawyer From Antiquity to Modern Times*. St Paul, MN: West Publishing Co.

Priest, George L. 1993. "Lawyers, Liability, and Law Reform: Effects on American Economic Growth and Trade Competitiveness." *Denver University Law Review* 71: 115-149.

Raiffa, Howard. 1982. *The Art and Science of Negotiation*. Cambridge, MA: The Belknap Press of Harvard University Press.

Rasmussen, Jacqueline M. and Paul M. Sedlacek. 1999. "Paralegals: Changing the Practice of Law." *South Dakota Law Review* 44: 319-339.

Ribstein, Larry E. 2010. "The Death of Big Law." *Wisconsin Law Review* 2010: 749-815.

Rosen, Robert E. 2010. *Lawyers in Corporate Decision-Making*. New Orleans: Quid Pro Books.

Rosenthal, Douglas E. 1974. *Lawyer and Client: Who's in Charge?* New York: Russell Sage Foundation.

Rosenthal, Douglas E. 1980., "Comment on "Obstacles to the Study of Lawyer-Client Interaction: The Biography of a Failure." *Law and Society Review* 14: 923-929.

Rostain, Tanina. 2008. "General Counsel in the Age of Compliance: Preliminary Findings and New Research Questions." *Georgetown Journal of Legal Ethics* 21: 465-490.

Routh, Paul J. 1984. "Liabilities of Tax Preparer: An Overview." *Capital University Law Review* 13: 479-519.

Rowe, Claude W. 1955. *How and Where Lawyers Get Practice*. Durham, NC: The Judiciary Publishing Co.

Sarat, Austin and William L.F. Felstiner. 1986. "Law and Strategy in the Divorce Lawyer's Office." *Law and Society Review* 20: 93-134.

Sayre, Paul L. 1926. "The Law—Business or Professional? By Julius Henry Cohen." *Indiana Law Journal* 1: 295-296. http://www.repository.law.indiana.edu/ilj/vol1/iss5/7.

Scheffer, Thomas. 2010. *Adversarial Case-Making: An Ethnography of English Crown Court Procedure.* Leiden: Brill.

Schlegel, John H. 1989. "American Legal Theory and American Legal Education: A Snake Swallowing its Tail." In *Critical Legal Thought: An American-German Debate,* C. Joerges and D. Trubek (eds.), Baden-Baden: Nomos.

Schon, Donald A. 1983. *The Reflective Practitioner: How Professionals Think in Action.* New York: Basic Books.

Seron, Carroll. 1996. *The Business of Practicing Law: The Work Lives of Solo and Small-Firm Attorneys.* Philadelphia: Temple University Press.

Slater & Gordon. n.d. http://www.slatergordon.com.au/the-firm/our-history/.

Slovak, Jeffrey S. 1979. "Working for Corporated Actors: Social Change and Elite Attorneys in Chicago." *American Bar Foundation Research Journal* No. 3: 465-500.

Smigel, Erwin. 1969. *Wall Street Lawyer: Professional Organization Man.* Bloomington, IN: Indiana University Press.

Spangler, Eve. 1986. *Lawyers for Hire: Salaried Professionals at Work.* New Haven: Yale University Press.

Speiser, Stuart M. 1980. *Lawsuit.* New York: Horizon Press.

Starbuck, William H. 1993. "Keeping a Butterfly and an Elephant in a House of Cards: The Elements of Exceptional Success." *Journal of Management Studies* 30: 885-921.

Starr, Paul. 1982. *The Social Transformation of American Medicine: The Rise of a Sovereign Profession and the Making of a Vast Industry.* New York: Basic Books.

Sterling, Joyce. S. and Nancy Reichman. 2010. "So, You Want to Be a Lawyer? The Quest for Professional Status in a Changing Legal World." *Fordham Law Review* 78: 2289-2314.

Stevens, Mark. 1987. *Power of Attorney: The Rise of the Giant Law Firms.* New York: McGraw Hill.

Stevens, Robert. 1983. *Law School: Legal Education in America from the 1850s to the 1980s.* Chapel Hill: University of North Carolina Press.

Stewart, James B. 1983. *The Partners: Inside America's Most Powerful Law Firms.* New York: Simon and Schuster.

Stinchcombe, Arthur L. 1965. "Social Structure and Organizations." In *Handbook of Organizations,* J. March (ed.), Chicago: Rand McNally.

Strong, Philip. 1979. *The Ceremonial Order of the Clinic: Parents, Doctors and Medical Bureaucracies.* London: Routledge and Kegan Paul.

Suchman, Mark C. 1994. "On Advice of Counsel: Law Firms and Venture Capital Funds as Information Intermediaries in the Structuration of Silicon Valley." PhD diss. Stanford University.

Susskind, Richard. 2010. *The End of Lawyers? Rethinking the Nature of Legal Services.* Oxford: Oxford University Press.

Swaine, Robert T. 1946. *The Cravath Firm and Its Predecessors, 1819-1947* (2 vols.) New York: Ad Press.

Tamanaha, Brian Z. 2012. *Failing Law Schools*. Chicago: University of Chicago Press.

Terry, Laurel S. 2010. "From GATS to APEC: The Impact of Trade Agreements on Legal Services." *Akron Law Review* 43: 675-984.

Thrift, Nigel. 1990. "The Making of a Capitalist Time Consciousness." In *The Sociology of Time* J. Hassard (ed.), London: Palgrave Macmillan.

Tolbert, Pamela S. and Robert N. Stern. 1987. "Clans and Hierarchies: Governance Structures of Major Law Firms." Unpublished paper presented at Midwest Sociological Society Meeting, Chicago.

Travers, Max. 1997. *The Reality of Law: Work and Talk in a Firm of Criminal Lawyers*. Farnham: Ashgate.

Twining, William L. 1968. "Lawyers Under the Microscope." Unpublished public lecture. Queen's University Belfast.

Twining, William L. 1985. "Taking Skills Seriously." Unpublished paper presented at American Bar Foundation London Symposium.

U.S. Bureau of the Census. 1975. *Historical Statistics of the United States, Colonial Times to 1970*. Washington, DC: U.S. Bureau of the Census.

U.S. Bureau of the Census. 1986. *Statistical Abstract of the United States*. Washington, DC: U.S. Bureau of the Census.

Wald, Eli. 2008a. "The Rise and Fall of the WASP and Jewish Law Firms." *Stanford Law Review* 60: 101-165.

Wald, Eli. 2008b. "The Rise of the Jewish Law Firm or Is the Jewish Law Firm Generic?" *University of Missouri-Kansas City Law Review* 76: 1-56.

Wald, Eli. 2010. "Symposium: The Economic Downturn and the Legal Profession: Foreword: The Great Recession and the Legal Profession." *Fordham Law Review* 78: 2051-2066.

Warkov, Seymour with Joseph Zelan. 1965. *Lawyers in the Making*. Chicago: Aldine Publishing Co.

White, D. Robert, 1983. *The Official Lawyer's Handbook*. New York: Simon and Schuster.

Whyte, William Hollingsworth. 1967. *The Organization Man*. Garden City, NY: Doubleday.

Wieder, D. Lawrence. 1974. *Language and Social Reality: The Case of Telling the Convict Code*. The Hague: Mouton.

Wilkins, David B. and G. Mitu Gulati. 1996. "Why Are There So Few Black Lawyers in Corporate Law Firms? An Institutional Analysis." *California Law Review* 84: 493-625.

Wilkins, David B. and G. Mitu Gulati. 1998. "Reconceiving the Tournament of Lawyers: Tracking, Seeding, and Information Control in The Internal Labor Markets of Elite Law Firms." *Virginia Law Review* 84: 1581-1681.

Williamson, Oliver E. 1979. "Transaction-Cost Economics: The Governance of Contractual Relations." *Journal of Law and Economics* 22: 233-262.

Zeeman, E.C. 1977. *Catastrophe Theory: Selected Papers 1972-1977*. Reading, Ma: Addison-Wesley.

Zemans, Frances Kahn and Victor G. Rosenblum. 1981. *The Making of a Public Profession*. Chicago: American Bar Foundation.

Zerubavel, Eviatar. 1979. *Patterns of Time in Hospital Life*. Chicago: University of Chicago Press.

Zerubavel, Eviatar. 1999. *Social Mindscapes: An Invitation to Cognitive Sociology*. Cambridge, Ma: Harvard University Press.

Zimmerman, Don H. 1969. "Record-keeping and the Intake Process in a Public Welfare Agency." In *On Record: Files and Dossiers in American Life*, S. Wheeler (ed.), New York: Russell Sage Foundation.

ABOUT THE AUTHOR

JOHN FLOOD is Professor of Law and Sociology at the University of Westminster in London. He is also Visiting Professor of Law at University College London where he is responsible for Law Without Walls, a global legal education program. He is presently a Leverhulme Research Fellow researching the new legal services market in its global context.

Flood has focused his research on legal profession, globalization of law, and the regulation of the legal services market with occasional forays into legal education and legal aid. His research is distinctive for the different types of methods he employs. He started with ethnography, of which this book is one example, and mutated into qualitative interviewing as full-time teaching jobs intervened. Projects include studies of large law firms, lawyer-client interaction, and the globalization of bankruptcy. His most recent research has been based on oral history of lawyers which he has been doing with Peter Lederer, former senior partner of Baker & McKenzie and now Practitioner in Residence at the University of Miami School of Law.

Since 2010 Flood has been a member of the Research Strategy Group of the Legal Services Board, the new oversight regulator of legal services in England and Wales. He also consults for the New York City Bar Association International Task Force, which is attempting to deal with the new threats of a liberalized legal market in the UK against the resistance of most US lawyers.

More information, including downloadable publications, can be found at *www.johnflood.com*.

Visit us at *www.quidprobooks.com.*